Writing problems
p 10, p 23
p 18 writes awk

14

21 recours
awk
undigested
17.7
191 awk
194 awk
writing

COSMOPOLITICAL CLAIMS

Cosmopolitical Claims

TURKISH-GERMAN LITERATURES

FROM NADOLNY TO PAMUK

B. VENKAT MANI

UNIVERSITY OF IOWA PRESS IOWA CITY

University of Iowa Press, Iowa City 52242
Copyright © 2007 by the University of Iowa Press
www.uiowapress.org
All rights reserved
Printed in the United States of America
Design by Richard Hendel
No part of this book may be reproduced or used in any form
or by any means without permission in writing from the publisher.
All reasonable steps have been taken to contact copyright holders of
material used in this book. The publisher would be pleased to make suitable
arrangements with any whom it has not been possible to reach.
The University of Iowa Press is a member of Green Press Initiative
and is committed to preserving natural resources.
Printed on acid-free paper

LCCN: 2006937995
ISBN-10: 1-58729-584-9
ISBN-13: 978-1-58729-584-3

07 08 09 10 11 C 5 4 3 2 1

TO APPA

1942–2002

for life lessons in
political claims

CONTENTS

Acknowledgements ix

INTRODUCTION
Cosmopolitical Claims 1

ONE
Thus Spake the *Gastarbeiter*:
Sten Nadolny's *Selim oder die Gabe der Rede* 44

TWO
Slouching Histories, Lurking Memories:
Emine Sevgi Özdamar's *Seltsame Sterne Starren zur Erde* 87

THREE
Authentic Hybrid? Feridun Zaimoğlu's *Abschaum*:
Die wahre Geschichte von Ertan Ongun 118

FOUR
Turkish-German Reattachments:
Orhan Pamuk's *The New Life* 146

AFTERWORD
Minorities, Literatures, and Recursive Leaps of Faith 183

Notes 201
Bibliography 219
Index 239

ACKNOWLEDGEMENTS

First of all, I would like to thank the staff at the University of Iowa Press. My special thanks to Joseph Parsons, acquisitions editor, for his kindness, professionalism, and enthusiasm for this project. John Joerschke's meticulous copy editing skills came right in time to help me dot the i's or occasionally undot them.

Ideas for this book were initiated, facilitated, processed, and written over the past five years at the University of Wisconsin–Madison. Funds provided by the Graduate School have been the major source of funding this project. The Department of German and Dutch, the Center for German and European Studies, the Center for European Studies, the Institute for International Studies, and the Global Studies Program provided other research and travel grants. The Language Institute, UW–Madison funded the workshop "Cosmopolitan Cultures, Cosmopolitan Histories" in spring 2005; the Center for the Humanities, UW–Madison sponsored the interdisciplinary Mellon Workshop "Cosmopolitan Cultures, Cosmopolitan Histories" (2005–2007). These workshops made it possible for me to present parts of my work and to develop and discuss ideas with colleagues and graduate students from a variety of disciplines. The DAAD provided the opportunity of presenting my work at two conferences on globalization: Berlin 2003 and Birmingham, UK, 2005. The Department of Germanic Studies, Indiana University, invited me to discuss my work under the aegis of the Leser Lecture Series (2003). The Max Kade Institute at UW–Madison and the Kansas Association of Teachers of German made it possible to discuss my research and teaching interests with high-school teachers of German. I thank these institutions for financial and intellectual support.

A number of individuals have inspired and encouraged me since I first started working on this project. I am uniquely beholden to Russell A. Berman, Valentin Y. Mudimbe, Kamakshi P. Murti, and Karen J. Kenkel for believing in this project, in addition to their critical comments and suggestions. I wish to express special gratitude to Leslie Adelson, Deniz Göktürk, Kader Konuk, and Azade Seyhan for presenting new challenges for scholars working on Turkish-German studies. I thank the two anonymous reviewers for offering constructive criticism that helped me to strengthen and fortify my arguments. This project has immensely benefited from discussions and arguments with Vinay Dharwadker and Rebecca Walkowitz. Their energy, enthusiasm, and commitment to cosmopolitan dialogues are simply amazing; I thank them.

I am thankful to all of my colleagues in my home department—scholars of literature and linguistics—for their encouragement and professional support over the last five years. While I cannot name all of them here, I want to convey my sincere appreciation to all. I do want to mention and thank Cora Lee Kluge for the time and effort she put into editing some of the very first drafts of chapters. I am honored to have been able to work with Klaus Berghahn and Jost Hermand, friends and colleagues, who constantly reinforced my interest in politics beyond aesthetics. They generously shared their knowledge and experience and provided invaluable comments and criticisms.

Also, here's a "shout out" to my undergraduate students from the seminars "Honors Introduction to German Literature," "Identifying the New Europe," and "Das andere Deutschland" offered in 2005–2006. You were awesome!

My brief but stimulating interactions with Homi Bhabha, Rey Chow, Gayatri Chakravorty Spivak, and John Tomlinson invigorated my desire to look beyond self-congratulatory multiculturalism. Paul Michael Lützler reinforced the significance of postcolonial theory in contemporary German literature. Elizabeth Bernhardt-Camille and Michael Camille are the best mentors one could ever wish for.

I was blessed to have extremely competent editorial assistance from Adam Woodis. Daniel Rosinsky-Larsson has been a fantastic research assistant. Nielke Wagner came to my rescue whenever I needed materials from Berlin, and at times at a very short notice. I thank them all for their time and patience.

"Back in India," I first want to thank my extended family. My special thanks to Shri Jawaharlal Jetli, my surrogate grandfather and a pillar of strength in my family for two generations. Laksmi and Vijayaraghavan Aiyangar, Maithili and Srinivasan Aiyangar, Kamlesh and Somnath Kwatra, Mrs. Chandrakala Mittal, Ganga and Anil Penna, Kalpakam Penna, Madhuri and Ramchandra Pundir, Shri Kedar Puri, Varsha and Prakash N. Srivastav, Sukhveer Kaur and Jasmail Singh Sidhu extended unflinching support when I needed it most; I thank them all.

Valliamma and Vishalakshi, my late grandmothers, taught me the value of education. It will remain an everlasting regret that my father, Balaji Vishwanath could not be physically present to see the completion of this book. I dedicate *Cosmopolitical Claims* to him. I am forever indebted to my elder aunt, Radha, for introducing me to the wonderful world of languages and literature. I thank my younger aunt, Nirupama, and my mother, Savitri, for the gift of literacy and the quest for knowledge. I thank Suryakiran Rai "Bahadur" Thapa for taking such good care of my family. A very special thank you to my darling sisters, Gauri and Mahima, for taking time from their own feminist battles to support me in my intellectual endeavors. This book could not have been written without them. My brother-in-law Sandeep has kept my spirits high by singing Ragas on the phone.

My dear friends: Anu and Neel Kohli, Hema and Mickey Rance, Sukhpal and Pratap Sidhu, Jay and Jacqueline Truesdale, Vishakha and Sudhir Prasad, La Nitra and Matthew Berger, Jirawan and Uday Varma, Shilpa and Sanjay Verma, Naveen Bhatt, Huma Dar, Anshul Puri, Nicole Schulz, and Mark Skvarça have extended warmth, hospitality, and generosity across three continents. Esperanza Alfonso, Deborah Bernhardt, Simon May, Mihaela Cabulia, Alfonso Moreno, and Lorraine Piroux offered support, advice, but also wonderful distractions from this book. Antonio Rauti made sure that this book got written. I thank all of them for their gift of friendship.

Todd Michelson-Ambelang, my friend, critic, and partner-in-crime, kept me sane throughout the writing of this book. I thank him for registering his claims on my time and my life.

COSMOPOLITICAL CLAIMS

INTRODUCTION
Cosmopolitical Claims

*The literature of guest workers ... offers the possibility to see
our problem not as the individual problem of a Mustafa from Istanbul
or a Jannis from Kilkis, but as a collective problem of over 4 million, yes,
60 million citizens of the Federal Republic.*
FRANCO BIONDI AND RAFIK SCHAMI, "LITERATUR DER BETROFFENHEIT"

*Europe is the reflection of my countenance, and contrariwise:
I am the reflection of the countenance of Europe. My speechlessness is
that of its own. My search for a new language contributes to the fact that it
[Europe] can resolve its speechlessness at the borders of the language.*
ARAS ÖREN, "DANKREDE ZUR PREISVERLEIHUNG"

At the 2002 Tanner Lectures on Human Values at Yale University, Salman Rushdie returned to evaluating frontiers.[1] "The frontier is an elusive line," he claimed, "visible and invisible, physical and metaphorical, amoral and moral.... To cross a frontier is to be transformed" (*Step across This Line* 352). Rushdie proceeded to call the frontier "a wake-up call," "the physical proof of the human race's divided self," the place where the "world's secret truths move unhindered every day" (ibid. 353).

Through these pronouncements, Rushdie becomes the purveyor of the bittersweet irony of frontiers that marks the beginning of the new millennium. Rushdie makes his statements in what has come to be known as the Post-9/11 World, a world where frontiers, boundaries, and borders dividing nations, cultures, religions, ethnicities, and languages have suddenly reacquired visibility and clarity. Reacquired, I emphasize, because in the early 1990s, as the iron curtain came down and silicon drapes went up, the information highway created the illusion of a connected, unified, and glorified global village, a postnational view of the world. Furthermore, in the wake of mass migration from Asia and Africa, metropolitan centers of Europe and North America were optimistically envisaged as miniature versions of this global village; peaceful coexistence of heterogeneous populations was promoted by intellectual and political investment in multiculturalism. The terms *global-* and *multi-* prefixed our imagination of varied cultures and communities peacefully coexisting in close proximity, purportedly breeding (hybrid) lilacs out of the dead sand of tolerance, mixing hopes and desires of natives and foreigners alike. UNESCO's *World Culture Report, 2000* is a classic document of how illusions of cultural diversity and pluralism continue to raise the hopes of blurring cultural frontiers and national boundaries, even as the ill-treatment of immigrants of color or with Muslim(-sounding) names is business as usual at ports of entry into Europe and North America.

After the reinitiation of the brown–white racial divide in 2001, as the United States prepared itself for the great ideological bifurcation of the red and blue states—to be uncovered in the presidential election of 2004—the continent of Europe was in a bid to redefine its internal boundaries. Disregarding U.S. Secretary of Defense Donald Rumsfeld's divisive distinction of "old" and "new," Europe was well on its way to celebrating manifestations of its economic and political unity, barring, of course, the difficult subject of cultural unity. Europe shared with the United States, its transatlantic partner, unease about the presence and participation of non–Judeo-Christian immigrants in its unified composition. This unease had been manifested before in terms of a threat to the enlightened, secular character of Europe immediately following the fatwa on Salman Rushdie in 1989; in terms of the headscarf debate in Germany and France in the late 1990s and the early years of the twenty-first century; and through the threat of Islamic terrorism in Europe and the United States—even more intensely palpable after the bombings in London in July 2005 and various uncovered terrorist plots since then. As the war on terror acquired the new appellation of a "global struggle against violent extremism" (Packer 33), once again in Rushdie's terms, invisible frontiers became visible again, and lines dividing human races reacquired their traditional qualifications: national, religious, racial, ethnic, linguistic.

The resurgence of these metaphysical and moral frontiers since the beginning of the new millennium might have seemed the source of an inescapable pessimism. Yet for an author like Rushdie, the possibility of escaping their boundaries presents itself in literature in stepping across linguistic, geographical, and cultural lines, forming new affiliations while retaining the old ones, redefining the traditional and the modern, and thus transforming oneself. In the second part of his lecture, Rushdie zoomed in on language as a frontier. He described the "crossing of borders, of language, geography, and culture; the examination of the permeable frontier between the universe of things and deeds and the universe of the imagination ... at the 'heart of the [his] literary project'" (*Step across This Line* 373). Rushdie describes the crossing over of the language frontier as a journey that "involves a form of shape-shifting or self-translation" (ibid.).

The epigraphs at the beginning of this chapter—which predate Rushdie's utterances by about two decades and find their first echoes in Europe—stand in solidarity with Rushdie's hope and determination to step across ethnic, linguistic, and national boundary lines. They were written in German by authors of Italian (Franco Biondi), Syrian (Rafik Schami), and Turkish (Aras Ören) heritages. These authors came to Germany in the early 1960s during the *Gastarbeiterbewegung* (guest-worker movement) and crossed the frontiers of their first languages to document their experiences in German, the majority-language of their country of residence.[2] By the mid-1980s, a substantial body of poems, short stories, and novels had appeared on the German literary scene. A number of these writings bore marks of ethnic or religious discrimination, social isolation, and cultural alienation in Germany, albeit not always accompanied by a continued sense of nostalgia for the authors' countries of birth. These literary works gave contours to the neologism *Gastarbeiterdeutsch*: an in-between, "almost-German" language with all the unorthodoxies and deviances picked up by workers on construction sites and in factories, thus rendering audible the accents of the workers. A slightly different German in a relatively heterogeneous Germany became the core of scholarly recognition of these authors. The immigration status of the workers became the qualifier of the literature by and about them, and this body of literature came to be known as *Gastarbeiterliteratur* (guest-worker literature).

The occasions when the epigraphs were spoken deserve a special mention. They symbolize not only the acknowledgement of the contribution of authors of non-German heritages to German literature but ultimately the recognition of the slow and steady changes in the cultural, ethnic, religious, and linguistic composition of Germany in the 1980s. Biondi and Schami made their joint statement at one of the first conferences in Germany on *Gastarbeiterliteratur* at the Evangelische Akademie in Iserlohn. Ören's words are from his 1985 speech accepting the first Adalbert von Chamisso Prize, a literary award conferred upon German authors of non-German ethnic heritage. The arrival of foreigners in Germany in the late twentieth century was part of the larger mass migration of people from the non-West to the West.[3] Literary accounts of *Gastarbeiter* in Germany after 1945 were radically different from those of Chamisso, who arrived in Germany from

France in the early nineteenth century. From Chamisso's short story about the bourgeois, albeit homeless antihero *Peter Schlemihl* (1814), literature of migration had come a long way to document the hopes and desires of a working-class racial minority in postwar–Western Europe. At the moment of the arrival of the *Gastarbeiter*, it was difficult to foresee that there would be a time when authors who began their careers writing under the imposed rubric of *Gastarbeiterliteratur* would win prestigious literary honors, one of which would be named after Chamisso himself.[4] Biondi won the Chamisso Prize in 1987, Schami in 1993.

As Biondi, Schami, and Ören acknowledge the institutional recognition of their works and react to their initial fame as bearers of Chamisso's legacy, they demonstrate their reluctance to be promoted only as guest-worker authors, thus registering an acute awareness of the dangers of marginalization through singularly ascribed affiliation. By choosing the phrase "Literatur der Gastarbeiter" (literature of guest-workers) over *Gastarbeiterliteratur*, Biondi and Schami emphasize the inadequacy of the latter term and criticize the efficacy of the word *guests*—a peculiar status attributed to authors. Through this gesture, they question whether this guest status of authors indicates their temporary inhabitancy of the language of their literary production and whether calling them guests alludes to their limited residency in literary production. Furthermore, by presenting the problems of a Turkish (Mustafa) or a Greek (Jannis) immigrant as problems that concern all citizens of Germany, Biondi and Schami emancipate themselves from confined allegiances to and affiliations with a single social group, ethnicity, culture, or nationality and assert their claims in the larger political reality and cultural citizenry of Germany. The geopolitical cartographies of Istanbul and Kilkis thus metaphorically merge into those of the German cities where the guest workers live and labor.

In tandem with Biondi and Schami, Ören claims his insider status in Germany but goes one step farther. Instead of perceiving his writings as just *Gastarbeiterliteratur*—or for that matter minority literature, multicultural literature, hyphenated (Turkish-German) literature, or simply German literature—he presents his work as part of the larger European space: a geopolitical space that, after the Second World War, was increasingly being inhabited by immigrants; a politico-cultural space that was undergoing a shape-shifting through works of immigrant authors. In calling Europe a reflection of his face and vice versa, Ören registers the changing face of the European continent—indeed, the new color of the face that Europe acquired at an accelerated pace due to mass migration from Asia and Africa. More importantly, Ören prompts his audience to ask if a specific kind of speechlessness pertains to an author who is perceived as a guest in a particular language. If yes, what is the nature of that speechlessness? How is it connected with that of the continent of Europe? How is this speechlessness resolved at the borders of a language? What does it mean to be a German *and* a European author in the late twentieth century, especially when the author is affiliated—by birth and language—with a purportedly non-European cultural space?

The efficacy of cultural and political affiliation with, and literary interventions in, a nation and its national culture—touched upon by Schami, Biondi, and Ören—resonates through literary works by many other authors living in countries that are not their countries of birth, writing in languages that might not be their first languages. Their questions hold currency in contemporary Germany. Since the arrival of the first guest workers in Germany in the late 1950s and early 1960s, the Berlin Wall has come down (1989) and the new German citizenship law has come into effect (2000), and a third generation of people of non-German ethnic heritages resides in Germany today. Over two million of them are Turks, and Berlin has slowly gained the reputation of being the third-largest Turkish city after Istanbul and Ankara. German literature today is replete with contributions from authors of non-German ethnicities, and some of the most famous of these authors were either born in Turkey or born in Germany of Turkish parents. Emine Sevgi Özdamar and Feridun Zaimoğlu, for example, have sutured tales of migration from Turkey into Germany with stories of inhabitation in Germany; so has Sten Nadolny, a (non-Turkish) German author, who wrote one of the first detailed accounts of a Turkish character in a novel published in 1990.[5] These authors push the boundaries of the German language and transform its grammar and vocabulary both literally and figuratively. More importantly, through metareflections on the scope and the limits, the ambitions and restrictions of their writings—ideas that I particularly wish to unfold in my readings of their novels—these authors stake their claims in contemporary Germany and Europe in idioms hitherto unfamiliar and unique. The stories these authors tell register their thinking and feeling through and beyond the German nation. The work of their imagination delimits itself from the confined spaces of Germany or Turkey and resists the limitation of their intellectual and political affiliations to one of the two nations.

In Turkey, similar crucial issues of affiliation to the dominant, populist, and often state-sponsored imagination of the nation, class, and religion are brought to light by the 2006 Nobel Prize winner Orhan Pamuk.[6]

Pamuk is neither an author whom one would associate with *Gastarbeiterliteratur* nor one who belongs to the community of Turkish (immigrant) authors in Germany. He lives in Turkey and writes in his first language, Turkish. But not unlike the authors mentioned previously, through his unorthodox use of the Turkish language, through his sharp criticism of homogenous conjectures of the Turkish nation and national culture, and through his stimulating probe of the notion of belonging, of frontiers, of divisive lines within a nation-state, a continent, and the larger political world, Pamuk innovatively decodes and recodes cryptic equations between the geocultural spaces marked as East and West, non-European and European. Pamuk makes incisions in the larger European and trans-European cultural space, and through these incisions he calls for a reconsideration of the very definition of Europe and its cultural heritage.

Nadolny, Özdamar, Zaimoğlu, and Pamuk, to use Rushdie's words again, examine "the permeable frontier between the universe of things and deeds and the universe of the imagination." The gravitas of their works, the force of their claims, lies in their cosmopolitan moorings—their multiple attachments, their constant and conscious problematization of their immediately identifiable national, linguistic, ethnic, and cultural affiliations. They defy easy categorization into a national, an ethnic, a cultural, or even a transcultural literature. The cosmopolitanism of these authors—a term I shall consider later in this introduction—does not manifest itself in a complete absence of identification with a nation, ethnicity, or culture and certainly not in declarations of absolute detachment or rootlessness. These authors are very much residents and political subjects of their cosmos. They are astutely cognizant of the cultural and political geographies of their polis, but they are not hesitant to unsettle and radicalize the definition of belonging to that very cosmos and the polis through their writings. Admittedly, Nadolny, Özdamar, Zaimoğlu, and Pamuk vary in their modes of engagement with national, cultural, and ethnic difference in metropolitan locations such as Berlin and Istanbul. However, their works intersect as they promote critical and reflective distance from, and at times a dissent against, what are perceived as their immediate linguistic, ethnic, religious, national, and class affiliations. These affiliations are not denigrated or diminished. In fact, they are presented as simultaneous, circuitous, and constellated. While the novels of Özdamar and Zaimoğlu present these simultaneous affiliations (and disaffiliations) as marked by migratory or minoritarian experiences and related political claims in a different linguistic and cultural home (the country of residence), those of Nadolny and Pamuk tell stories that challenge the ideological bases of a homogenous, ethnocentric nationhood in their countries of birth. Literary claims registered by these authors in their novels are *cosmopolitical claims*.

This book aims to isolate and explore literary claims of multiple and simultaneous affiliations and disaffiliations through four novels that depict complexities of engagement between Turkey and Germany since 1990. This study demonstrates that recent German and Turkish novels upset normative perceptions of dominant cultural production in a nation, its language, and its literature through new forms of imaginative expressions. Central to this book is the argument that through these new expressions emerge palpable resurgences of not singular, but multiple, simultaneous affiliations. The work of interventionist imagination thus resists crude proverbial assimilation to and co-optation by legislations of hegemonic culturalisms, regardless of whether these culturalisms are prefixed by mono- or multi-. While this study explores such expressions in literary works that bear specific marks of migratory experiences characteristic of the late twentieth century, it makes a case for parallel explorations of these expressions in nonmigratory contexts through the inclusion of Orhan Pamuk's *The New Life*. Most importantly, this book accounts for narrative complexities that register problems of representations of multiple affiliations. What sets *Cosmopolitical Claims* apart from previous studies is its commitment to think through difference without indulging in the triumphant vocabularies of multicultural inclusions or the defeatist critiques of monocultural exclusions. *Cosmopolitical Claims* explores aesthetic and political claims that unsettle concepts of home, belonging, and cultural citizenship in four Turkish-German novels, whereby the cultural hyphen signals at best a sustained criticism and a sustainable scrutiny of affiliations to Germany or to Turkey.

An understanding of these claims requires an acknowledgement of the ever-present and clearly delineated political and cultural boundary lines, imaginary as well as real. These delineations surface and resurface in the political climate of Europe, where the harmony of the European anthem is lost time and again in cacophonic assertions of national specificities. The crisis in the European Union that led to the rejection of the proposed constitution in referenda in France and Holland in the spring of 2005 reflects various anxieties, not the least of which is the entry of Turkey into the European Union.[7] At stake is a complex interplay of cosmopolitan aspirations and what is often presented as a clash of civilizations. This constellation has been explored with intensity in Germany, home to Europe's largest Turkish minority, where the vocabularies of clash and confrontation have been part of the bureaucratic and media discourses. The inescapability of metaphysical frontiers, borders, and boundary lines has been noticeable in the resistance to Turkey's entry into the European Union, the source of the resistance often locatable in Germany itself. Such resistance comes shrouded in vocabularies of cultural—if not always religious—difference. Lorenz Jäger, sociologist, literary critic, and editor of the "Feuilleton" section of the *Frankfurter Allgemeine Zeitung*, registers his opposition in terms of the lack of an Enlightenment or counter-Enlightenment tradition in Turkey:

> But there is no Turkish philosophy, neither of Enlightenment nor of counter-Enlightenment, which could have participated in this process, or could have made itself heard in the conversation about Europe. Whoever listens to Sibelius or Puccini knows how far Europe extends. He listens to the borders—also when he does not want to admit to it intellectually. On none of the possible cultural maps of Europe is Turkey to be found.[8]

Forty years of the presence of Turkish immigrants in Germany notwithstanding, cultural borders are drawn very clearly. Apparently Europe exists only as far as north as Jean Sibelius's *Finlandia* (1899) and as far south as Giacomo Puccini's *La Bohème* (1896) can be understood and appreciated. One hundred years after the creation of these compositions, Turkey is instantly dislodged from the "cultural" maps of Europe, nowhere to be found. The cultural inheritor of Sibelius and Puccini *and* European Enlightenment is capable of recognizing this absence, even if "he," as Jäger presents it, does not admit to it intellectually. Perhaps, if I may add facetiously, due to "his" distaste for Wolfgang Amadeus Mozart's "*Rondo alla Turca*" (1783).

This book admits to Turkey's intellectual presence in Europe and, therefore, locates claims of belonging and the clamor against exclusion—as registered in literary works—not outside or beyond, but along, within, and across ethnic, national, and linguistic lines and frontiers. This book asserts that such literary claims hitherto have been idealized at the margins of a homogenous imagination of the nation or valorized at the center of the national culture as appendages or as artifacts of a minority culture or have been panegyrized between the center and the margin *only* as testimonies of pluralist multiculturalism or yet, especially in the case of Pamuk, as documents of a world-cultural internationalism. Against such prevalent perceptions, the current study argues that these claims inscribe themselves both within and outside the confines of political and cultural boundaries that divide ethnicities within a nation and national collectivities from each other. How are these inscriptions to be read and understood? What happens *after* linguistic, cultural, and political borders have been crossed or blurred? What kind of critical approaches can assist us in reading literary works that reflect on the permanence of crossing frontiers without indulging in a romanticized denial of divisive frontiers in order to assert itinerant and dissident subjectivities? How are we to understand literary works that express frontiers of ethnicities, nations, and cultures while rendering those very frontiers porous and permeable, not just through identification with ethnicity or with the nation but through difference and distance from ethnicity and the nation? What are the registers of assertions of ethnic and cultural difference in works of literature? What are the complexities and difficulties that accrue in representing differential affiliations?

These questions are central to this introduction, which lays the foundation of the book's investigation of modes of imagining individual and collective affiliations in homogenous and heterogenous distinctions between the national (majoritarian), the ethnic or multicultural (minoritarian), and the cosmopolitan. To this end, I first underline the process of imagination of national collectivities in the German context with glimpses of two historical textual moments: one from the height of German nationalism in the late nineteenth century and another from the period of crisis in German national self-assertion after the Second World War. Next, I move to recent theoretical contestations surrounding the position and ambition of literature written in German by and about Turkish minorities. Through these discussions, I wish to spell out the issues at stake in recent debates on Turkish-German literature. In the end, I inaugurate this book's larger ambition of rethinking what we have come to understand as minor and minority literatures through a discussion on cosmopolitanism and cosmopolitics.

"Every nation has its others, within and without," observes the noted thinker Seyla Benhabib in the introduction to her significant study *The Rights of Others* (18). As Benhabib lays the foundation of her investigation of political membership as imagined and practiced by modern nation-states, she pursues the "conceptual gap in the legal construction of the constitutional state" (ibid.). Citizenship and political membership thus become "rituals through which the nation is reproduced spatially" (ibid.). Before proceeding to a discussion of the significance of Kant's cosmopolitan right in contemporary discussions on immigration, asylum, and the rights of noncitizens (ibid. 25–48), Benhabib identifies "historical contingencies, territorial struggles, cultural clashes, and bureaucratic fiat" (ibid. 18) as factors that collaborate to define nationality and citizenship of peoples around the world.

At the core of Benhabib's argument is an assessment of modes through which distinctions of us and them, citizens and aliens, could be reconceptualized both in the principle and practice of modern nation-states. She unfolds such practices under the rubric of "Democratic Iterations" (ibid. 171–212), as "complex processes of public argumentation, deliberation, and exchange through which universalist rights claims and principles are contested and contextualized, invoked and revoked, posited and positioned throughout legal and political institutions, as well as in the associations of the civil society" (ibid. 179).[9] As an example of such iteration, Benhabib discusses a law passed by the provincial assembly of Schleswig-Holstein, according to which any person over eighteen with a residency that exceeded three months was eligible to vote. Benhabib further mobilizes the use of the expressions *Inländer* ("cohabitants," trans. Benhabib) and *ausländische Mitbürger* ("our co-citizens of foreign origin," trans. Benhabib) to illustrate the possibilities of defining political membership in a nation-state in vocabularies other than those of citizenship—indeed, as examples that articulate the desirability of immigration in Germany in the 1990s. The law passed by the assembly of Schleswig-Holstein, the ruling of the German Constitutional Court in 1990, and the position of the city-state of Hamburg appear in Benhabib's analysis as steps that became part of the discussions and debates toward future changes in the German citizenship law of 2000, which replaced the antiquated *jus sanguinis* dating to 1913 and established *jus soli* as the basis of political membership to the German nation-state.

Underlying Benhabib's discussion of changing forms of citizenship is a renewed examination of the relationship between *demos* and *ethnos*. *Demos* are "authors as well as the subject of the laws" upon which democratic sovereignty is based (ibid. 216); "members of the demos are entitled to have a voice in the articulation of the laws by which the demos is to govern itself" (ibid. 20). *Ethnos* is a "community of memory, fate and belonging . . . something one is born into, although as an adult one may renounce this heritage, exit it, or wish to alter it" (ibid. 207). By way of discussing democratic iterations, Benhabib argues, "the demos and the ethnos do not *simply overlap*" (ibid. 207, my emphasis).

vs. Benhabib?

Although Benhabib's axiom pertains directly to constitutional pronouncements of the relationship between the *demos* and the *ethnos* vis-à-vis deliberative democracies, I read it both as an admonition and a suggestion for imagining connections between the native and the naturalized, the inherited and the inhabited, the fated and the willed. Benhabib's formulation provides pointers to investigate the relationship between *demos* and *ethnos* when the two are not explicitly stated in constitutional terms and yet conjecture the schism between belonging through accidents of birth and affiliation through acts of engagement. *Demos* and *ethnos* might not simply overlap, but they might overlap in complex ways, or they might accrue other forms of engagement rather than overlap: partial attachment, partial detachment, reattachment, and many more. In other words, the unsimple nonoverlap of *demos* and *ethnos* merits attention in extraconstitutional contexts, which nonetheless act as rituals that produce the spatiality of a nation, with or without an inherent acknowledgement of the desirability of immigration. However, before getting too enthusiastic about imagining the complexities between the inherited and the inhabited, the fated and the willed, it is fruitful to cast a sober glance at instances that have presented the inherited *as* the inhabited, the fated as the willed, the native as the natural—perhaps not simply, but in equally complex ways. A desire to unfold these complexities informs the following invocation of two textual moments of imagining Germanness.[10]

In 1878, the February issue of *Bayreuther Blätter* carried an article, "Was ist Deutsch?" (What is German?), Richard Wagner's attempt to locate and define the German essence and spirit. Starting with an investigation of the peculiar German impulse to attribute nouns such as *Tiefe* (depth), *Treue* (fidelity), and *Ernsthaftigkeit* (earnestness) to Germanness, Wagner moves to a history of various German groups that came to be known as the German race. By citing Jacob Grimm's proposition about the shared etymology of the words *Deutsch* (German), *deuten* (to point out, indicate), and *deutlich* (clear), Wagner illustrates the representative power of the word *Deutsch* for people who speak a mutually comprehensible language. Very soon in the course of his argument, he abandons the idea of mutual comprehensibility in favor of familiarity generated by lineage. All that is clear (deutlich) must be "the familiar, the habitual, that which has been passed on from our fathers, or one which has sprung from our soil" (Wagner 40). Wagner's subsequent observations on the heterogeneity of folk groups that would later fall under the rubric German are eclipsed by his organic idea of German nationhood: Deutsch/German becomes the name for people who speak one language and are geographically located on one side of the Rhine.

For Wagner, an original homeland, a singular language, and later, a singular religion (Christianity) become the criteria that define an exclusive collectivity known as German. An unflinching attachment to these criteria, he writes, is the reason why Germans—unlike the Franks, the Goths, and the Lombards, who adopted foreign languages and cultures, thus neglecting their own languages and customs—never feel at home abroad. He points out the "shameful truth" of Germans living under foreign domination in Italy and the Slavic countries, where they are hated for their loyalty to their languages and customs.

As Wagner rearranges the archives of the German-speaking people, he criticizes the self-glorification of German history under the Holy Roman Empire. For him, this period of the Germans' authority over the non-Germans is fatal to the German essence. He ridicules the German mourning of the Holy Roman Empire, insisting that the very fall of the Empire signaled the birth of the German spirit. Religious, racial, and linguistic homogeneity in the original homeland (disrupted during the Holy Roman Empire) appear as prerequisites for the development of the German spirit. In Wagner's essay, this is precisely the point of entry of the Jew, "an utterly alien element" known for his "invasion of the German nature" (ibid. 46). Unlike the "Germanic races which, upon their natal soil, retained their speech as customs" (48), the Jew has neither home nor customs and stands outside "seeking nothing but his own profit" (53). Wagner's essay starts with a desire to challenge self-glorification of Germans, but rather speedily turns into a treatise on the pride and the superiority of the Germans over the "phlegmatic" and "Oriental sloth" (53).

Close to a century after the publication of Wagner's article, after his return to Germany from exile in the United States, Theodor W. Adorno revisited Wagner's question. Trying to capture the complex political atmosphere of post–Second World War Europe in his essay "Auf die Frage, 'Was ist Deutsch?'" Adorno identifies the "bird which soils its own nest while those who complain about this bird tend to be birds [of] a feather that flock together" (Adorno 121). Writing at a time when the historical sensitivity of the German-speaking world was traumatized by the National Socialist ordeal, the German-Jewish thinker, unlike Wagner, is in no position to recount the superiority of the German essence and spirit. His philosophical agenda is very much directed toward a refutation of Wagner's contention. In order to achieve a nuanced understanding of the German collective subject, Adorno announces at the outset that there can be no immediate answer to this question, for the question itself is "burdened by those smug definitions which assume as the specifically German not what actually is German, but rather what one wishes it were. The ideal suffers at the expense of the idealization. The very form of the question already desecrates the irreparable experiences of the last decades. It presupposes an autonomous collective entity, 'German,' whose characteristics are then determined after the fact" (ibid.). Given the specificity of assertive modes of national identity during and after the Second World War, Adorno's reflections on a damaged existence in modernity find extension in a critical evaluation of collective subjects. As politicians in Europe and North America realign power axes, Adorno questions the autonomous status granted to collective identities such as German, Russian, or American. In an attempt to disclose certain inherent contradictions, inconsistencies, and incongruities that inform an individual's position in the collective, Adorno declares the "fabrication of national collectivities" as "the mark of a reified consciousness hardly capable of experience" (ibid.). Having witnessed how stereotypes about national collectivities—propagated in abundance both by individuals as well as by the state—tend to dominate human interactions, he asks for an inquiry into the shallow narcissism of autonomous collectivities. Pleas for the revival of German self-confidence on the one hand and ostracism felt by certain Germans on the other hand motivate Adorno to call for a critical self-reflection. Throughout his essay, Adorno accentuates the heterogeneity of collectivities. For him, "the True and the Better in every people is much more likely that which does *not* adapt itself to the collective subject, but, wherever possible, even resists it" (ibid., original emphasis).

Adorno's essay was published in the politically turbulent Germany of the late 1960s. The ideological bifurcation of the two German nation-states had already been symbolically completed through the construction of the Berlin Wall in 1961. Between the assassinations of Benno Ohnesorg and Rudi Dutschke, the student revolution had reached its zenith and its nadir, and the conundrum of the nation's National Socialist history was being questioned in all public forums, including cinema, literature, and of course, the print media. During this revitalization of the German national collective through a *Vergangenheitsbewältigung* (coming to terms with the past), a new present of the nation was being written by the newly arrived immigrants. This rewriting of the nation happened figuratively in the social text of the nation and more literally through literature and the print media. Another collective was being created under various names such as *Gastarbeiter, Ausländer, Fremden,* and others, defined almost entirely against the self-referentiality of the German nation. This segregation of collectivities was closer to the determinant vocabulary of Wagner and farther from the productive ambiguity of Adorno's syntax. I provide a longer discussion of these terms in Chapter 1. Here, it suffices to state that it is important not to lose sight of key moments that conflate the *demos* and *ethnos*, as signified by Wagner. But, along with Adorno, it is equally important to remember the tensions caused by a simplistic overlapping of the two. Remembering the contexts that these two texts offer will also assist in understanding the debates over positioning of the Turkish *ethnos* against the German *demos* and *ethnos* in literary scholarship, to which I now turn.

Scholarship on Turkish-German literature has long foreshadowed and accentuated cultural and ethnic difference, even though difference itself is often forestalled and attenuated. In the civic space, such simultaneous accentuation and attenuation of difference occurs through vocabularies of cultural presence, cultural participation, cultural assimilation, cultural integration, and similar concepts. In discussions of literature the success of these civic questions has long been measured in terms of ethnic or cultural (collective) identity formation, identitarian negotiation, identitarian assertion, cultural transference, and cultural transmittance, to name only a few. In other words, as identity conveys its antagonism to difference, interactions between Germans and Turks—as depicted in literary works—are either theorized in adversarial vocabularies of "writing back," or they are configured in the more harmonious descriptions of formulaic negotiations of identity in pluralist registers of multiculturalism. In short, the imagination of Turkish-German literature as a body of literary works by and about Turkish minorities in Germany has for the longest time revolved around questions of exclusion and inclusion: of Turks in the German nation and of Turkish-German literature in the German national canon. Since the inception of the word *Gastarbeiterliteratur*, the history of scholarship in Turkish-German literature has been fraught with discussions and debates on the best-suited classifications and appellations. These appellations can be summed up as follows: 1) the use of the term *Gastarbeiterliteratur* as literature written by and about guest workers between the 1960s and the 1980s[11]; 2) the replacement of this term by a multitude of others, such as *Ausländer-* or *Fremdenliteratur* (literature of foreigners),[12] *Literatur der MigrantInnen* (literature of migrants), and *interkulturelle Literatur* (intercultural literature)[13] toward the late 1980s into the 1990s or, in tandem with Anglo-American scholarship, an ethnicity-oriented *Türkisch-Deutsche/Deutsch-Türkische* (or *Griechisch-Deutsche/Deutsch-Griechische*, etc.) *Literatur, multikulturelle Literatur* (multicultural literature), and *Minderheitenliteratur* (literature of minorities) from the mid-1990s to the present. In more recent discussions, the "bridge" appears as a structure that replaces the "wall" that limits Turkish accessibility to Germany and helps extend an intercultural dialogue.[14]

A cursory glance at these appellations suggests their alliance with multiculturalism and political recognition through inclusion, possibilities of cross-cultural exchanges through an intercultural dialogue, and the assertion of group identities of minority cultures against the majority culture. These appellations and the discussions surrounding them are thus deeply ensconced in the vocabularies of democratic deliberations, promoting egalitarianism through recognition and representation of a minority culture in literature and in the nation. A statement by Hinrich Seeba captures the idea central to such modes of literary criticism. German literature, Seeba wrote, "highlights the very problems of discord it was believed to have resolved. . . . The project of national literature can now serve as a particular cultural practice of coping—or avoiding to cope—with a collective sense of loss and deficiency in a historical context from which it can no longer be separated" (Seeba 364f.). Seeba thus asks future Germanists to "take a careful and critical look at the concept of 'national literature'" and to "rethink its role for the future [by] shifting their focus from ethnic unity to cultural diversity" (ibid. 365).

A shift of focus in imagining the composition and constitution of German literature has, indeed, occurred in the past decade. Through their astute analyses of literary texts and methodological issues, scholars such as Leslie Adelson, Claudia Breger, Tom Cheeseman, Petra Fachinger, Ülker Gökberk, Deniz Göktürk, Nilüfer Kuruyazıcı, Mary McGowan, Azade Seyhan, Katrin Sieg, Sargut Sölçün, and Karin Yeşilada—to name just a few—have slowly altered the definition of German literature to include writings by authors of non-German ethnic and linguistic heritages. Gökberk boldly spelled out the need to move away from a mere listing of stereotypes in representations of the cultural Other. Breger, Cheeseman, Göktürk, Sieg, and Sölçun have effectively critiqued problems of self-representation in works by ethnic minority authors. Fachinger, Kuruyazıcı, and Yesilada have unsettled the notion of German national literatures as a body of canonized texts into which a nation's collective sense of imagined history is believed to be inscribed in images that invoke historical continuity and social unity. Kader Konuk has positioned

Turkish-German literature in the larger constellation of other literatures of displacement. These scholars have pertinently revealed the inherent problems of readings that merely essentialize cultural diversity and turn Turks into purveyors of a unidirectional address to the center of the German nation. Instead of rehearsing the arguments of all of these scholars, I suggest an engagement with two recent discussions, whereby some of the aforementioned appellations and reading strategies have been rethought and others—interculturalism in particular—have come under stringent criticism. Two scholars in particular, Leslie Adelson and Azade Seyhan, have pushed the critical agenda beyond descriptive assertions of group identity in literature to sustained analytical engagements with confluence and congruence (Adelson), and intermittence and intersections (Seyhan). The following discussion identifies and embraces some of the newer questions and challenges that emerge from these scholars' recent works.

In her new study, *The Turkish Turn in Contemporary German Literature*, Leslie Adelson stresses the necessity to develop a "new critical grammar of migration," one that innovatively reimagines the location of Turkish-German writings within German literature and the position of the Turk in literary works. Adelson's study prompts attention to the "riddle of referentiality" (*Turkish Turn* 17). "What are the figures in reference to which literary tales of migration are told?" asks Adelson; "by what means are these figures constituted?" (ibid.). While imagining the constitutive elements of Turkish characters, Adelson dismisses the "rhetorical conceit" that places Turkish migrants on a "bridge between two worlds," arguing that it "signals both a German world embedded in a European world and a Turkish world with its proper place outside Europe" (ibid. 6). The rhetorical conceit, Adelson argues, acquires the form of a "cultural fable" (ibid. 20). Positioning her analytical and critical agenda beyond this conceit, Adelson diagnoses a "broader Turkish turn [that] began to acquire critical mass in German-language fiction in the 1990s" (ibid. 15). As an inquiry into this "Turkish turn," Adelson introduces "the concept of *touching tales* as an alternative organizing principle for considering *'Turkish' lines of thought*" (ibid. 20, original emphasis). With this "heuristic device," Adelson aims to depart from "a model of incommensurable difference to stress a broad range of common ground, which can be thicker or thinner at some junctures" (ibid.). Her readings of works by Nadolny, Özdamar, Zaimoğlu, and others aim to bring together "affective dimensions that shadow the literature of Turkish migration, which in varying configurations reflects German guilt, shame, or resentment about the Nazi past, German fears of migration, Turkish fears of victimization, national taboos in both countries, and Turkish perceptions of German fantasies" (ibid.). Adelson's study thus aspires to open new "lines of thought" (ibid. 21) to conceptualize the presence of Turkish culture in German society at the end of the twentieth century.

Adelson delineates these "new lines of thought" through two foundational steps. First, in order to release the Turkish character from the literary narrative as a representative figure of the larger Turkish community, Adelson carefully scrutinizes the concept of referentiality, "a conjoined effect of literary figuration and narrative development" (ibid. 17). Adelson's discussion of Katrin Sieg's definition of referentiality—"the representation of clearly recognizable social and ethnic milieux" (Sieg *Ethnic Drag* 10, and Adelson *Turkish Turn* 19)—serves to illustrate Adelson's criticism of a "referential presumption" that "dovetails easily with the perception that public figures of Turks represent self-evident categories of cultural difference, social unassimilability, or incommensurable strangeness" (*Turkish Turn* 16) and the perception of Turks "as and on ... *the face of things*" (ibid., original emphasis). Second, to stress the significance of historical references from Germany, Adelson focuses on narratives that intervene "in the German national archive" rather than "the Turkish national archive, transnational literatures with an 'accent' ... or even postcolonial difference" (ibid. 12). Her attempts to illustrate the inadequacies of models that only emphasize "self-evident" differences, unassimilabilities, and strangeness then culminates in her elaborate critique of the two-worlds theory of interculturality (ibid. 23–26).

Adelson's critique of interculturality and the efficacy of postcolonial difference requires more detailed comments, to which I shall return. Here I wish to isolate two claims that Adelson makes: 1) "the literature of Turkish migration is not anchored in a politics of identity" and 2) "the cultural effects of Turkish migration to Germany manifest themselves variously in medium-specific ways" (ibid. 20).

These claims stand in sharp contrast to those of Azade Seyhan in *Writing outside the Nation*, a study of "allegorical transfiguration, and inscription of new identities" (20) in Chicano/a and Turkish-German literatures. To this end, Seyhan recontextualizes "social ruptures caused by displacement, migrancy, and exile [that] lead to an impoverishment of communal life and shared cultural histories" (ibid. 15). Her work delimits the imagination of Turkish-German literature by locating the authors and their works not just within Germany but, rather, in a transnational space inhabited by migrant subjectivities. Seyhan's book is a multifaceted comparative examination of cultural assertions of two geographically distanced communities of displacement: one in Germany, the other in the United States. She identifies her project as an "investigation of stories and histories that recuperate losses incurred in migration, dislocation, and translation, those deeply felt signs and markers of our age" (ibid. 4). Locating such signs and markers at "border crossings" of languages and literary traditions, Seyhan ventures to explore in select literary works "expressions of contemporary sociopolitical formations [that] offer critical insights into the manifold meanings of history" (ibid. 5). The novelty and ambition of Seyhan's enterprise can be accredited to her relentless and astute awareness of the visuals and acoustics at the "horizon of language" (ibid. 6), as she lays bare literary imagination that captures "identity, agency, and solidarity" (ibid. 7) in narratives "born of crisis and change, suffering alternatively from amnesia and too much remembering, and precariously positioned at the interstices of different spaces, histories, and languages" (ibid. 4). As Seyhan unsettles multiple layers of memory and forgetting in works of authors such as Rafik Schami, Emine Sevgi Özdamar, and Maxine Hong Kingston, her focus remains on the specifics of "cultural memory" embedded in literary works and retrieved through representation (ibid. 16). The brilliance of Seyhan's project lies in her capability to necessitate and demonstrate the retrievable nature of elements of specific history and cultural memory otherwise embedded in aesthetic expressions of migratory experiences. Her attentiveness to "elliptical recollections of ancestral languages, cross-cultural idioms, and mixed codes" (ibid. 17) facilitates her inquiry of the modes through which a "self-consciously fragmentary memory intimates the virtual existence of a longer collective narrative of a nation, ethnic group, or class" (ibid.).

Seyhan and Adelson differ in their techniques of mobilization of national, cultural, and linguistic frameworks. Seyhan's readings highlight the recuperation of lost tongues and idioms through the migratory experience; Adelson emphasizes the gains that are made when migratory tales signal interventions in the history and culture of the host nation. Seyhan pursues an investigation of difference through "paranational communities and alliances" (ibid. 10); Adelson reveals that literature of Turkish migration is deeply embedded in German history and literary history. And while Seyhan researches "allegorical version[s] of modern Turkish history" (ibid. 20) in "unauthorized biograph[ies] of a nation" (ibid. 150), Adelson argues that the "cultural space in question" (i.e., Germany) "is not always accurately captured by references to the national culture of Turkey" (*Turkish Turn* 25).

Calling for a move beyond paradigms of unassimilability and incommensurability of the Turkish minority in Germany—which she argues that mosaic multiculturalism and interculturalism have influenced and propagated—Adelson situates her readings of literary works in historical referents such as the Holocaust, the Cold War, and the taboo of Armenian genocide. These historical events then become spaces where Turkish and German characters gain referentiality past their "clearly recognizable" social or ethnic milieu. Seyhan does not insist on persistent incommensurability or unassimilability through unchanged referentiality of the Turkish or Asian or Eastern European subject as a literary character. Indeed, her readings of literary texts unravel many a careful consideration of "ambiguities of referentiality" (*Writing* 83). In addition, while arguing for intercultural dialogue as the source for unleashing the "demons of history" (ibid. 4) by illuminating the interstices and interruptions of dialogue in and through the polyvocal registers of the authors she archives, Seyhan conjectures some of the most inspired interrogations of the concept of translatability.

Since multiculturalism, interculturalism, and the category of minority literatures shape and inform the critical alternatives that these scholars offer, some explications in the specific context of Turkish-German literature are in order. I offer these comments in the spirit of refreshing our memories of the political significance of multiculturalism, interculturalism, and minor/minority literatures before we declare all of them obsolete in search of new theoretical paradigms.

First, literary scholarship that aligns itself to political recognition of visible and palpable ethnic, religious, or cultural difference and delineates such difference in registers of multiculturalism and identity politics needs to be debated but cannot be entirely debunked. In *Rethinking Multiculturalism* Bhikhu Parekh defines multiculturalism as "identity and difference . . . embedded in and sustained by culture" (2). It is true that such literary recognition of multiculturalism did limit itself to a mere disembedding of identity and difference lodged in the cultural corpus, thus propagating irreconcilable difference and a disconnected existence of various cultures next to each other, often in armed truces. It is equally true that in the wake of debates on multiculturalism, which echoed in the Anglo-American universities in the 1980s, German literature departments mobilized themselves to undertake reforms in their own curricula. The conference "New Ethnic Minorities in European Culture" at Cornell University (1988) and the publication of a special issue on minority cultures and literature by the journal *New German Critique* (1989) are two significant moments that signal this change. Russell Berman, coeditor of the issue, asserted that Germanistics had hitherto given priority to the "white boys of Weimar" and that it was high time to redesign German Studies in the United States. Azade Seyhan emphasized the need to embark upon a discussion of the "cultural vitality generated by the ethnic presence in West Germany" (Introduction 7) and the necessity of recalling Germanistics in the United States from its self-imposed isolation, thus moving it into a dialogue about multicultural politics with other disciplines. Thus began an ongoing conversation on the impact of immigration on the racial, ethnic, and religious composition of Germany and the valences of minority issues within the context of Germany, as well as on the future of the discipline of German studies in the United States.[15] However, this effort to recognize literatures of and about ethnic minorities in Germany does not limit itself to a mere recognition of minorities in literary works. This is reflected in the Methodological Postscript to the issue, where Jeffery M. Peck admonishes future scholars about the risks of conducting minority studies:

> Any discussion of minority culture or discourse has traditionally assumed a majority against which it is defined. Without making explicit the epistemological dimensions of a subject-object split, such a discussion presupposes a notion of majority grounded in a dubious binary opposition. Unfortunately this positioning often reinforces images of oppressor and the oppressed, or simply proceeds positivistically by amassing an abundance of facts around an "objective" position imagined to be separate from our constitution of it. (Peck 204)

Peck's admonition brings me to my second point. The uncritical transformation of the term *minor* into a demography-oriented term *minority* can be easily identified as one of the reasons for this clear demarcation between majority and minority literature and the celebration of the "authentic" voice of the minority, usually always oppressed by the majority. Discussions on multiculturalism and literature in the American academy in the late 1980s and early 1990s often carry a covert or overt engagement with Gilles Deleuze and Felix Guattari's innovative interpretation of Franz Kafka's writings on minor literature. Deleuze and Guattari define "minor literature" as the work of a minor author in the language of the majority, with three distinct characteristics: "the deterritorialization of language, the connection of an individual to a political immediacy, and the collective assemblage of enunciation" (*Kafka* 18). The authors propose the term *minor literature* for any literature—written outside the sites of power in a given language—that liberates itself from any stagnant projects of uniform, homogenous, national cultures; a literature that is by its very nature deterritorialized. Kafka, almost a synonym for twentieth-century German literature—literate in Czech, Yiddish, and Hebrew, though writing in German in Prague—is reintroduced by Deleuze and Guattari in the light of his linguistically and geographically marginalized beginnings. Deleuze and Guattari draw attention to the deterritorialized nature of the writings of Kafka, an author who emancipated a language from the boundaries of nation-states. They focus primarily on a German writer in Prague but expand the idea of minor literature and offer it as applicable to literature written within any established major literary tradition and suggest that minor literature is always implicated in the political constituencies of an assertion of collectivities. Although the emphasis in Kafka's diary entry from December 11, 1925—on which Deleuze and Guattari base their proposition—was on language and not on ethnicity, the collapse of the idea of minor literature into literature of and by ethnic minorities becomes the norm. Minority literature thus comes to represent a static category that would, perhaps, increase in size with the growing number of contributions from writers of ethnic and religious minorities and yet a body of literature that could never aspire to become part of the national literature of the nation about which it is written, reasserting the notion that national literatures are always monolingual and written by authors who belong to the ethnic majority of a nation.[16] While the political credence attributed to works by authors who belonged to an ethnic or linguistic minority remains undeniable, an uncritical reliance on this term reinstates the idea of these works and authors as always already marginalized, situated at the periphery of a national culture.

Third, while interculturalism as a mode of literary criticism conveys the sense of in-betweenness and—as Adelson demonstrates—views cultures first as insulated units to then imagine a coming together of the two through a *simplified* dialogue, intercultural practices connote an amelioration of tensions between central and peripheral, hegemonic and marginalized cultures. The possibility of transcending the binaries between us and them in order to foster egalitarian exchange between the communities and cultures is at the heart of intercultural dialogue. Bhikhu Parekh asserts this as he points out a number of crucial problems—from female circumcision to Sikhs wearing turbans—as issues that must be considered through the "Logic of Intercultural Evaluation" (*Rethinking Multiculturalism* 264–65). In addition, Seyla Benhabib herself argues for a "complex cultural dialogue" as recourse to "cultural seperatism and balkanization" (*Claims of Culture* 70) or "cultural enclavism" (ibid. 71). The transformation of Hans Georg Gadamer's hermeneutical proposition of *Horizontverschmelzung* (fusion of horizons)—from one between the reader and the object of analysis to one between two different cultures—is, indeed, a debilitating mode of arranging both texts and cultures. I submit to Benhabib's critique of Gadamer, whereby she points out that "a melting together and into one another" may offer "tragic alternatives ... in which opting for one language and pattern of interpretation may require excluding the other" (ibid. 35). Thus, *intercultural* need not persistently mean "an encounter between communitarian traditions taken to replicate what Benhabib decries as the figure of 'seamless wholes,' even if scholars allow for the heterogeneity of a given tradition considered in isolation," as Adelson suggests (*Turkish Turn* 23).[17] Intercultural readings such as those of Seyhan take into consideration the difficulty of such a dialogue precisely because "heterogeneity of culture is not a given, but is predicated on interaction, contestation, and possibly confrontation" (*Writing* 4). Thus intercultural readings need not be necessarily reliant on Gadamer's proposition of *Horizontverschmelzung*. Literary interpretations centered on the optimism of an intercultural dialogue at best imagine the possibility of cross-cultural exchanges through literature. In literary criticism, if indeed the dialogue is simplistically imagined as the one between two cultures that are seamless wholes, transferring traditions through contact and melting into each other, interculturalism would only promote reified views of cultures, binaries between us and them, where the *them* ultimately is co-opted by the *us*. As Seyhan aptly remarks, "Although Gadamer maintains that the desire for understanding originates in the self's experience of its otherness ... and understanding is always the interpretation of the other, the realization of historical understanding takes place in the fusion of familiarity and foreignness. *And this fusion comes very close to consuming the foreign*" (*Writing* 6, my emphasis).

I offer these rejoinders to my juxtaposition of Adelson and Seyhan to remind us of the significance of multicultural, intercultural, or minority studies that today appear to be redundant and obsolete due to the modes in which they stunted their own growth: through the sole focus and reliance on visible difference, through the accentuation of difference alone, or through the resolution of difference through fusion. If debates on Turkish-German literature have centered on questions of inclusion and exclusion, it is due to the combined effect of all three of these modes of thinking; each of them carries the critical burden of tacitly becoming an instrument of exclusion in its efforts to promote inclusion.

However, at the core of Adelson and Seyhan's methodological differences are not just labels of multicultural, intercultural, or minoritarian reading strategies. If these scholars carve new spaces from which newer questions emerge, these questions pertain to historicity, spatiality, locality, translatability, and the manifestations of all of these through fictional representations in multiple national and cultural contexts. These concepts and their contestations do not limit themselves to the field of Turkish-German literature; they pervade discussions on works of fiction that connote difference, whether that difference be marked by the presence of multiple languages, varied skin colors, diverse and divergent histories, nations, or cultures of characters. The task of a (professional) reader of literatures that give contours to difference lies precisely in thinking through the combinations and permutations in which historicity, spatiality, and locality converge and diverge in those works of literature to facilitate or impede translatability. The predicament lies in examining and evaluating how "clearly recognizable" markers of difference are accentuated but also attenuated, defied, or deferred through subtle interruptions and impediments in the narrative. If these complex examinations are to be conducted with any success; indeed, if difference is to be understood not merely as an agency of radical incommensurability and unassimilability but, rather, as a set of democratic markers that promotes what Benhabib identifies as a "complex cultural dialogue," our understanding of ethnic, linguistic, cultural, and national differences will have to be reconsidered but not entirely jettisoned. Taking cue from, but also parting company with, Adelson, other lines of thought need to be followed; drawing upon Seyhan, other spaces need to be marked to demonstrate the distance from both "home and host culture" (*Writing* 10), whereby difference is accounted for not as a self-evident, preeminent, presumptive, and preemptive reference but, rather, as a mode of critical vigilance that necessitates its own surveillance.

A useful strategy to think through difference is offered by Arjun Appadurai in his seminal study, *Modernity at Large* (1996). Reflecting on the schism between the noun *culture* and the adjective *cultural*, Appadurai observes that "much of the problem with the noun form has to do with its implication that culture is some kind of object, thing, or substance, whether physical or metaphysical" (*Modernity* 12). The substantialization of culture, Appadurai argues, aligns it with the idea of race, turning it into a biologism, a kind of "sharing, agreeing and bounding" (ibid.) through which culture appears to "discourage attention to the worldview and agencies of those who are marginalized or dominated" (ibid.). The adjective *cultural*, however, "moves ... into the realm of differences, contrasts, and comparisons" (ibid.). Before expanding further on his distinction between culture and cultural, Appadurai makes a short, but crucial, stop on the word *difference*:

> Although the term *difference* has now taken on a vast set of associations ... its main virtue is that it is a useful heuristic that can highlight points of similarity and contrast between all sorts of categories: classes, genders, roles, groups, and nations. When we therefore point to a practice, a distinction, a conception, an object, or an ideology as having a cultural dimension (notice the adjectival use), we stress the idea of situated difference, that is, difference in relation to something local, embodied, and significant. This point can be summarized in the following form: culture is not usefully regarded as a substance but is better regarded as a dimension of phenomena, a dimension that attends to situated and embodied difference. Stressing the dimensionality of culture rather than its substantiality permits our thinking of culture less as a property of individuals and groups and more as a heuristic device that we can use to talk about difference. (*Modernity* 12f.)

Appadurai's explication thus allows us to construe the limitations of the noun *culture* as a conglomerate of rites, rituals, language, and other forms of shared knowledge into which one is initiated before any other—*ethnos*, or the community of fate, as Benhabib expresses it—and which one inherits due to one's accident of birth. The adjective *cultural* derives its own delimitation from initiation and inheritance. It could, therefore, be mobilized to understand other kinds of initiations, and reinitiations, or iterations. The cultural, when refracted from culture through the prism of difference, absolves us of the obligation to perceive both *culture* and *difference* as always already reified, unchangeable, a priori, given, and necessarily in an adversarial relationship with other cultures (substantiated).[18] This model of the cultural brings it closer to Benhabib's concept of the *demos*—willed, inhabited, naturalizable. Difference itself has to be obviated through its manifestations, for it is less to be *perceived* in its situated substantiality: a particular text allows us to discuss difference not merely because the author or a character's ethnicity, language, gender, or sexuality is different. Difference has to be *pursued* through situational dimensionalities; a particular text allows us to discuss difference because a *dimension*—a feature, a standard, a level of conscience, a coordinate, a magnitude, a reality—has an unsettling impact on our conforming perception of gender, ethnicity, sexuality, language, or nation in which it was thought to be or to have been situated. It is not surprising that Appadurai's distinction serves as an apt precursor to his definition of ethnicity, which also ceases to serve, like race, only as a biologism. Rather than resting his definition of ethnicity in Weber's "primordial idea of kinship" (*Modernity* 14), Appadurai presents it as one that "takes the conscious and imaginative construction and mobilization of differences at its core" (ibid.).

Appadurai's seminal study of "*cultural* dimensions of globalization" (*Modernity* 12, original emphasis) thus highlights, on the one hand, the flexibility of cultural affiliations and, on the other hand, assists us in thinking through ethnic or cultural difference not just as an inheritance but as a practice. When considered along with Benhabib's distinction of *ethnos* and *demos*, Appadurai's discussion further facilitates a novel imagination of the position of the migratory subject: part of a different *ethnos*, politically incorporated into a different *demos*, marked by difference that is not just obvious and substantial but, rather, dimensional and situational. Conjecturing this kind of difference on the intersecting points of nations and cultures means not just locating it in the duality of the two; it signifies the responsibility to conduct a more ambitious enterprise of thinking through the situationality of these differences across, and in reference to, more than the two given and inherited contexts. It requires a refraction of the substantial through the dimensional. Indeed, it calls for a reconsideration of the national through filters of what unsettles and upsets the national. It means a rethinking of the foreign through the native and vice versa. It implies the necessity to reimagine the relationship between the *ethnos* and the *demos* away from simplistic overlaps. For Benhabib, such reimagination in constitutional contexts becomes the harbinger of cosmopolitan federalism; for Appadurai, the dimensionality of cultures of globalization manifests itself in newer forms of cosmopolitanism.

But what is the place of difference in cosmopolitanism? Aren't the terms *difference* and *cosmopolitanism* mutually incompatible? I want to approach these questions by making note of a recent article that highlights the limits of the word *cosmopolitan*. In his article "Diaspora and Nation" (2003), the noted scholar Andreas Huyssen discusses the "troubling affinities" between "memory formations" of a diaspora within a nation (Huyssen 150). I will return to the specifics of Huyssen's reflections on memory in Chapter 2. Here, without meaning to do injustice to his insightful analysis of diasporic memory, I wish to extrapolate Huyssen's astute reflections on the relationship between diaspora and the nation in times of accelerated human mobility.[19] Huyssen explains the traditional understanding of diaspora as a "minority culture within a larger majority culture organized around nation and state" with a "tenuous and often threatened status within the majority culture" (ibid. 149). Commenting on "the changing nature of nationhood and of diaspora under global conditions," Huyssen writes: "If diaspora means loss of a homeland combined with the unfulfilled desire to return, then the shuttling of whole migrant populations between host nation and homeland today may require some new conceptual language" (ibid. 151). At the beginning of Huyssen's article, the word *cosmopolitan* remains beyond the limits of the new conceptual language in thinking about diasporic memory. Arguing against "one global memory" or a "cosmopolitan memory," Huyssen further observes: "International human rights discourses and their legal practices based on universal claims can be characterized as cosmopolitan, but memory discourses remain tied to the specific memories of social groups in time and place" (ibid. 148). It would be unfair to completely dislodge Huyssen's observations from his discussion of memory and the Holocaust, which is central to his argument. However, the limitations of the word *cosmopolitan*—which, as Huyssen reveals, prevent its inclusion in the "new conceptual language" for thinking about contemporary diasporas and minority cultures—are highly instructive. Huyssen does not explicitly criticize cosmopolitanism in his article, but his brief comment serves as an apt point of departure to think through the efficacy of the word *cosmopolitan* for our discussion. Embedded in Huyssen's brief comment are two of the many normative perceptions of cosmopolitanism: attached to the cause of egalitarianism through universalistic order and regulation and at the same time detached, not tied to a group in time and place.

The first implication can be traced back to the idea of perpetual peace through regulation and control. As Stephen Toulmin explains in his book *Cosmopolis*, the Stoics conceived cosmopolitanism as an order that arises out of a commingling of natural and social order through the power of reason (68). Furthermore, while imagining the possibility of adherence of political units to a commonly defined and executed legal order, Kant in his essay "Perpetual Peace" spelled out two kinds of rights: *hospitality*, "the right of a stranger not to be treated with hostility when he arrives at someone else's territory" (105) and the "*right of resort*, for all men [sic] are entitled to present themselves in the society of others by virtue of their right to communal possession of the earth's surface" (ibid. 106, original emphasis). At the core of Kant's propositions for "Perpetual Peace" is an acknowledgement of foreignness and strangeness. This acknowledgement self-necessitates the aspiration to configure modes of multiple affiliations through a perpetual attentiveness to a political worlding of the world beyond local, regional, and national boundaries, without a total effacement of such boundaries. The Cosmopolitan Right (*jus cosmopoliticum*)—the right to hospitality and resort—therefore logically emerges in Kant's essay only after the ethical responsibility—that is, the duty to affiliate and associate with the foreign without the use of aggression—has been amply emphasized in the first section of the essay. Kant inaugurates an imagination of world citizenry that transgresses associations marked *only* by identitarian similitude. The necessity to affiliate with the world beyond native and filiative markers does not bear the noblesse oblige of philanthropy; it is a right, with corresponding duties and responsibilities.[20] Whereas Kant's Universalism purportedly prevaricates cultural difference,[21] contemporary discussions on cosmopolitanism debate the accountability of difference and diversity through filters of immigration and globalization.

The second implication in Huyssen's article, detachment and severance from any particular group, has also accrued centrality in debates on cosmopolitanism in the last decade or so. Kant's essay significantly defines the terms and conditions of these discussions. The idea of an order of attachment to the world as citizens was at the center of Martha Nussbaum's much discussed book *For Love of Country* (1996). Combing the idea of world citizenship from the Stoics to Kant to the Bengali poet Rabindranath Tagore, Nussbaum defined *cosmopolitan* as "the person whose allegiance is to the worldwide community of human beings" (4). Situating the need to rethink cosmopolitanism in an age where globalization insinuated a unification of the world while differences and distinctions remained indispensable, Nussbaum called for empathy and understanding through allegiance to humanity and worldwide citizenship (ibid. 3–17). Nussbaum's view of cosmopolitanism has been sharply criticized, especially by David Hollinger, who calls Nussbaum "the most visible voice to the 'universalist left' of new cosmopolitanism" (Vertovec and Cohen 232). In addition, in his book *Postethnic America*, Hollinger criticizes the term *rooted cosmopolitanism*, stressing that, "As 'citizens of the world,' many of the great cosmopolitans of history have been proudly rootless" (5). Hollinger privileges postethnicity to convey "the critical renewal of cosmopolitanism," rejecting rooted cosmopolitanism as "a label recently adopted by several theorists of diversity whom I take to be moving in the direction I called postethnic" (ibid 5). In his essay "Political Belonging in a World of Multiple Identities" (Vertovec and Cohen 25–31), Stuart Hall identifies the advocacy of a "non-communitarian, post-identity politics of overlapping interest and heterogeneous or hybrid publics" as attributes of recent discussions on cosmopolitanism (ibid. 25). In "The Class Consciousness of Frequent Travellers" (Vertovec and Cohen 86–109), Craig Calhoun discusses "actually existing" cosmopolitanism, critiquing cosmopolitanism as a "discourse centered in the Western view of the World" (ibid. 90), "a third way between rampant corporate globalization and reactionary traditionalism or nationalism" (90) as a reflection of "an elite perspective on the world" (ibid. 91).

The issue of allegiance to the world as a citizen of the world who is equal but also different, connected but also detached, is indeed a challenge without an easy solution. John Tomlinson's insightful study *Globalization and Culture* resonates this challenge. Tomlinson describes globalization as "ever-densening networks of interconnections and interdependeces" (*Globalization* 2), and he probes "the sense in which culture is actually *constitutive* of complex connectivity" (ibid. 22, original emphasis). Toward the end of his examination of cultural implications of socioeconomic globalization defined by connectivity and proximity, Tomlinson attempts to imagine the "Possibility of Cosmopolitanism"—the title of the last chapter of his book—and raises two questions: "How are people even to *think* of themselves as belonging to a global neighborhood? This is the problem I want to explore: what does it mean to have a global identity, to think and act as a 'citizen of the world'—literally as a 'cosmopolitan?'" (ibid. 184, original emphasis). Tomlinson's questions are significant for our discussion for two reasons. On the one hand, they encapsulate and confirm the essential associative vocabulary that escorts the term *cosmopolitan*: world, global, belonging, identity, citizen. On the other, the emphasis on the word *think* and the use of the word *literally* open the possibility of the existence of cosmopolitanism first as a realizable abstraction and next as an inscribable, legible, and decipherable text. The legislative source and the executive force of this idea and its script is what Tomlinson terms a "cosmopolitan disposition" (ibid. 184), a disposition to distance oneself from the local in order to associate with the global. Tomlinson's efforts to unfold this disposition immediately bring him into debate with Ulf Hannerz's problematic demarcation between locals and the cosmopolitans ("Cosmopolitans and Locals" 237). Tomlinson engages with Hannerz's important formulation on cosmopolitanism as a cultural perspective: "a willingness to engage with the Other. It is an intellectual and aesthetic stance of openness toward divergent cultural experiences, a search for contrasts rather than uniformity" (Hannerz, "Cosmopolitans and Locals" 239; Tomlinson, *Globalization* 185).

I read the above-cited quotes of these scholars as equations that explain the torque between abstraction and realization, the tension between the idea and its script that has shaped discussions and debates on cosmopolitanism in the last decade. While Tomlinson succeeds in drawing attention to the constitution of cultural locations in times of global connectedness, Hannerz's provocative dismissal of cosmopolitans as individualists with stronger relationships with the para- and the metalocal necessitates a rigorous evaluation of openness toward divergent cultural experiences and the intellectual and aesthetic stance of practitioners of such openness.

In the specific context of our discussion of migratory contexts, two distinct, albeit mutually reciprocal, sets of questions emerge from this brief recapitulation. The first set relates directly to the investment in and commitment to the locative culture of origins in the specific context of deterritorialization and displacement, indeed the very position and ambition of a literary figure and an author as a local or native informant. Does thinking and acting as a citizen of the world always already jeopardize one's relationship with one's original locations? Does a critical distance acquired from the city or country of birth necessarily demote one's power of intervention in that country of birth? If that is the case, does that distance automatically empower one's intervention in the country of residence as an autonomously recognized and acknowledged equal? If that is not the case, does that intellectual and aesthetic stance toward the world beyond the place of birth, that literal cosmopolitanism, qualitatively compromise an individual's investment in the native as well as the naturalized cultural location?

The second set of questions pertains to the terms and conditions of willingness to engage with the Other and to the idea of openness to divergent cultures. Does engagement with the Other necessarily mean an abnegation of the inherited culture? Is the desire to privilege contrast over conformity while engaging with the Other always preconditioned by the zeal to dominate the Other? And if not, does the openness and willingness to engage with the Other always result in an instant establishment of the Other as the native informant of this or that divergent culture? Does the hospitality offered to the Other also extend to privileges of intervention and argument of the Other? Or in the name of difference, does the Other remain a marginalized guest, a resident with few if any claims over the old local and the new global neighborhood?

These issues penetrate the larger issues of displacement, dislocation, deterritorializations, questions of home, belonging, citizenship, and the right to argue and intervene equally and effectively in cultures of origin and residence in the contemporary contexts of transnational connections. These are questions of per-formance and in-formance that urge consideration through but also outside of the lived realities of migratory experiences. These questions thus resonate with problems that have perturbed discussions on immigrant minorities and their political and aesthetic representation—*Darstellen* and *Vertreten*—under the rubric of multiculturalism over the past two decades. Rey Chow explains these struggles as "an outcome of shifting historical relations of representation" (*Protestant Ethnic* 1), whereby ethnicity emerges as an "observable and hence manageable unit" (ibid. 2). Chow assesses the politics of minority interventions through a reevaluation of alliance with ethnicity as the authoritative source of cultural difference. Chow's argument against a perpetual validation of authenticity of minoritarian self-representation resonates in Spivak's rightful criticism of self-marginalization and self-consolidation of a migrant as a "native informant" (*Critique* 6). These two scholars argue against discursive modes that have reduced and limited the politics and aesthetics of cultural difference to philanthropy of cultural nativism.

The strife among ethnicity, class, and gender overtly and covertly interrupts the naïve optimism often espoused by globalization and multiculturalism. The need to account for such strife and interruptions necessitates reconsideration of purportedly progressive teleologies of multicultural and globalizing discourses and their repercussions on minority politics, as well as minority aesthetics. The accountability of these realities becomes even more crucial when discussing literary works that refuse to elide such realities but exercise restraint in establishing a single political reality as the source of their creative enterprise.

Delimiting the right to acknowledge and practice cultural difference from a benevolent cultural pluralism that ultimately legitimizes native affiliations has, indeed, revealed the need to rethink cosmopolitanism through a politics of representation in terms of cosmopolitics. In his introduction to the anthology *Cosmopolitics: Thinking and Feeling beyond the Nation*, Bruce Robbins elaborates on cosmopolitics as an "effort to describe, from within multiculturalism, a name for the genuine striving toward common norms and mutual translatability that is also part of multiculturalism" (Cheah and Robbins, Introduction I 12). Extending Robbins's argument, Pheng Cheah, in his separate introduction to *Cosmopolitics*, emphasizes the need to "turn our critical focus to the mutating global field of political, economic, and cultural forces in which nationalism and cosmopolitanism are invoked as practical discourses. . . . The *cosmopolitical* is an apposite term for this global force field of the political" (Introduction II 31, original emphasis).

These two foundational statements carry the premise of discussion and debate through a wide range of interdisciplinary explorations of cosmopolitics. Robbins's and Cheah's own contributions echo questions and concerns about cultural difference, its accountability and responsibility. In his essay "Comparative Cosmopolitanisms" (Cheah and Robbins 246–64), Robbins takes issue with the neoconservative allegations of pressure from minority constituencies for curricular recognition in the academy through an inclusion of minority "cultural exhibits" (246). Responding to such allegations, Robbins calls for "shifting criticism's whole sense of intellectual enterprise" (247), for a "new transnationality of intellectual work" (255). Boldly eliminating the possibility of the "optional extension of the canon" (247), Robbins proposes a cosmopolitanism that distances itself from a narrow promotion of cultural particularism.

Pheng Cheah's essay "Given Culture: Rethinking Cosmopolitical Freedom in Transnationalism" (290–328) extends Robbins's argument by locating and testing it in the context of migrants in a (Western) metropolis (300). Cheah questions the validity of migrants as the sole purveyors of cosmopolitanism. In his engagement with Homi Bhabha's hybrid conjectures of culture that touch on the potential of cultural negotiation, Cheah effects a cautionary distinction between migrant metropolitans and "those postcolonials for whom postnationalism through mobility is not an alternative" (302). Moving away from a celebratory stance toward an all-pervasive postcolonial cosmopolitanism that feeds off a constant rejection of the national, Cheah puts the "national-in-the-cosmopolitical" (303) to test. "Cosmopolitical Freedom," therefore, emerges not as a prerogative of the migrant minority and its situationally privileged negotiations of cultural identity; it avails itself of and requires careful rethinking in nonmigrational contexts in non-Western metropolitan locations.

Robbins and Cheah thus provocatively illustrate—to return to Tomlinson's terms—the complexities of connectivity that influentially alter and moderate our normative understanding of new cosmopolitanisms. Instead of reading cosmopolitanism as the harbinger of a postnational, postethnic, postlinguistic (i.e., postcollective) individualism, these scholars relax the very boundaries that simultaneously distill and desediment perceptions of connectivities and proximities. Cosmopolitanism today, as Robbins states, is not just about "the old cosmopolitan ideal of transcending the distinction between strangers and friends" (introduction I 3). In lieu of presenting intellectual investment in the nation as an antithesis to cosmopolitanism, Robbins formulates the "test and invitation offered by cosmopolitics" (ibid. 4) as "less than kin or friendship but a good deal more than polite or innocent nonrelation" (ibid. 3). Cosmopolitics, while remaining attached to universal human rights, thus emerges as located, situated, tied to various different groups and places.

★

"Cosmopolitanism is, to reach a formula, universalism plus difference," writes Kwame Anthony Appiah in his essay, "Cosmopolitan Reading" (202). Appiah reaches this formula by way of a thought-provoking anecdote about a class discussion on race, during which the varied ideas and assumptions about Shakespeare's *The Tempest* unfold. The students identify *The Tempest* as the appropriate text for a discussion of race in Shakespeare, even while Appiah reminds them that the word *race* occurs only once in the play; "it's used by Miranda to refer to Caliban" (ibid. 197). During the course of the discussion, which Appiah briefly reconstructs in his essay, further misgivings present themselves, including one about the Miranda's use of the word *demi-devil* for Caliban (ibid.). The punchline of this anecdote comes in the form of a series of questions put forth by a student: "Excuse me . . . but would you mind telling me, what are we talking about? This play of Shakespeare's, this *Tempest*, what happens in it? Who are Prospero and Miranda and Caliban? Why are they on this island?" (ibid. 198).

Appiah does not use this anecdote to illustrate the alleged ignorance of his students, of their inability to knowledgeably reference a text that was not "required reading" (ibid. 198) for the course. This anecdote becomes a point of departure for Appiah's discussion of the very definition of shared literature (ibid. 199), the parameters of which, he remarks, have dramatically changed since the political discussions about inclusions and exclusions in the canon (201). Because required readings define and dominate conversations about literature and stipulate forms of shared knowledge, the universal familiarity promoted by the hierarchical superiority of texts by Shakespeare or Sterne, Appiah admits, seems more diffused than ever before. However, Appiah's discussion of Shakespeare does not stop at the shared aspects of well-known texts. The difference in contemporary perceptions of difference—registered, among other measures, through changes in syllabi—leads Appiah to think through the normative understanding of cosmopolitanism *as* universalism defined by familiarity with shared knowledge. Instead of reinforcing a cosmopolitanism that utilizes similarity to escape ranking, Appiah draws attention to familiarity with difference.

Appiah's formulation captures the significance of difference in its bearing upon contemporary imagination of cosmopolitanism. The changing definition of that which is shared as a culture of literacy, and our access to fellow readers, can be implicitly or explicitly defined through textuality. While the familiarity invoked by shared textuality creates a universe inhabited by readers, the parameters of readership, the litany, the central texts, must take into account the inherent differences in what shapes and influences that litany. And the definition of the *shared* that brings the fellowship together must account for the unshared, the uncommon, the contested.

While Appiah's formulation prevents cosmopolitanism from being perceived only as an investigation of what is shared, the suspicion of the definition of what is shared in literature comes from Timothy Brennan. In his book *At Home in the World* (1997), Brennan vehemently criticizes what he identifies as cosmopolitan writing (*At Home*, 38). While imitations of "metafictional extravaganzas and the multilingual and multiracial cross-dressing of work from non-European countries" is one feature of cosmopolitan writing (38), "unity and complementarity" as opposed to "cultural dissonance and mutual incomprehensibility" (39) is another. "Assimilationism with dignity" (40), "reinforce and significantly extend already established aesthetic criteria" (40), perception of culture as "literacy, education, and hygiene" (40), salability of politics (41), and last but not least, an expansion of knowledge through the "intermediary" and "ushering-in" role of the third-world writer "critiquing the West" (41) sum up "cosmopolitan writing."

I mention Brennan's sharp criticism of cosmopolitan writing as a reminder that the predicament of cosmopolitan readings is not just to express the claims of the unshared, the uncommon, the contested, as described by Appiah, but also to reveal the contestability of such claims. These include assertions, declarations, and agreements, but also accusations, allegations, disputations, refutations, and contentions. This is what I try to bring forth in my cosmopolitan readings of four novels, three of which directly concern Turkish migration to Germany and the fourth of which engages with Germany in a nonmigratory context. In performing these cosmopolitan readings, my effort is not to merely isolate gestures of multiple attachments, detachments, and reattachments through difference as represented in the novels, but to demonstrate and discuss the difficulties of such gestures. As I embrace Robbins's description of cosmopolitics—"Less than kin or friendship but a good deal more than polite or innocent nonrelation" (Introduction I 3)—I do not consider the authors and characters as "simply" cosmopolitan. Their cosmopolitanism requisites consideration—to borrow from Appadurai again—not substantially as a list of attributes that form the normative understanding of their cosmopolitanism but, rather, dimensionally in relation to the specific geopolitical and cultural locations they inhabit and in which they intervene. As I deliberate upon the authors and their characters' transgression of boundaries, crossing into oft-forbidden territories, stepping across lines, I remain attentive to the multifaceted relationship between *ethnos* and *demos* through which nomenclatures of kin- or friendships are aspired to or acquired. My readings, therefore, highlight the noninnocent, assertive, satirical, interrogative, at times aggressive and at other times downright impolite claims of these authors and their characters. Overcoming "innocent and polite nonrelation," *Cosmopolitical Claims* attempts to circumnavigate the singularly divisive politics of segregation, as well as the total effacement of difference.

This study investigates what Sheldon Pollock, Homi Bhabha, Carol Breckenridge, and Dipesh Chakrabarty have identified as "minoritarian modernity (*as a source for contemporary cosmopolitical thinking*)"(Breckenridge et. al 6, emphasis added). The editorial introduction to their anthology, *Cosmopolitanism*, registers the inadequacy of grouping "refugees, peoples of the diaspora, and migrants and exiles" in "a vocabulary of victimage" that presents them as constituents of "the problem of multiculturalism to which late liberalism extends its generous promise of a pluralist existence" (ibid.). The "well-intentioned" benevolence offered by cultural pluralism, the editors argue, "fails to acknowledge the critique of modernity that minoritarian cosmopolitanisms embody in their historic witness to the twentieth century" (ibid.). *Cosmopolitical Claims* arises out of the parenthetical description of minoritarian modernity as cited above. It thus pursues "ways of . . . being different beings simultaneously, of seeing the larger picture stereoscopically with the smaller" (ibid. 11) and looks for "unanimity in consensual dissensus" (*Cosmopolitanism* 13). More specifically, this book aligns itself with Walter D. Mignolo in a pursuit of "critical cosmopolitanism from the exteriority of modernity" (ibid. 160). In his essay, "The Many Faces of Cosmopolis" (ibid. 157–87), Mignolo explains the necessity of reexamining Kant's cosmopolitanism from the perspective of "the outside that is needed by the inside" (ibid. 160). Mignolo's perspectives on imagining the terms and conditions of inclusion are particularly significant for *Cosmopolitical Claims*:

> Today, silenced and marginalized voices are bringing themselves into the conversation of cosmopolitan projects, rather than waiting to be included. Inclusion is always a reformative project. Bringing them-

selves into the conversation is a transformative project that takes the form of border thinking or border epistemology—that is the alternative to separatism is border thinking, the recognition and transformation of the hegemonic imaginary from the perspectives of people in subaltern positions. Border thinking then becomes a "tool" of the project of critical cosmopolitanism. (*Cosmopolitanism* 174)

However, in aligning myself with Mignolo's proposition of border thinking and border epistemology, I subject the very form of border thinking and border epistemology to critical scrutiny. If mass-migration and international mobility—nonnative, noninherited, inhabited, and naturalized cultures and traditions—pervade our conceptualization of the world today, then the difficulty of conversation and the subaltern position of the perspectives of people who become the source of border thinking necessitate discussion. In the specific contexts of Turkish-German literature, thinking through relationships between residence and immigration, the local and the global, the here and the elsewhere, the national self and the foreign Other requires reconfiguring the position and the ambition of—to borrow from Adelson—the "figure of the Turk." Pushing the discussion beyond debates of inclusion and exclusion of Turks in Germany and Turkish-German literature into German (or Turkish) literature requires revaluation of representational strategies that facilitate or impede our access to such positions and ambitions.

Looking beyond separatism, my readings investigate, along with Seyhan, multiple and simultaneous "paranational alliances" that signal a critical distance from "both the home and the host culture" (*Writing* 10). With Adelson, I try to decode the "cultural fable" initiated and promoted by the rhetorical conceit of "in-betweenness" (*Turkish Turn* 17). However, my pursuit of the means of constituting literary figures in the Turkish-German narrative zooms in on the very constitution of the subaltern perspective through the native informant, whom I present and discuss as the purported epistemological disseminator of migratory experiences, the curious perpetrator and victim of cultural nativism and cultural pluralism, the thought at the center of border thinking, with alliances and allegiances recognizable within and beyond immediate collectivities defined by ethnicity and nationality. My readings of literary works strive to convey the establishment of the native informant as the allegedly reliable and gullible purveyor of minoritarian modernity and border epistemology in order to then destabilize and disrupt that establishment by highlighting the circuitous and complex politics of literary representation. These ideas form the methodological core of this study, wherein I 1) destablize the locationist authenticity of the figure of the Turk, questioning its establishment as the native informant of Turkish traditions or German and European modernity; 2) delimit but not dislodge the Turkish figure and its author from Turkish and German national, ethnic, cultural, and linguistic affiliations; 3) delineate the interventionist claims of multiple affiliations and strategic disaffiliations in the novels as cosmopolitical claims, and most importantly, 4) demarcate and discuss the complexities of literary representations of such claims. I shall provide brief illustrations of these tasks in the context of my literary readings shortly. Here some of the terms that direct my methodological trajectory warrant immediate explication.

Through my use of the term *native informant*, I embrace the arguments of two critics of postcolonial theory: Aijaz Ahmad and Gayatri Chakravorty Spivak. In his essay "Languages of Class, Ideologies of Immigration" (*In Theory* 73–94), Ahmad criticizes the "institutionalized symbiosis between the Western scholar and the local informant ... between the contemporary literary theorist of the West, who typically does not know a non-Western language, and the indigenous translator or essayist, who knows one or two" (ibid. 79). The thrust of his critique is specifically aimed at the context of literary translations from non-Western languages into English and the concept of "Third-World literature." However, Ahmad directs his polemics toward the descriptive denominators of race and ethnicity that have contributed to the conceptualization of categories such as Third-World and Minority, through which the "elite immigrant intelligensia" have privileged "the writings of immigrants ... to be the only *authentic* documents of resistance in our time" (ibid. 91, original emphasis). Ahmad's critique resonates in another provocative statement that Spivak offers in *A Critique of Postcolonial Reason*. Beyond her larger project of thinking through the foreclosure of the "native informant,"[22] Spivak comments, "an unquestioning privilege of the migrant may also turn out to be a figure of the effacement of the native informant" (*Critique* 18). Spivak's admonition against the "self-marginalizing postcolonial masquerading as a native informant" (ibid. 6) is situated in the polarized evaluation of cultural affiliations, which she decries as the "Scylla of cultural relativism and Charybdis of nativist culturalism" (ibid.).

Both Ahmad and Spivak point toward the complicity of the metropolitan intellectual in establishing the migrant as the native informant. Not a mere admittance of this complicity, however, but a persistent engagement with it shall unfold the political claims at stake. Questioning the counter-canonical significance of Turkish-German or minority literature will not occur without questioning the establishment of the Turkish figure itself as the representative figure of all Turks in Germany: traditional and modern, discriminated and isolated, token of cultural diversity, the most reliant and competent observer of contemporary German history and literary history, the interpellator of knowledge for Turkish issues and politics in Germany and in Turkey, the glorified figure between the East and the West, the assumed, stylized, and self-styled purveyor of cultural difference. The same argument holds currency for the term *subaltern*. As I explain in Chapter 1, I borrow this term from subaltern studies as a useful descriptor that stresses urgent considerations of subjectivity and ideology refracted through differences of class, gender, and in the case of the novel, nationality and ethnicity in narrative representation.

With my engagement with the terms *subaltern* and *native informant*, I am neither suggesting the easy availability of an analogy that defines the relationship between Turks and Germans as postcolonial subjects in the colonialist metropolis, nor am I establishing a colonial relationship between Turkey and Germany in retrospect.[23] The lack of an immediate colonial relationship between Germany and Turkey, Germany's sparse presence as a colonial power in Asia and Africa in the nineteenth century, the repercussions of this in the German cultural space in the second half of the twentieth century, and most importantly, the political realities of German colonialism in the nineteenth century cannot be easily dismissed.[24] In other words, research on Europe-wide repercussions of the special kind of redistribution of labor through mass-migration of people from Asia and Africa after the Second World War deserves recognition. The division of labor in the moment of postcolonialism was historically very differently defined for Britain and France than for Germany. Due to the absence of an immediate colonial relationship between Germany and Turkey, writings of Turkish immigrant authors in Germany have carried their own specific marks that distinguish them from their counterparts in France or Great Britain. A conflation of authors of non-German heritages in Germany with immigrant authors from ex-colonies in England and France merits criticism. However, postcolonial theory's critical investment in demonstrating the epistemological imbalance in European representations of non-European subjects or immigrant minorities deserves sincere engagement.

To sum up, in its attempt to discuss "minoritarian modernity (as a source for contemporary cosmopolitical thinking)" (Breckenridge et. al 6), this study explores claims of difference that the Turkish figure registers as a problematic of his or her representation as a foreigner, ethnic minority, native informant, hybrid, and subaltern. This study reveals the modes in which the Turk ruptures and disturbs normative perceptions of the politics of identity: ethnic, linguistic, and political (migrant/citizen/resident). The complexities of relationship between the *ethnos* and the *demos*, dimensionality of difference, connectivities and proximities, noninnocent relationship between citizens and immigrants/residents, and multiple affiliations and disaffiliations are at the core of my imagination of cosmopolitics. In the literary representations of cosmopolitcs, this study focuses on interrogating and unsettling the ascription of subalternity to border epistemology.

To this end, I first analyze three novels that directly address issues of Turkish migrants in Germany: Sten Nadolny's *Selim oder die Gabe der Rede* (Selim or the Gift of Speech), Emine Sevgi Özdamar's *Seltsame Sterne Starren zur Erde* (Strange Stars Stare toward the Earth), and Feridun Zaimoğlu's *Abschaum: Die wahre Geschichte von Ertan Ongun* (Scum: The True Story of Ertan Ongun). I then shift the focus from Germany to Turkey. With my reading of Orhan Pamuk's *Yeni Hayat* (The New Life), I examine registers of cosmopolitics in a nonmigratory context.

The first chapter centralizes subalternity as part of the difficulty of conversation that I mentioned in my discussion of Mignolo's essay. My reading of Nadolny's *Selim* focuses on understanding the struggle between the represener and the represented—the narrator, Alexander, and Selim, the subject of his narration as a substructure of an emerging recognition of the two as integral parts of the same polity. As I engage with Nadolny's narrator's struggle with writing about a guest worker, I explore Spivak's question "Can the Subaltern Speak?" alongside Derrida's "question of the foreigner" in his essay "Of Hospitality." In addition, I discuss Homi Bhabha's invocation of the Turkish guest worker in his essay "DissemiNation." In order to understand the modes in which the narrator acknowledges his incapability to write and represent, I introduce the term *narraphasia*, a kind of narrative aphasia, whereby the narrative is interspersed with the narrator's self-interrogation.

The second chapter presents the political claims of memory. Through my discussion of Özdamar's *Seltsame Sterne* in the second chapter, I investigate the narrator's documentation of a brief period in the cultural history of the GDR in an autobiographical novel. I explore how the cultural legacy of the former East Germany is rehearsed by an aspiring actress who carries with her specific burdens of Turkish history's totalitarian moments from the early 1970s. By prefacing my discussion of the novel with Gayatri Chakravorty Spivak's essay "Acting Bits/Identity Talk," I try to understand

Spivak's expression "slouching of history" in origins. Through an engagement with Dipesh Chakrabarty's essay "Minority Histories, Subaltern Pasts" alongside Andreas Huyssen's "Diaspora and Nation," I attempt to comprehend the narrator's leading the reader to certain subordinated pasts through a combination of recuperation and *recherché*.

Hybridity and its cryptic claims to authenticity are central to the third chapter. I contextualize Zaimoğlu's reception as a model minority in the German print media in order to interrogate the tense descriptions of a conforming, assimilating minority, from which Zaimoğlu purportedly emancipates himself as a practitioner of cultural hybridity. With a discussion of Pheng Cheah's critique of hybridity in his essay "Given Culture" parallel to Rey Chow's concept of self-referentiality, this chapter explains the purloining of ethnicity in hybrid narratives and the consequent disingenuousness of an incessant valorization of the hybrid subject as the authentic native informant.

I end my consideration of literary texts with a discussion on the Turkish writer Orhan Pamuk. This chapter discusses Homi Bhabha's conception of the pedagogical and the perfomative in "DissemiNation" alongside Pheng Cheah's critique of Homi Bhabha in "Given Culture." I present Pamuk's *The New Life*—a Turkish road-novel inspired by an aphorism from the German Romantic author Novalis—to discuss literary exchanges that occur outside of migratory contexts. I pursue the novel's challenge to reflect on the banality of debates on the Western origins of the novel, on indigenous forms of expression, and on the contestations of national identities. I juxtapose the novel with an essay by the renowned Turkish social thinker and Atatürk's confidante, Ziya Gökalp, in order to centralize the unsettling of allegiance to a nation and its national culture.

In my afterword, "Minorities, Literatures, and Recursive Leaps of Faith," I discuss the critical agenda of this book in conjunction with the current political and theoretical issues that seem to mar the project of multiculturalism. Through a juxtaposition of the Pakistani poet Faiz Ahmad Faiz with Jacques Derrida, this afterword provides concluding statements on the discursive significance of cosmopolitanism in rethinking questions of hospitality and tolerance within and outside of literary studies. In addition, it presents my own intellectual and personal itinerary in envisaging, conceptualizing, and materializing this project.

In "Explanation and Culture: Marginalia" (*Other Worlds* 103–18), Gayatri Chakravorty Spivak comments, "The only way I can hope to suggest how the center itself is marginal is by not remaining outside in the margin and pointing my accusing finger at the center. I might do it rather by implicating myself in that center and sensing what politics makes it marginal" (107). This idea is at the core of this book. The essence of a national collective cannot be determined by a familiarity that is a function only of the lineage, ethnicity, or nationality of authors. The significance of physical and virtual migrations and new inhabitations needs to be accounted for in order to provide analytical specificity and argumentative clarity to cultural difference. A sustained vigilance for the adjectives *national*, *multicultural*, and *cosmopolitan* therefore accompanies my endeavors to detach literary criticism from an uncritical engagement with the ethnicity of authors or their minority or immigration status within a nation or a national literary tradition. This book aspires to highlight the interruptions, discontinuities, and differences that accompany—to borrow from Mignolo again—cosmopolitan conversations and border epistemology. It is in those discontinuous, indefinite, different, and self-interrogating moments of German and Turkish national literatures, in the sutures that connect and at times threaten to disconnect the majority/national and the minority/peripheral, I argue, that literature by and about itinerants in Germany and Turkey makes its spatial claims. By focusing on novels, I want to investigate how the novel itself is transformed from its role as the cornerstone of the edifice of the nation in the nineteenth and early twentieth centuries to that of the scaffolding that holds and supports this national edifice during reconstruction and remodeling in the late twentieth and early twenty-first centuries.

While exploring the aesthetic modes in which the Turkish figure does not just represent an easy insertion into the national or the multicultural imagination, but simultaneously enjoys and struggles with the multitude of associations and dissociations, affiliations and disaffiliations, attachments and detachments, this book benefits from the critical agenda of two recent studies: Amanda Anderson's *The Powers of Distance* and Rebecca Walkowitz's *Cosmopolitan Style*. Anderson defines detachment as "a set of practices of the self" (7) in order to examine the "dialectic between detachment and engagement, between a cultivated distance and newly reformed partiality" (ibid. 6) in the context of Victorian authors from George Eliot to Oscar Wilde. "Irony, performance, and negative freedom" thus become "favored forms of detachment" (ibid. 27). Walkowitz embarks upon her investigation with Oscar Wilde, placing him on the same bookshelf as Joseph Conrad, Virginia Woolf, Salman Rushdie, and W. G. Sebald. "Naturalness, triviality, evasion, treason, mix-up and vertigo" (32) are elements of "cosmopolitan style" that Walkowitz identifies in her study.

Although the novels I have chosen for examination differ from those of Anderson and Walkowitz, these scholars offer cosmopolitanism as a disposition and as an intellectual practice in order to then configure the referential quotient of cosmopolitan thinking in literary works. However, their formulations inform my imagination of Turkish-German literature. Along with Robbins and Cheah, I suggest that this literature is best understood as a literature of stepping across lines, across—not just beyond—encodings of ethnicity, as a literary practice that strives for comprehensibility and translatability within and beyond the German and Turkish nations. In this striving to render the incommensurable commensurable, along with Anderson and Walkowitz I contend that its practitioners (the authors) simultaneously attach themselves to and detach themselves from both the nation and their ethnicities and, thus, transform themselves. This simultaneous attachment and detachment, affiliation and disaffiliation, the transformation of works and authors, of conceptualizations of allegiances to nations and national literature define the agency of the text and become the reference and register of *Cosmopolitical Claims*. The hyphenated term *Turkish-German* thus transcends the mere invocation of biculturalism or dual-citizenship. It is in the distance between one adjective and the other that the embedded existence of the two in the national/ethnic vocabulary, and yet the yearning to overcome this embedded existence, becomes clear. The purpose of this book is, therefore, not to offer *cosmopolitan* or *cosmopolitical* as another adjective to describe Turkish-German literature. The cosmopolitical readings of texts that I propose imply a complete negation neither of cultural/ ethnic/gendered/national identities nor of the frontiers of cultural difference. However, my readings refrain from seeking identitarian repair through mere assertion of cultural difference at the frontiers. The novels that I examine in this book are laden with frontiers; the authors transform themselves with these frontiers, sometimes through another word, at other times through another world. In the novels that I have selected for discussion, narrative aphasia, distanced and partially engaged registers of memory, convoluted conjectures of hybridity, and concomitant allusions to multiple literary traditions shape and inform the aesthetics of *Cosmopolitical Claims*.

At the beginning of this introduction, I presented the yearning of three immigrant authors to step across confinements of language, ethnicity, and nationality in order to insert themselves into the larger social and cultural text of Europe. After the long walk through the imagination of Germany as a European nation, the tensions between *demos* and *ethnos* that determine political entitlement, the dialectics of exclusion through multicultural/intercultural readings of texts, and the establishment of the immigrant as the local/native informant, I have tried to highlight the need for new modes of reading literature. Throughout this exercise, the reader must have noticed my own use of national and ethnic qualifiers to describe authors, scholars, and literary works. I attribute this to an unsurpassable inescapability imposed by these terms. I acknowledge this inescapability because its critical cognition is important in order to overcome the limits these terms impose. The recognition of preexisting appellations of boundaries as such is essential. Reading itself is a crossing over of a threshold, of a line, a passing through a door. This crossing over by invitation is dependent on the hospitality extended to the guest by the host. Hospitality alone indeed gives rise to familiarity, a requisite for mutual understanding between guests and hosts, immigrants and residents, peoples of different ethnic, religious, and national backgrounds. If the word *Gastarbeiter* can teach us something, it is precisely this relationship between guests and hosts.

As I invite my readers to enter this book, the literary works of my study become at times blurred, and at other times double-visioned, eyewitness accounts of the effects of multiculturalism and globalization on the cultural texts of the late twentieth and early twenty-first centuries. Some of these accounts are mutually contradictory, and that is precisely how they help us understand their difference and multiplicity. An understanding of their *cosmopolitical claims* comes with the cognition that legends of multiculturalism do not necessarily espouse a joyous, hybrid closure. In fact, they always incarnate an element of turbulence caused by exclusion. In laying bare this turbulence, I hold on to the optimism that it should not necessarily sanction the death of tolerance. The epidemic of contempt, caused by estrangement, can only be eradicated by breeding familiarity within today's globally connected communities.

These thoughts underlie my curiosity to think through the position and ambition of literary works in a world that is still struggling with frontiers, even as it likes to pretend that there are fewer frontiers than ever before. The imagination of the world for the past decade has been one where the global flow of capital, technology, and dominant electronic media have shrunk the gaps between communities and cultures. For *New York Times* columnist Thomas L. Friedman, one of the most significant manifestations of globalization is the moment when "The Berlin Wall came down, the Berlin Mall opened up, and suddenly some 3 billion people . . . walked on to the flattened global piazza" (*World Is Flat* 182). At first go, this line seems to indicate the beginning of the opening up of all borders and boundaries: the focus of Friedman's study is, after all, the leveling of the world, the flattening of the global piazza as it were, through the accelerated pace of technological exchange that brings the world together. However, the book ends with a curious analysis of post-9/11 Islamic resurgence, unwillingly, if half-consciously, positing a contradiction. On the one hand, the vigor of Eastern capitalism is presented as an ersatz to the late-capitalist technological fatigue of the West; on the other hand, the rise of religious fundamentalism is reinforced in the social fabric of the East. The great hope of capitalist egalitarianism and meritocracy inaugurated by the fall of the Berlin Wall seems to dissipate very quickly in the specific contexts of cultural differences that also exist in the same world. Instead of celebrating the bangs and thuds that accompanied the fall of the Berlin Wall, in search of a polyglot clamor that echoes through the global piazza I turn now to literature. Whether or not literature flattens the globe is for us to decide.

ONE

Thus Spake the *Gastarbeiter*
Sten Nadolny's *Selim oder die Gabe der Rede*

*I was always able to speak, when I spoke about Selim.
While writing it turned out: he was a phantom.
I had conceived of him more than I had understood him.
That does not disturb me. The fallacy was probably
better than the reality.*

Who should read it? Selim! Selim should read it.
STEN NADOLNY, SELIM

In his volume *Of Hospitality*, Jacques Derrida contemplates the "Foreigner Question." At the very outset, he asks if "the question of the foreigner" is not indeed "a foreigner's question? Coming from the foreigner, from Abroad?" (3). He shifts the accent of his interrogation: "*the* question of the foreigner" becomes for Derrida "a question *of* the foreigner, addressed *to* the foreigner" (ibid. 3). While registering the presence of foreigners in Plato's *Sophist*, Derrida reminds us that it is the foreigner, indeed, who asks the first question (ibid. 5). The arrival of the foreigner signals the birth of the question. "The Foreigner carries and puts the fearful question," Derrida asserts, "he sees or foresees himself" (ibid. 11). As he moves from the *Sophist* to the *Statesmen* to *The Apology of Socrates*, Derrida elaborates upon Socrates' enactment of a foreigner in front of the Athenians: "a foreigner accused in a language he says he does not speak, a defendant required to justify himself, in the language of the other" (ibid. 17). Derrida underlines the notion of "the foreigner (*hostis*) welcomed as a guest or as enemy" (ibid. 45). The question of the foreigner is thus established as the question of hospitality and hostility, of acceptance and accusation, of judgments and justifications. Derrida complicates the distinction between guests and hosts, arguing that the question *of* the foreigner *as* a foreigner's question emerges from the interstices of equations of guest and host, enemy and friend. In the naming of the foreigner, calling him or her *xenos, hostis,* or *l'étranger,* the polis defines itself, and the foreigner defines the polis by way of presenting his question. The foreigner acknowledges the assignment of being a foreigner simultaneous to offering the polis a predicament of willingness to engage with the foreigner. The foreigner is willing to defend himself in a language that is not his own, as the interpretative polarities of guest, host, enemy, and friend seek signification through enunciation. The foreigner empowers himself through enunciation and interrogation in the language of the polis where he is a guest. Derrida's reflections on the fragile relationship between the citizen and the foreigner mark two distinct possibilities, one more obvious than the other. The bidirectionality of the question, the necessary exchange between the host and the guest, provides political credence to the foreigner: the foreigner might not initially be perceived as a juridical or epistemological equal of the host, and yet he emerges as a subject of the polity. In addition, the foreigner presses the question of his epistemological and juridical equivalence by enunciating his question in the language of the host; the guest transforms his culpability as a foreigner into a capability.

Derrida's reflections unsettle the ontological stability that might be accrued to the foreigner—for there isn't a clear trajectory one can follow from an inferiorized, disempowered status of the foreigner to an empowered emergence of the foreigner as a subject of the polity. The possibilities that I list above remain as such; the questions of the foreigner are not necessarily answered. The enactment of foreignness by speaking the language of the host does not instantly provide clues to his acceptance. The foreigner emerges neither as a captive of his foreignness nor as an entirely emancipated and, therefore, equitable subject of the polity.

I inaugurate my discussion of representation of a Turkish guest worker in a German novel with Derrida's "Foreigner Question," not to reenact the long march from captivity to emancipation, from disempowerment to empowerment of a foreigner through a narrative. Derrida's reflections underline issues of acceptance and accusation, judgments and justifications, epistemological and juridical inequities, culpability and capability, and most importantly, silence and enunciation that infiltrate and accompany invocations and associations of the very word *Gastarbeiter*—a guest, whose primal familiarity to the German nation is through the justification of his existence as a laborer, but whose familiarity as a guest is at once belabored by foreignness, *Fremdheit*. The guest must labor to learn the language of the host to make himself be known, to present his question. The host claims benefits of the labor of the guest; the guest claims the hospitality of the host—hostility and hospitability, allowance and restriction simultaneously defining their mutual relationship.

It is helpful to consider this restrictive entitlement to the political imagination of or participation in a nation with Benedict Anderson's elaboration on "seriality." In his insightful essay "Nationalism, Identity, and the World-In-Motion: On the Logics of Seriality" (Cheah and Robbins 117–33), Anderson theorizes the formation of collective subjectivities through a distinction between "unbound" and "bound" serialities. He locates unbound serialities in the print market and identifies "nationalists, anarchists, bureaucrats, and workers" as its exemplifiers. Bound seriality originates in governmentality, and its confined and restricting character is exemplified in the finitude of terms like "Asian Americans, *beurs*, and Tutsis" (ibid. 117). It is through the contrast between these two kinds of serialities, Anderson claims, that the "lineaments of two kinds of politicization and political practice emerge, both of which, however, show how basic seriality always is to the modern imagining of collectivity" (ibid. 127). Anderson argues that the politics of entitlement in a nation are a function of a bound seriality generated by practices of state-sponsored numeration (e.g., census), whereas through the unenumerated, unbound seriality, the otherwise unentitled members of a collective stake their claims within and beyond the national imaginary. This distinction serves as a pointer and a framework for the following discussion of *Gastarbeiter*, Turks, and other foreigners in the German press since their first arrival. Although the official governmental designations for foreigners, that is, bound seriality in the Andersonian sense, will be mentioned only as they appear in the press, my focus on the unenumerated and politically unentitled foreigners should highlight the lineaments that separate national collectivities of citizenry from their noncitizen Others.

As is well known, during the formative years of the establishment of the German nation-state, in order to realize Adenauer's vision of the *Wirtschaftswunder* (economic miracle), the Federal Republic of Germany signed *Anwerbeabkommen* (recruitment agreements) with Italy (1955), Spain and Greece (1960), and Turkey (1963). As Anna Picardi-Montesardo points out, Germany's historical peculiarity with respect to foreign workers played a central role in the coinage of the term *Gastarbeiter*. During the industrialization of Germany in the late nineteenth century, *Wanderarbeiter* (moving, or migrant, workers) recruited from various eastern (and some southern) European countries worked in Germany. Around 1907, about 125,000 *Wanderarbeiter* were employed in German factories—including Turkish workers, who were primarily employed in the tobacco industry. Between 1939 and 1945, 7.5 million foreign workers from the German-occupied territories in France, Poland, Czechoslovakia, and the Soviet Union, among others, were forced to work in Germany as replacements for workers who were fighting for the Nazi army. These workers were known as *Fremdarbeiter* (foreign workers). This was the primary reason why the term *Fremdarbeiter* could not be used again in the post-War era without invoking historical guilt. So a safer term, *Gastarbeiter*, was introduced, not only to imply that these workers would not be treated as the *Fremdarbeiter* in Nazi Germany but also to indicate that their stay in Germany would be temporary.[1] In other words, the *Gastarbeiter* were expected to return to their homelands once Germany decided that they were no longer needed. The guests were expected not to overstay their invitation, but the length of the invitation was rendered ambiguous through the distribution of renewable work permits.

The first frontiers of division between us and them in German society started with the undetermined and yet renewable length of the invitation extended to the *Gastarbeiter*. These workers came from a Europe that was very different than Germany. The cultural peculiarity and linguistic incomprehensibility of the *Gastarbeiter*, their darker skins, the preexisting and prevalent notions of subjugation through headscarves for women and sexual promiscuity, dishonesty, and slyness of men—in short, German society's unfamiliarity with these workers—slowly led to anxieties about the safety and stability of Germany's national culture.

It is important to remember that a number of initial reports on *Gastarbeiter* in the German press were not entirely negative. National and regional newspapers tried to educate readers about the newcomers in Germany. In 1964, the Düsseldorf-based conservative newspaper *Die Rheinische Post* conducted a survey among its readers, "Wie stehen Sie zu den Gastarbeitern?" (How do you perceive the guest workers?). In the results published in November 1964, the newspaper had the following to report: "Most of the answers to our question, 'How do you perceive the *Gastarbeiter*?' appear to be explicitly positive. Clichéd conceptions—unclean, loud, women-chasers, knife-heros—were repeatedly questioned. [The readers] enthusiastically pleaded that the *Gastarbeiter* should not be considered and treated as second-class human beings" (Jung et al. 54). Other newspapers followed suit. From the Hamburg-based *Die Welt* to the Munich daily *Süddeutsche Zeitung*, press coverage in the 1960s focused on the necessity of *Gastarbeiter* in the economic and industrial reconstruction of Germany. Leading newspapers also reported on the wretched conditions in which the *Gastarbeiter* lived and worked. *Die Zeit*, for example, stated in an editorial in May 1965, "they voluntarily take up all difficult and dirty jobs which must be done, but for which there is no one to find among us" (op cit.).

This positive, affirmative, and tolerant discourse underwent a change around 1967–68, as Germany felt the first waves of an economic crisis since the end of the Second World War. As a result of the worldwide oil crisis, Germany declared an *Anwerbestopp* (recruitment freeze) in 1973. The word *Gastarbeiter* immediately became compounded with other nouns and appeared in the news media as *Gastarbeiterproblem*, *Gastarbeiterwelle* (wave), and *Gastarbeiterlawine* (avalanche), all referring to the alleged overpopulation of guest workers in Germany. The late 1960s and the early 1970s were precisely the years when a debate about integration and assimilation of Islamic guest workers in the primarily Protestant German society gained currency. Cultural difference, which until 1966 was championed by newspapers as a factor to be reckoned with, turned into a moral issue. In the 1970s, the religious difference of Turks from the Germans was not merely recognized and acknowledged; it was debated, contested, and presented as a force threatening the very fiber of German society. The Federal Republic seemed divided on the idea of integration, although the social isolation of guest workers and visible racial discrimination did not go unnoticed.

As a means to curb this growing distance between Germans and Turks, cities with a long history of industrial working classes like Berlin, Hamburg, Bielefeld, and Essen took steps to promote the integration of guest workers and their families into German society through special language classes in schools or through the support of social initiatives by the *Ausländerbeauftragte* (foreign directorates). Some states, such as Bavaria, condemned these initiatives, even actively resisted them. In December 1979, Hans Maier, the cultural minister of Bavaria, denigrated the initiatives of the city administration of Berlin by calling them *Zwangsgermanisierung* (forced Germanization). This accusation created a wave of articles in all major national newspapers, including the *FAZ*, the *Frankfurter Rundschau*, and the newsmagazine *Der Spiegel*. Participants in the debate were against any kind of forced Germanization or even the use of the term, but the importance of linguistic training and inclusion of children of the *Gastarbeiter* in German schools was recognized by most of the media. This style of negative reporting continued all the way up to 1982, when on October 13, 1982, Chancellor Helmut Kohl declared his plans to reduce the number of guest workers in Germany during his tenure.[2]

These debates culminated in the passage of the *Ausländerintegrationsgesetz* (bill for the integration of foreigners) in 1988. The bill included an elaborate social and financial plan for the betterment of guest workers and their children. However, this development did not come without its critics. The former Chancellor Helmut Schmidt wrote in *Die Zeit*, "We Europeans together are strongly marked by a culture emanating from the lands of Judeo-Christian traditions; the Turks as a largely Islamic nation belong to a completely different cultural sphere, which has its home in Asia and Africa, but not in Europe" (Schmidt 7).

After the reunification of Germany in 1990, economic disparity and unemployment turned the Turks into the latest scapegoats in the history of blaming the cultural Other for a society's shortcomings. In the early 1990s, right after German unification, the burning of two hostels in Mölln and Sollingen with a majority of Turkish residents by Neo-Nazis was a manifestation of a brewing sentiment against the Turks. Udo Steinbach, director of Deutsche Welle, the radio and television channel, expressed his reaction quite succinctly:

> The migration of Turks into Germany, which created a physical nearness, one that had not existed in the past, should be seen as a catalyst of a process of segregation, which has largely accelerated since the beginning of the 90s. The good comrade "far away" has over the time become an exotic entity, soon enough a troublemaker. Recruitment freeze, complaints that the Turk is very difficult to integrate, visa requirements, and last of all even residence permits for Turkish children born in Germany—these are just a few stations of segregation—so to speak at the lower levels of the society. (Steinbach 35–36)

Steinbach's statement came in the wake of the 1993 immolations, but as early as the 1960s, artists and authors had been reacting against discrimination against foreigners, against the finitude of the *Gastarbeiter*'s entitlement to belong in the country of residence. Max Frisch was one of the first authors to register such a reaction. As resistance to guest workers became visible through the political and social rhetoric in Germany in the 1960s, a parallel outcry was heard in another German-speaking country, Switzerland, with an admittedly multilingual, multiethnic, and multireligious composition. The first uproar against the growing number of foreigners (Italians) was registered in the early to mid-1960s through the term *Überfremdung* (overforeignization), the topic of the annual conference of the Vereinigung der Kantonalen Fremdenpolizei (Association of Districts of Immigration Police) in 1965. In his sharp reaction, Frisch urged the Swiss to refocus on the plurality of their nation. His speech offers a stringent critique of the word *Gastarbeiter*: "Guest workers or foreign workers? I am for the latter: they are not guests, whom one serves, in order to earn from them, they work in a foreign land, because they cannot amount to anything in their own country" (Frisch 100). Frisch's perspective on the word *Gastarbeiter* cannot be read as an articulation of mere verbal unease; he highlights a crucial dichotomy in his differentiation of the two terms. It is impossible to read the quote above without noticing the presence of the verbs *bedienen* (to serve) and *verdienen* (to earn, deserve—here: "*an ihnen zu verdienen*," to make money off of), both of which are also related to the German noun *Dienst* (service). Furthermore, through another pithy and now oft-cited formulation in his speech, Frisch addresses the neglect of the human aspect of *Gast/Fremdarbeiter* and criticizes the prevalent image of immigrant workers as mere tools and machines used to construct buildings, wash dishes, and clean toilets: "man hat Arbeitskräfte gerufen, es kamen Menschen" (ibid. 100).[3] The following words of Yüksel Pazarkaya, one of the pioneers of *Gastarbeiterliteratur*, resonate Frisch's sentiment: "The Turks . . . came to the offered jobs in Germany; in no way did they come as only workforce. They came: on their feet the dirt of the Anatolian earth, on their bodies the collarless Anatolian shirt, the Anatolian hat on their heads, in their hands or in the pockets of their jackets the rosary, in the wooden baggage or in a bag white beans, wheat, rose-water and a bottle of Rakı" (Pazarkaya, "Stimmen" 16).

Frisch and Pazarkaya comment respectively on two different groups of guest workers: Italians in Switzerland and Turks in Germany. In these descriptions by Frisch and Pazarkaya lie many a story of a nascent stage of economic globalization in Europe after the Second World War—stories that do not limit themselves to middle- and upper-class professionals, intellectuals, and businessmen for whom movement between countries and across borders is a privileged choice. One of the lead actors in the drama of globalization in the twentieth century is the immigrant laborer at the assembly line in a factory, in a fruit-orchard, at the kitchen sink, or in the bathroom, who—as Pazarkaya reconstructs—carries a portion of his or her rural past from the country of birth to the metropolitan present in the country of residence.

Indeed, in German literature the hardships of these journeys and the tensions between a rural past and a metropolitan present were first recorded by Turkish, Italian, Syrian, and Greek authors. Italian guest workers began to arrive in Germany as early as 1955 and were the first to publish their experiences in Germany in newsletters toward the end of the 1960s.[4] While the guest worker as a literary character claims centrality in a body of literature that came to be known as *Gastarbeiterliteratur*, marginality through sporadic visibility and limited mobilizing power over the narrative mark his presence in works by authors of German ethnic heritage: Heinrich Böll's *Gruppenbild mit Dame*, Rainer W. Fassbinder's film *Katzelmacher*, and Botho Strauß's *Rumor* being just a few examples. Sten Nadolny's novel *Selim oder die Gabe der Rede* stands out for many reasons. In writing *Selim*, Nadolny had come a long way from his first novel, *Netzkarte*, which detailed train journeys through West Germany—by way of his second novel, *Die Entdeckung der Langsamkeit*, about the travels of John Franklin, the English researcher of the geographical poles—to recount the journeys of a Turkish guest worker, Selim, and his "gift of the speech"[5] as narrated by Alexander, a young German student.

With the friendship between Selim and Alexander at its center, the novel encompasses accounts of lives of a diverse group of people: a Swiss nun, an experimental filmmaker, a young Turkish woman activist, and numerous Turkish guest workers, crossing paths with shorter and longer engagements with each other against the backdrop of the political events of Germany from the early 1960s to the late 1980s. Nadolny's *Selim* is exceptional because it raises the question of the guest/foreigner as central to the host-citizen. Through the narrator Alexander's constant reflections on the struggle to narrate the questions and claims of the foreigner, the novel is replete with cryptic struggles of subjectivity, ideology, and epistemic privilege that simultaneously facilitate and impede the narrator's access to the subject of his narration, his friend Selim, a Turkish guest worker. Apart from Selim, other guest workers in the novel emerge not merely as tokens of ethnic diversity at the periphery of German society; their role is not limited to that of recipients of a labor migration process who stay at the sidelines of Konrad Adenauer's "Economic Miracle." Rather, they are participants vital to Germany's political realities after the Second World War. Simply stated, the guest workers register their presence in Nadolny's novel as characters conscious of their roles as strangers, guests, workers, friends, as purported cultural enemies, as both hospitable and hostile entities, central to but also marginalized in German society.[6]

Selim has been much written about and discussed since its publication in 1990. *Selim* won almost instant adulation from major German newspapers; critics received it as a significant intervention in the minority by a member of the majority.[7] The intervention is conscious and consistent in *Selim*; the narrative is interspersed with vignettes: diary-entries of the protagonist, Alexander, in which he expresses his desire to write a novel about Selim, a Turkish guest worker who slowly becomes his friend. The narrative proceeds through frequent self-interruptions, through which Alexander reacquaints the readers with his inability to write about Selim. A selective combination of the constitutive elements of the novel—cross-cultural representation, reflective metafiction, incorporation of discussions on German history after the Second World War—have featured centrally or marginally in a number of academic discussions. Nadolny's *Selim* was at the center of a stimulating debate in German studies in the United States. Sabine von Dirke, Leslie Adelson, and Ülker Gökberk examined and disputed modes of representation of a Turk in a novel by a German author. This scholarly debate denoted three distinct methodological positions: an evaluation of the nature of images—positive, negative, Orientalist, Western—and a reconstruction of differences between East and West through a rushed application of Said's *Orientalism* (von Dirke); a careful employment of Homi Bhabha's concept of hybridity as a methodological escape from the simplistic binary of the hegemonic European against the non-European Other (Adelson, "Opposing Oppositions"); a supplication for the reconsideration of the hermeneutical model of studying the cultural Other as developed in Germany by practitioners of *interkulturelle Germanistik* (Gökberk).[8] With a range of theoretical underpinnings and largely different evidential archives created from the novel in support of their respective arguments, these three scholars revealed the tensions inherent in critically evaluating the representation of the guest worker, a member of the underclass whose status as an Other was prompted by differences of ethnicity and religion. Integral to their discussions of the novel was a critique of cultural stereotypes: von Dirke exposed stereotypes about Turks in the novel, declaring Nadolny a dyed-in-the-wool Orientalist; Adelson tapped the potential of the text to oppose binary constructions and stereotypes of East and West; Gökberk highlighted the recursion to truth claims and stereotypes both in the novel and in Adelson's reading.

Other discussions on *Selim* revolve around some of the aspects identified as central to the novel. In his study of images of Turks in German literature between 1970 and 1990, Nazire Akbulut criticizes Nadolny for his reliance on "archaic" cultural elements that the Turks come to represent in the novel (Akbulut 197). Manfred Durzak emphasizes the intercultural dialogue enabled by the protagonist Alexander's engagement with Turkey (Durzak 297f.). Nilüfer Kuruyazıcı's reading focuses on the biculturality of the novel, which characterizes the coming together of two separate worlds of Germany and Turkey ("*Selim*" 21–31). In a more recent discussion, Aglaia Blioumi investigates the novel's success in promoting cultural understanding and applauds it for its "dynamic cultural understanding" through an intentional use of stereotypes ("Interkulturalität und Literatur" 33). Other scholars, such as Thomas Überhoff ("Sten Nadolny"), have attempted to view the novel in the larger context of Nadolny's writings, which harbor his affinity for epic narration. Still others, such as Dieter Hoffmann, have combined an identification of postmodern narrative structures in the novel with their investigation of interculturality. Leslie Adelson's recent commentary on the novel focuses on the moments of dialogic interaction between Alexander and Selim to explain how the historical particularity of the Auschwitz trial "transforms the rhetorical figure of Selim into a German story that Alexander struggles to tell by weaving himself and the Turkish migrant into the fabric of the national narrative simultaneously" (*Turkish Turn* 36). Adelson writes, "Alexander's reflections on Selim's gift of speech situate the figure of the Turkish migrant at the core of a decidedly German cultural dilemma" (ibid. 35).

My concerns here are of a different nature. I neither aim to evaluate Nadolny's success in initiating or facilitating cultural understanding nor am inclined to identify narrative structures in the novel at length as postmodern. While my interests partially coincide with those of Adelson in following the situation of the Turkish migrant and Alexander's inclusion of Turks in the novel with references to German history after the Second World War, I wish to highlight the challenges Alexander faces and acknowledges in trying to weave the Turkish migrant into the national narrative. My reading, therefore, focuses on understanding the struggle between the representer and the represented—the narrator, Alexander, and Selim, the subject of his narration (the citizen and the foreigner in the specific contexts of this novel, respectively)—as a substructure of an emerging recognition of the two as integral parts of the same polity. While I consider stereotypes and narrative strategies as important to our understanding of situating the Turkish migrant in the German national narrative, my considerations are animated by imbalances of power over the narrative created by the narrator's dependence on the one who is narrated. The narrator's acceptance of this dependence and of his epistemic privilege are further complicated by various manifestations of difference: linguistic, ethnic, cultural. Instead of obviating these differences, I ask, what is the nature of the signification of the figure of the Turkish guest worker? What are the frameworks through which we can best understand the narrator's struggle with epistemic privileges? What are the questions of the foreigner, and how do these questions help us understand   to borrow from Seyla Benhabib again—the complicated relationship between the *ethnos* and the *demos*? I pursue these questions to elucidate dilemmas that are directly related to questions of representation and the significance of enunciation—more specifically, to locution and interlocution. Before I arrive at my discussion of the novel, I want to explicate the significance of my questions through a commentary on a much-debated figure of the Turkish guest worker.

★

An unnamed Turkish guest worker appears in Homi Bhabha's discussion on "Foreignness of Languages" (164ff.) in his influential essay "DissemiNation: Time, Narrative, and the Margins of the Modern Nation" (*Location of Culture* 139–70). Bhabha borrows this figure from John Berger's *A Seventh Man* to "give way to the *vox populi*: the relatively unspoken tradition of the people of the *pagus*—colonials, postcolonials, migrants, wandering people who will not be contained within the *Heim* of national culture and its unisonant discourse, but are themselves the marks of a shifting boundary that alienates the frontiers of the modern nation" (ibid. 164). Bhabha views in these "migrants, colonials, postcolonials" the capability to "split the patriotic voice of unisonance," which they achieve "by speaking the foreignness of their language" (ibid.). A little later in Bhabha's discussion, "*Heim*" is identified as a "lost object" (ibid. 165); it is "repeated in a void that at once prefigures and pre-empts the 'unisonant' that makes it *unheimlich*." Through these conjectures, Bhabha's Turkish guest worker, qua John Berger, exemplifies the enthusiasm of splitting the patriotic voice of the unisonance while simultaneously becoming a somber reflection on an "oral void" that "emerges when the Turk abandons the metaphor of a *heimlich* national culture" (ibid.). Due to the "opaqueness of words" and the "opacity of language," the Turk becomes the Other that renders the metropolis "strangely familiar": "in the process by which the paranoid position finally voids the place from where it speaks," Bhabha observes, "we begin to see another history of the German language" (ibid. 166).

Bhabha's commitment to give way to the *vox populi* through the foreignness of the language of the migrant, the dissonance in the patriotic language, the loss of the homeland for the migrant, alienation of the frontiers of the modern nation, the abandonment of the metaphor of the *Heim*, the opacity of language, opaqueness of words, the oral void—when considered together—at first seems to impede rather than facilitate the way of the *vox populi*. Bhabha's inclusion of the Turk as an emphatic particle in the "desolate silences of the wandering peoples" (ibid.) seems to belie any optimism of splitting the unisonance of the patriotic language.

Furthermore, his mobilization of John Berger's account of the experiences of Turkish *Gastarbeiter* to represent "the silent Other of gesture and failed speech" (ibid. 166) and "the radical incommensurability of translation" (ibid.) seems to defy the interventionist articulation of Whiskey Sisodia, a character in Salman Rushdie's *The Satanic Verses*.[9] These impediments have invited criticism by scholars: Deniz Göktürk expresses regret at Bhabha's representation of a Turk as "an incommensurable, alienated, speechless victim without any voice" ("Turkish Delight" 4). The sociologist Levent Soysal criticizes Bhabha for centralizing silence in the narrative of Turkish migration ("Labor to Culture" 500). Leslie Adelson's reading focuses on the "oral void" as well: "Whatever oral void this Turk is made to represent, its figurality represents a particular and early moment in the history of Turkish labor migration" (*Turkish Turn* 89). Adelson centers her explanation around Bhabha's use of Rushdie as a counterpoint to the Turkish guest worker; she observes, "Rushdie articulates the disjunctive structure of modernity that the incoherent Turkish guest worker can only represent and embody" (ibid. 90). While Adelson attempts to clarify Bhabha's "narrative of nineteenth century migrations within Europe to his story of transcontinental labor migration, diasporic exile, and postcolonial ambivalence in the latter half of the twentieth century" (ibid. 88), she identifies the "strategic centrality" of the Turkish figure in the "constitutive disjunction between the actual loss of home for many migrants in the nineteenth century and the imagined restitution of home through the metaphor of home on which the modern nation-state in Europe relies" (ibid. 89).

The denigration of the Turkish laborer as a victimized foreigner alien to a Western nation-state through the invocation of a purportedly outdated reference, and the debilitation of the Turk through silence, versus the privileging of Rushdie's power to articulate "disjunctive structures of modernity": these three points inform the thrust of these critiques. While Göktürk and Soysal are spirited by their defiance of stereotypes that the silenced minority invokes, Adelson interprets the centrality of the Turk by distinguishing Bhabha's metaphor of the home in the nineteenth and twentieth centuries. These insightful critiques hold validity. However, if only these frameworks are validated, the turbulence that Bhabha's passage engenders can be seen easily as a misappropriation, a failed example, the weakest link in Bhabha's larger investigation of the temporality of a nation as a "time-lag," the "'meanwhile' . . . the present as a succession without synchrony" (*Turkish Turn* 159). Bhabha's Turk (qua Berger), like Appadurai's Turkish guest workers, watching "Turkish films in their German flats"

(*Modernity* 4), invokes a particular image that either upsets or pacifies political sensitivities. Bhabha's discussion of the Turkish guest worker can be debunked for its exceeding authentication of victimization. The Turkish guest worker can easily be set aside as a stereotype or as an anachronism, as Soysal observes ("Labor to Culture" 500).

Perhaps not so easily. There exists another framework that grants a new dimensionality to Bhabha's interpellation of the figure of the Turk at the disjuncture of a modern nation-state. When read in conjunction with the discussion of cultural difference that precedes the section on foreignness of languages in Bhabha's essay, the Turkish figure underscores a very specific kind of incommensurability and intranslatability: one that differentiates co-optation from incorporation, homogenization from inclusion, and assimilation from integration in the narrative of a nation. The nature of this differentiation is not a simple or simplistic articulation of adversarial positions. "Cultural difference," Bhabha writes, "does not simply represent the contention between oppositional contents and antagonistic traditions of cultural value" (*Location of Culture* 162). The predicament of difference is to "transform the scenario of articulation—not simply to disclose the rationale of political discrimination" (ibid.). That is the interventionist aspect of the "analytic of difference" (ibid.), which behooves the "logic of articulation" to consider the "topos of enunciation" (ibid.). Cultural difference then rearticulates the "sum of knowledge ... where adding *to* does not add up but serves to disturb the calculation of power and knowledge, producing other spaces of subaltern signification" (ibid., original emphasis). Bhabha does not provide a definition of subaltern signification in this particular passage, but earlier in the essay "DissemiNation" subalternity appears adjacent to subversion: "forces of social authority and subversion or subalternity may emerge in displaced, even decentered strategies of signification" (ibid. 145). Bhabha's enthusiasm for the decentered, displaced, and therefore, subversive potential of the subaltern echoes in his discussion of subaltern historiography and agency (ibid. 237).

If a general outline can be drawn from these two passages and the passage leading up to the phrase, then subaltern signification implies an avoidance of superficial accounts of social contradictions and antagonisms, to consider knowledge and practices that exist beside each other, in order to render intelligible the incommensurable as a subversive agency from outside the centers of hegemonic power. Even by anticipation, it seems like a tall order. But it deserves pronouncement precisely because subaltern signification provides clues to Bhabha's imagination of the Turkish guest worker. The silence of the guest worker is not his lack of speech. The Turk is not speech-impaired; it is his language that the host nation is both literally and figuratively incapable of understanding. The untranslatability of the foreignness of the Turk's language does not immediately signal his culpability to be excluded from the narrative of his host nation in modernity—it is the inability of the host nation to comprehend the analytic of difference that creates the logic of articulation as incommensurability. Bhabha's imagination through the Turk of the *vox populi* as the desolate silence of wandering peoples does not vouch for victimization through authentication of suffering or merely rest on the literal silence of the Turk as an outsider in the late-capitalist economy of mass migration. The irresolute nature of subaltern signification induces incommensurability; the seemingly incommensurable resists being turned into an incommensurable sign; the challenge needs to be met by the one who is engaged in the signification of the incommensurable in the analytic of difference and the constitutive disjuncture of a nation-state. The Turkish guest worker is incommensurable, not merely due to the foreignness of his language or his silence. While he may offer the possibility of being perceived as part of the nation-state where he is a migrant or a foreigner, he cannot be written *into* the logic of a nation-state or into any available histories or presents with alacrity.

In other words, Bhabha's discussion of the Turkish figure is problematic, but the problem lies not just in his specific mobilization of an archive offered by Berger. The problem of analyzing and mobilizing an archive in order to give way to the *vox populi* has enriched the field of subaltern studies since its beginnings in 1982, as Dipesh Chakrabarty elucidates in his essay "A Small History of Subaltern Studies" (*Habitations* 3–19). While detailing the specifics of the project in the context of Indian history is beyond the scope of this chapter, it seems relevant to mention the point central to Chakrabarty's essay. Commenting on the Indian historian Ranajit Guha, Chakrabarty explains the problems inherent to Guha's project of thinking of the subaltern as the purveyor of his autonomy. Guha's commitment to histories of peasant rebellions in India, Chakrabarty writes, was aimed at demonstrating "that, instead of being an anachronism in a modernizing colonial world, the peasant was a real contemporary of colonialism and a fundamental part of the modernity to which colonial rule gave rise in India" (ibid. 9). While Bhabha does not quite mark the space where the Turkish guest worker can be the maker of his own destiny, his attempt to grant contemporaneousness to the silent migrant by locating him at the center of late-capitalist economy echoes the problem central to the subaltern studies project: the problem of naming, cognizing, and translating the subaltern. Bhabha's invocation of the subaltern makes the signification even more problematic, as Bhabha offers all migrants, postcolonials, and wandering people as part of a single syntax. If Bhabha's Turkish guest worker becomes the anathema and apologia of the very process of subaltern signification, it is because of the conundrum specific to rendering commensurable the hitherto incommensurable in the narrative of a nation.

★

Does Selim appear in Nadolny's novel as an autonomous, fully self-conscious member of the German polity? By virtue of his gift of speech, does Selim emerge as the nemesis of John Berger and Homi Bhabha's silent Turk, lost in the foreignness of his language? Or does Selim, the foreigner, by his acquisition of German, demonstrate his capability to formulate the foreigner's questions and claims to equity? Does Selim master the craft and skill of articulation in order to unfold the disjuncture of the West German nation-state? Does Selim's relationship to labor elevate itself to a programmatic consciousness that adds up to a "knowledge of work and labor" lacked by Bhabha's silent "automaton" (*Location of Culture* 165)?

If Dipesh Chakrabarty's remarks are indicative of problems inherent in pursuing what Bhabha formulates as subaltern significations through an analytic of cultural difference—the latter explained more specifically by Bhabha than the former—this interrogative mode of setting up adversarial models does not hold much currency. In the specific context of migrant workers of ethnic minorities, the analytic of cultural difference merits consideration away from a simplistic recognition or acknowledgement of difference, or even through a mere authentication of the foreigner. What can be asked, however, is if Nadolny's novel offers us the possibility to trace some of the problems inherent in the attempts to represent the Turkish guest worker, Selim? Are there any specific facilitations or impediments to subaltern signification that can be identified in the novel? As I have just demonstrated, presenting the sovereign voice of the people, conceiving them as Others—whether peasants or migrant workers or ethnic minorities—"letting the people speak," constructing them as conscious subjects of polity calls for vigilance in interpretative contexts of difference. Therefore, it is first necessary for me to explain my use of the term *subaltern* in my exploration of processes through which a Turkish guest worker undergoes subjectification and signification in Nadolny's *Selim*. My use of *subaltern* to reflect on a Turkish guest worker does not entail a celebratory inflation of a migrant industrial worker in late-capitalist globalization through a curious ahistorical conflation with the peasant as a subject of colonial-postcolonial historiography. I am borrowing this term from subaltern studies as a useful descriptor that stresses urgent considerations of subjectivity and ideology refracted through differences of class, gender, and in the case of the novel, nationality and ethnicity in narrative representation. This would be a good time to point out the hubris of the title of this chapter. My aim here is not to reinforce the subordinate status of the foreign guest worker and the manifestations of his or her subordination, but to probe if, and by what narrative or representational means, the significations of domination and subordination are rendered problematic and irresolute in fictional representations. Before the processes of subaltern significations in *Selim* are explored, the epistemological and ethical imperatives of naming, cognizing, and rendering the incommensurable commensurable merit attention. I propose to do so in two steps. First, I want to demonstrate the complexities of conceptualizing and representing the Other through a brief discussion of Gayatri Chakravorty Spivak's seminal essay "Can the Subaltern Speak?" Next, with a discussion of Rey Chow's analysis of the specific context of what she explains as cross-ethnic representations, I want to demonstrate that such conceptualizations and representations become even more complicated when those who are identified as ethnic Others become subjects of narration.

Gayatri Chakravorty Spivak questions political and artistic representations as she reconstructs and comments on the conversation "Intellectuals and Power" between Deleuze and Foucault. Spivak highlights several cryptic contours that depict the dynamics among power, desire, and subjectivity. She conducts a simultaneous examination of a) representation of the Third-World subject in systems of thought emanating from the geographical West, and b) intellectual and ideological endorsement of self-representation of the native subjects. In her detailed elucidation of the limits of representationalist realism, Spivak calls for a careful investigation of the ideological relations between the privileged and the underprivileged and the identification of the underprivileged as such. Having pronounced poststructuralist theory's predicament toward the Others of a society, Spivak is perturbed by the distance that Deleuze and Foucault suggest from what they conceive as an actual participation in the struggle of the Others and the theorization about such struggles. She challenges their contentions, calling instead for a redefinition of "concrete experience" as propounded by them, in order to unravel the complexities of the politics of *Vertreten* (political representation, speaking for) and *Darstellen* (artistic representation). By delineating the terrains of theorization and action, speech and struggle—which take center-stage in the conversation between Deleuze and Foucault—Spivak evaluates the significance of textual politics and appeals for a sustained vigilance on the part of the intellectual in the act of discursive representation of the subaltern. On the one hand, Spivak identifies the modes in which the native as a subaltern can be marginalized and disenfranchised along an un-self-critical "track of ideology" ("Subaltern" 272), in a discourse unaware of its desire for, and investment in, epistemic privilege. On the other hand, she analyzes the very processes of constitution of the subaltern masses as an alternative to disenfranchisement, thereby rendering doubtful the naïve valorization of self-representation of the subalterns in their "own" voices.

Spivak's poignant critique of Deleuze and Foucault's celebration of the self-representative power of the people, the masses, is anchored, however, in her promotion of vigilance toward those who represent. Throughout her critical engagement with Deleuze and Foucault, she categorically refrains from declaring the permanent inability of a Western intellectual to represent the non-Western native subject. This is especially evident in her timely invocation of Jacques Derrida. Reflecting upon *Of Grammatology*, Spivak notes how Derrida attempts "to keep the ethnocentric Subject from establishing itself by selectively defining an Other" (ibid. 292). That Derrida "discloses the vulnerability of his own desire to conserve something that is, paradoxically, both ineffable and nontranscendental" (ibid. 293) does not disconcert Spivak, a critical practitioner of postcolonial reason. To her, it is more important "that as a European philosopher, he articulates the European subject's tendency to constitute the Other as marginal to ethnocentrism and locates *that* as the problem with all logocentric and therefore also all grammatological endeavors" (ibid.). Derrida's subject would thus become the "blank part of the text" that will be ascribed to the Other. Thus, for Spivak, Derrida's call for "rendering *delirious* that interior voice that is the voice of the other in us" (ibid. 294) becomes the site of essentialist critiques of representation. Before finally spelling out the question "Can the Subaltern Speak?" Spivak will have suggested the usefulness of the "sustained and developing work on the mechanics of constitution of the Other" because that serves a "much greater analytic and interventionist advantage than invocations of the *authenticity* of the Other" (ibid. 293).

Spivak's acute awareness of the dangers of valorizing the authenticity of the Other and her pursuance of "the mechanics of constitution of the Other" become the source of the "analytic and interventionist advantage" of her later work, preeminently visible in the chapter "Philosophy" of her book *The Critique of Postcolonial Reason*. From her critique of the native-as-authentic in "Can the Subaltern Speak?" Spivak moves to the emergence of the native-informant-as-authentic in the *Critique*. Once again, Spivak abstains from the easy identification, construction, and valorization of the native informant. She "clears the native informant out" of the "cluster" of "self-marginalizing or self-consolidating migrant or postcolonial masquerading as a native informant" (*Critique* 6).[10] If in "Can the Subaltern Speak?" Spivak focuses on the loss of the native in the interstices of a philosophical dialogue, she comments in the *Critique* on the reemergence of the native informant as the authentic self-representative of the postcolonial condition, as the immigrant. In charting this itinerary of the native to the native informant, Spivak reconfirms the inherent ambivalence of the Other, which does not let itself be manipulated in absoluteness by a colonial/hegemonic narrative but will not, and cannot, entirely reveal him- or herself as a self-fulfilled subject through self-representation. She pursues what she calls a deconstructive reading, "unaccusing, unexcusing, attentive, situationally productive through dismantling" (ibid. 81).

Spivak's insistence on vigilance in modes of subjectification of the Other is visible in another context, in Rey Chow's study, *The Protestant Ethnic*. The Other acquires the explicit specificity of the ethnic subject, and otherness emerges as an "ethnic spectacle," whereby, as Chow convincingly argues, the uniqueness of ethnicity also becomes its confining, limiting element. Chow's important and multifaceted arguments pertaining to conceptualizations of ethnicity, ethnics, and the politics of representation will inform Chapters 2 and 3 of this book. Here I wish to spell out three important issues relevant to our discussion. First, akin to Spivak's admonition against any easy resolution of epistemic privilege that accompanies representation of the underrepresented, the subaltern, Chow argues against discursive practices that look for a clear trajectory from repression to emancipation in narrative representations of ethnics and ethnicity. "The commodified relations of ethnicity," Chow writes, "are underwritten by the conviction that the other is being held captive within his or her own culture . . . and that such captivity necessitates protest and liberation" (*Protestant Ethnic* 23). Second, similar to Spivak's emphasis on examining the "mechanics of constitution of the Other" ("Subaltern" 294), Chow evaluates modes through which the category "ethnic" itself acquires both objectification and subjectification through disciplinary and discursive practices. Commenting on "visible and observable" modes of rendering the world "knowable," Chow situates ethnicity in a "politics of cultural legitimation" (*Protestant Ethnic* 2). Most importantly, Chow reveals the circuitous nature of ethnicization that belabors subjectification and objectification of ethnicity and ethnics in literature and other media. Chow argues against a critical tendency that bases its evaluations on distinctions between negative/positive, affirmative/resistant, entrapped/emancipated and forces inquiry into modes of cross-ethnic representations in literature and other aesthetic media. This also serves as Chow's entry into a discussion of stereotypes, which form the core of such binaries. Defining stereotypy as "an objective, normative practice that is regularly adopted for collective purposes of control and management" (ibid. 54), Chow vouches for an inevitability of stereotypes and, therefore, urges a critical examination of their location in social text—as "effective, realistic, political weapons" (ibid. 59). Disputing the sanitizing of ethnic stereotypes from languages, Chow demonstrates the unique location of stereotypes between speculation and intelligibility, asking for alternative readings of stereotypes beyond politically correct Orientalism and ethnic *ressentiment*. Questioning the efficiency of accrediting an inherent potential of resistance to ethnic subjectivities and their narratives, Chow underscores the complexities that the category ethnic has accrued in the contemporary contexts of economic globalization and mass migration:

> The experience of migration . . . simply highlights and amplifies the connection between commodified labor and ethnicization—what I would call, more precisely, the *ethnicization of labor*—that takes place in a society even when there are no migrants, even when migrants have become citizens. . . . The point to note about the relationship between ethnicity and labor is therefore not the oft-reiterated one of the existential uprooting of the migrant worker from home (with all the sentimental trappings of the argument) but rather that the ethnic as such stands in modernity as the site of foreignness that is produced from within privileged societies and is at once defined by and constitutive of that society's hierarchical division of labor. A laborer becomes ethnicized because she is commodified in specific ways, because she has to pay for her living by performing certain kinds of work, while these kinds of work, despite being generated from within that society, continue to reduce the one who performs them to the position of the outsider, the ethnic. (34, original emphasis)

We have now reached the heart of the problem. As Derrida, Spivak, and Chow demonstrate, there exists an inherent ambivalence and fragility in the ontologies of the terms *foreigner, subaltern, ethnic*. These terms point out the difficulties involved in representing—in politics or in art—those who are categorized as such. These categories, therefore, cannot be easily called upon to serve as descriptors for a Turkish guest worker. What they do reveal is a necessity to think through their ambivalence and fragility in descriptions of a Turkish guest worker. If the figure of the Turkish guest worker in a novel by a German author is to be pursued beyond evaluations of cultural understanding, intercultural dialogue, critique of positive or negative images, or even beyond a critique of the critique of positive and negative images—as Ülker Gökberk brilliantly performed in her essay "Culture Studies"—narrative moments and strategies that reveal the fragility, rupture, and instability of foreignness, subalternity, and ethnicity merit credence. In other words, instead of fixing the Turkish guest worker into categories of subaltern, ethnic, foreigner, or Other, signification of Otherness, as well as moments that disrupt such signification, necessitate discussion. Bhabha himself has drawn attention to the fixity of the Other in his essay "The Other Question" (*Location of Culture* 66–84), where he approaches the processes of naming, cognizing, and rendering the Other commensurable with far greater caution than in his explications of the Turkish guest worker in "DissemiNation." Bhabha develops strategies for considering "Otherness," suggesting that the "point of intervention should shift from the ready recognition of images as positive and negative, to an understanding of the 'processes of subjectification' made possible (and plausible) through stereotypical discourse" (ibid. 67). Instead of acknowledging Otherness as a mere conglomerate of stereotypes, Bhabha asks for an examination of Otherness that is "at once an object of desire and derision, an articulation of difference contained within the fantasy of origin and identity" (ibid.). Furthermore, Bhabha warns us of the futility of the incessant purging of stereotypes as he writes: "Stereotyping is not the setting up of a false image which becomes the scapegoat of discriminatory practices. It is a much more ambivalent text of projection and introjection, metaphoric and metonymic strategies, displacement, overdetermination, guilt, aggressivity; the masking and splitting of 'official' and phantasmatic knowledges to construct the positionalities and oppositionalities of racist discourses" (ibid. 81f.). Bhabha sees stereotypes as a form of knowledge that vacillates between what is known and what must be repeated. He calls for a move beyond the "dogmatic and moralistic positions on the meaning of oppression and discrimination" (ibid. 67), asking the cultural critic to focus on the ambivalence of the stereotype rather than on its fixity in order to challenge "deterministic or functionalist modes of conceiving of the relationship between discourse and politics" (ibid. 66f.).

Although Derrida, Spivak, Bhabha, and Chow develop their own unique modes of mapping the "Othering" of the Other in hegemonic discourses, their projects intersect in that they destabilize normative ontologies and highlight the problems inherent in delineating, legitimizing, or pretending to give voice to (represent) that which has been named the Other. It is not too difficult to perceive an alliance between Spivak and Bhabha on the critique of representations. Both these scholars tend to agree on the intellectually restricting enterprise of the critique of representation backed by claims of truth. While for Spivak the European subject's acknowledgment of its tendency to constitute the Other as a marginal figure presents itself as a progressive move toward epistemic construction of the Other, for Bhabha the challenge cannot stop short at listing and evaluating positive or negative images.

What does all of this have to do with cosmopolitics and cosmopolitical readings? If cosmopolitanism embodies a willingness to engage with the Other, and cosmopolitics the way of understanding relations between natives and foreigners, I deem it important to revisit these thinkers because they offer challenging insights into the legitimacy of artistic representation of the Other. Although in the works discussed here these thinkers develop their arguments in specific colonialist-neocolonialist contexts—and none of the terms they use (the *subaltern*, the *Other*, the *Colonial*, the *Postcolonial*, the *Ethnic*) permits easy conflation with the term *guest worker*—their insights are beneficial for assessing the validity and legitimacy of artistic representations of cultural otherness in other narrative contexts where articulations of epistemic power are conspicuous; narratives are, therefore, more vulnerable to reproducing, if not necessarily intentionally and consciously propagating, stereotypes. Cross-cultural, cross-ethnic representation is one such rich force field, where, due to the political hegemony and power privilege of the majority, representations of minorities defined by caste, class, color, religion, or ethnicity are highly contested. As is known from the long history of colonialist or neocolonialist stereotypical narratives, the minority Other gets constructed simultaneously as a curiosity, a novelty, yet the very stereotypes that make the Other curious and novel become tropes of familiarity.

The critical discomfort that these cross-cultural representations invoke often results in the privileging of self-representation. This discomfort resonates in Satya P. Mohanty's persuasive "post-positivist realist" intervention as Mohanty raises the foundational question, "who can be trusted to represent the real interests of the group without fear of betrayal or misrepresentation?" (29). Mohanty stresses the importance of experience: cross-ethnic representations of the Other often lack concrete experience of the oppression of the Other. This is a valid line of critical inquiry. However, this is not the right occasion for an in-depth engagement with Mohanty or the scholars who engage with post-positivist realism, simply because my intention is not to assess, along with Mohanty and others, the truth-claims of identity through my reading of Nadolny's *Selim*. My interests lie in the claims of crossing over identitarian truth-claims, trespassing the legitimacy and validity of self-representation. It is, therefore, necessary to point out that in reclaiming identity, and in a bid to save identity from the eternal fluidity of the poststructuralist model, the distinction between authentic and inauthentic modes of representation is established once again, leaving little possibility of escape from accuracy and accusations. The loss of what Spivak accentuates as a "greater analytic and interventionist advantage" of "inauthentic representation" becomes palpable in critiques of representation where accuracy, adequacy, and appropriateness—which purportedly constitute authentic objectivity—become the only evaluating criteria. This debilitates reading in works of literature the freedom to play—to be ironic, to be self-critically incorrect—in order to be able to see the unseen or see the hitherto seen in a different way. Inculcation of this sensitivity for the ironic, I believe, could be a more productive critical approach for texts that consciously step across lines of class, ethnicity, and nationality.

This approach informs my reading of *Selim*, whereby I propose a move away from Orientalism and ethnic *ressentiment*. I wish to examine if Alexander, Nadolny's narrator, is able to render "delirious the voice of the Other" in himself; does *the* question of the Other/the foreigner/the guest worker also emerge as the question *of* the Other/the foreigner/the guest worker? In addition, by focusing on certain textual moments, I wish to highlight a much older discussion on belonging and citizenry that the novel offers its readers. The investigation of these moments cannot restrict itself to locating the silence or the articulation of the Turk; aphasia of the narrator needs equal attention. Instead of merely investigating locution, interlocution of the Turk by the narrator demands attention. And discussions of interlocution will not happen without accounting for stereotypes.

To this end, first I discuss at length the novel's central concerns and the narrative strategies Nadolny employs to articulate these concerns. This will assist in exploring the possibilities of a narrative about the minority/the cultural Other, where the Other is not always already victimized by the author, waiting to be saved by the privileged, multicultural, cosmopolitan critic. Second, by following the line of inquiry mentioned above, I attempt to move the scholarship beyond the traditional identification of and polemics against stereotypes. I want to argue that a careful use of stereotypes in a literary text can enable alternative reading strategies for majority representations of minorities. Finally, I want to show how a cultural interlocutor's acknowledgement of his or her dependence on the native informant and of the scope and limits of narration reveals the conundrum that accompanies efforts to let the guest worker speak as it unfolds the aphasia of the narrator himself. This idea continues in my investigation of the friendship between the narrator and the subject of his narration, an aspect central to the novel, which I connect with Derrida's important work on friendship as both emotional and a rational political alliance. Underlying this trajectory is my desire to demonstrate that in the multicultural, multilinguistic, multiethnic world of Nadolny's novel, the voice of the foreigner, the ethnic, the subaltern competes with the din of authorial domination. I propose to understand the narrator's aphasia through a heuristic device, narraphasia, to which I now turn.

In his influential work *Language in Literature*, Roman Jakobson expounds on the idea of aphasia, which he describes as "a language disturbance" that must be given due attention to understand "any breakdown of communications" (Jakobson 95). Drawing from cognitive sciences as well as from neurobiology, Jakobson names a kind of aphasia, a "contiguity disorder" (ibid. 106), that is marked not by a lack of words but an inability to "combine simpler linguistic entities into more complex units" (ibid.). This leads to a kind of "*agrammatism*" that "causes the degeneration of the sentence into a mere 'word heap'" (ibid., original emphasis). In Nadolny's novel, the impaired oral competence of Alexander, the first-person narrator, is similar to Jakobson's definition of aphasia, even if Alexander's condition cannot be exactly identified as such. At the very beginning of the novel, Nadolny writes, "when Alexander opened his mouth, confusion arose in his head, a light cacophony, a luminous landscape without a signpost" (*Selim* 7). Alexander's inability to speak well, which dominates the novel and impedes his role as an instructor of communication skills, is central to grasp his interrupted narration in the novel. Beyond its pathological implications, Jakobson's definition of aphasia, when modified in the context of a narrative, can lead to a richer understanding of Nadolny's novel. The narrator and the narrative in *Selim* do not suffer from, but are rejuvenated by, their narraphasia: a state of narration that occurs as a result of acknowledgement of the inherent insufficiency of narration, and acknowledgement of and engagement with the struggles and failures that accompany the process of narration. Narraphasia could also be imagined as a kind of narrative conundrum through which an author disrupts a linear narration, disorders the order of things, and thus engages rigorously not just with locution but also with the problem of interlocution. Thus, the narrator becomes the very agent of his or her own narraphasia, which he or she cultivates in order to break out of truth-claims. While narrating difference—cultural, linguistic, or ethnic—complex processes that code and recode interactions between the native informant and the interlocutor have to be registered by the interlocutor in order to accommodate the native informant in the narrative space with a consciousness of the narrative's desire to exercise power and domination over the informant.

Selim oder die Gabe der Rede has two beginnings. The first, *Vorspann* (prelude), is offered to the reader before she arrives at the meticulously enumerated chapters and sections. Nadolny's *Vorspann* consists of six fragments dated from 1965 to 1988. These fragments preview anxieties about narration, both oral and written, and register the conundrum of description and artistic representation that belabors the protagonist, Alexander, throughout the course of the novel. Alexander's anxiety about becoming a good speaker marks the beginning of the very first segment. On a snowy winter evening in the year 1965, Alexander stands on a bridge in the provincial Bavarian town of Rosenheim, identifying and analyzing faults in his oration (*Selim* 7). He attributes his lack of elocutionary prowess to his inability to discipline and streamline his thoughts. He remarks that his attempts at breaking his silence and entering speech result in a simultaneous emission of contesting ideas. In a passage that bears resemblance to a confessional, Alexander accepts that he is incapable of clearly perceiving the object he wants to describe and will never be able to find the right means to describe it. He briefly comments on his curiosity about truth-claims, "wie sich die Wahrheit bewegte" (ibid.), and in a moment of brilliant irony, immediately leaves the bridge to watch the matinee screening of the film *Lawrence of Arabia*.

An incapacity for clear perception and the resultant lack of optimal articulation are manifestations of Alexander's narraphasia. Alexander's concerns for truth and its troubled relationship to narration find extension in the next fragment, dated 1972. In an about-face, while reflecting upon composing manifestos, Alexander questions the value of theorizing about good oration. He reflects that there is no eternal truth, "keine Wahrheit für alle Tage" (*Selim* 8), confesses that he has believed in truth-claims for too long, and ruminates that speaking itself is a meta-activity; the act of speaking is an act of speaking about speaking. Having acknowledged the temporally limited validity of truth-claims, he inquires into the concept of understanding and reaches the conclusion that it is at best an illusion. Alexander expresses his dislike for courses on effective speaking, for they create and sustain the illusion that eloquence generates understanding without encouraging inquiry, and he seeks to move away from a systematic analysis of effective tools of speaking (ibid.).

It is at this very moment that the Turkish guest worker Selim enters Nadolny's narrative as the subject of study, and suddenly questions about quality, mode, and the (im)possibility of representation through narration gain contextual specificity. Alexander's casual comment about the curious nature of his profession (*Vertreterberuf*) as a sales representative for lexica, and his reflections about speaking and its relationship to truth, embody the conflict between temporality, subjectivity, and narration within Nadolny's larger story about Selim. Alexander makes the decision: "Selim [zu] studieren, er soll mein Lehrer sein, so etwas ein natürlicher Lehrer für Rhetorik" (ibid.). This passage is remarkable not because it declares Selim the natural teacher for rhetoric but because in the introduction of Selim, Alexander's promise to himself to observe (*beobachten*), to inculcate the desire to speak and listen to words (*Wörter-Sprechen* und *Wörter-Hören*), and to accomplish that by studying Selim, come together (ibid.). Alexander's valorization of Selim's rhetorical abilities is rather momentary and superfluous. Selim is not established as the Oriental guru of rhetoric: immediately after this confession, Alexander is ready to start a school for teaching how to speak.

The next three fragments, dated 1979, 1982, and 1983, are italicized diary entries that further testify to Alexander's desire to narrate Selim's story. The fragment from 1979 registers the progress of Alexander's school of rhetoric (*Redeschule*). This is the first diary entry of the novel, and the reader gets acquainted with Alexander's initial design for his novel. The plot of the novel in this entry has Alexander's school at the center and the two Turks only at the periphery ("darunter die beiden Türken") (*Selim* 9). But immediately in the second entry, from 1982, the reader knows that Selim is at the center of the novel. Alexander realizes that he imagined Selim more than he understood him.

The scattered, telegraphic, personal, and speculative mode of these fragments is very different from the assertive and confident style of the previous two. They provide the reader a glimpse into various modes of writing—dated sections, narration interspersed with diary entries—that Nadolny employs to depict Alexander's struggle with the subject of his cognition. Above all, as the fragment from 1982 declares, Alexander's narration of Selim can never be omniscient. The only solace for Alexander is the realization that Selim is a phantom, a project of his own imagination:

> 1982
> *Ich habe immer Reden können, wenn ich über Selim sprach. Beim Schreiben stellt sich heraus: er war ein Phantom. Ich habe ihn mehr erdacht als verstanden.*
> *Das stört mich nicht. Der Irrtum war vielleicht besser als die Wahrheit.*
> (ibid.)

Thus, by the end of the *Vorspann*—the prelude to a novel about a Turkish guest worker—the initial question about the acquisition of eloquence changes. Instead of just asking how to speak and write well, Alexander now asks himself how to speak and write well about Selim, the cultural Other. The reader is introduced to the complex relationship between the two protagonists, one German, the other Turkish. For Alexander, the Turkish guest worker becomes a teacher who surpasses all textbooks on rhetoric, indeed the best storyteller. Selim also becomes the hero of a novel that Alexander wants to write, though a hero who provides only limited access to his biography. The space between the narrator and the narrative is marked by strife and struggle, and Selim becomes a unique informant who mobilizes Alexander to change his questions about locution to those about cultural interlocution. A question that Alexander asks himself in his provincial German town acquires an international dimension. And just before the prelude to the novel comes to an end, Alexander expresses the dubious reliability of his informant and subject. He questions the whereabouts of Selim and expresses his vulnerability by accepting that his narration is dependent on Selim (ibid.). Thus, speaking, truth, narration, and the foreigner Selim all become part of one complicated question that drives the narrative: "Who was this Selim, who is he, above all, where? Where is he off to, instead of narrating to me?" (ibid.).

With the responsibilities of the informant and the interlocutor blurred at the outset, the novel invites the reader to uncover the tension caused by writing, a tension that arises from the narrator's dependence on and his limited access to the protagonist. This tension appears in the novel in numerous diary entries, wherein Alexander incessantly questions and critiques his own capability to write. It is essential to explore this paratext in

Nadolny's novel, for it has serious bearings on the narrator's desire to generate and amplify the speech of the subject of narration: the guest worker. Thus, along with Gayatri Chakravorty Spivak, in order to approach the pivotal query, "Can the Subaltern Speak?" it might be useful to first pose the question, can the interlocutor narrate? I will now address how the concerns raised in the *Vorspann* find extension in the novel, in order to show that the narrator's complex relationship with the process of writing creates a much larger room for the subaltern to speak. I concentrate on the vignettes, the diary entries that intersperse Nadolny's narrative, which are key to understanding the rich tension that makes the novel unique.

Alexander's tense relationship with writing about Selim begins in the *Vorspann*. In his diary entry from 1979, Alexander writes, "*You ask me, why I am writing the book. I have discovered narration, the substance of all speech. . . . The plot of the novel? A lot autobiographical; the pre-history of Alexander's* 'School of Rhetoric'*; Observations, how my generation speaks; all kinds of people who have to struggle,* among them the two Turks" (ibid., my emphasis). I emphasize the last phrase because its ambiguity could lead to a rather simplistic reading, one that implies that the Turks, per se, are not important for Nadolny or Alexander, with the exception of Selim and his (Selim's) co-worker and friend Mesut. Alexander's interest in the Turks does indeed start with his idealization of Selim's oratorical superiority, his gift of speech. But during the course of writing, especially during his reflections on his writings, Alexander works his way out of the idealization, and the novel turns into a larger statement about Turks in Germany. In addition, the sentence fragment emphasized in the above quote previews another important aspect of Alexander's writing about Selim: neither Alexander nor Nadolny ventures on a programmatic, institutionally systematized approach to promote cultural understanding through a multicultural novel. The novel begins with an unpretentious, if not entirely inclusive, attitude toward the Turks. Alexander does not claim to write the story of Selim in order to break the silence of a Turkish guest worker. Instead, his intention is to write a novel about the contemporary German social text, which *includes* two Turkish figures. Fairly early in the novel, he declares his commitment to Selim:

Selim ist eine Geschichte, die ich erzählen will.
Selim ist einer, dem ich verpflichtet bin. (*Selim* 47)

Alexander's identification of his first reader frames and complicates his relationship with Selim, as well as his relationship with writing/narrating about him.[11] Alexander's first attempts at writing the story of

Selim begin when Selim is in jail. The multiple conversations among other prisoners and their guests force Alexander and Selim to talk very loudly. Selim thus tells his story above the din of visitors and bureaucracy. Unlike Günter Wallraff—who, in his highly controversial book *Ganz unten*, documented stories of Turks from the very site of their exploitation—Alexander does not want to write a report or an exposé. Alexander questions the worth of his project of writing about Selim, whether it is even possible to begin with narration (*Selim* 160). Thus as Nadolny's novel proceeds, Alexander becomes increasingly uncertain of his novel. Alexander also registers that the protagonist of his novel is shaping up to be very different from his friend Selim. In the course of writing the novel, the informant becomes "*befremdet*" (*Selim* 252), a stranger to his own stories, and Selim will not be able to find himself in the novel that is about him (*Selim* 253). Alexander frustrates himself with his own idealization of Selim (*Selim* 272). He is anxious about whether Selim would ever read it, and he realizes that the novel he is trying to write is itself becoming more uncertain of its readership.

Alexander's conversations with his friend Olaf are further occasions whereby he recognizes the tension between the certainty and the uncertainty of his investment in writing, along with the anxieties about uncertainties that writing itself involves. These conversations inspire Alexander to review his own politics of representation. The first one takes place during the shooting of Olaf's film about Jews in Germany. Alexander finds it problematic that Olaf's film about Jews is called *Deutsche Konjunktiv* (German Subjunctive). He objects to Olaf's portrayal of the Jewish community as an integrated and, therefore, completely accepted social unit in Germany. Olaf refutes Alexander's opposition with an explanation and a question. He considers Jews and the subjunctive as subjects of hatred in German society and sees it as a coincidence that they both would appear together in a film. Olaf interrogates Alexander about the appropriateness of the presence of another minority, the Turks, in his novel. Alexander describes this as a pleasant coincidence: "Zufall . . . doch ein Glücklicher" (*Selim* 188). For Olaf, the appearance of "happy" Jews in a German film is a matter of the subjunctive—that is, wishful thinking; for Alexander, the presence of Turks might be a coincidence. What appears as a coincidence to Alexander qua Nadolny is registered in the novel, including narratives of oppression of the Turks and those of the Turks' struggle against their oppression.

The second conversation takes place during Olaf's shooting of a film on East Africa. Pointing out that Selim is providing Alexander only a restricted access to his life, Olaf claims that Selim is an unreliable native informant (*Selim* 321). Despite this accusation, Olaf alone is the one who gives apt expression to Alexander's relationship with Selim. His announcement that Selim and Alexander complement each other is, unbeknownst to him, uncannily appropriate. One is the *Suchender*, the searcher, and the other the object of research, apparently more complete but carrying the self-same insufficiencies, gaps, and lacunae (ibid.). Thus not only the interlocutor but also the native informant suffers from narraphasia. As narraphasia becomes a shared condition, the silence of the native informant becomes the silence of the interlocutor. And if they speak, they speak together. The blurring of responsibilities in the *Vorspann* now takes a material form. Both the interlocutor and his native informant simultaneously present themselves as agents of knowledge and narration.

The interlocutor's limited access to the native informant motivates a narrative whereby not every detail of the life of the native informant gets signified in order to fit the narrative. Alexander tries to speculate whether Selim's hometown, his origins, have a special significance. He fails for two reasons: he does not know much about Turkey and Selim gives him two conflicting stories about his origins. According to one, he comes from a family of teachers and midlevel government officials. According to the other, his parents were farmers (*Selim* 294). Alexander simply decides to include both versions in his narrative. Nadolny thus accommodates conflicting accounts, conveying that no singular narrative of the native informant perfectly fits into the story the interlocutor is trying to create. In addition, Nadolny diffuses the establishment of a unique native informant by accepting his temporary reliance on and valorization of Mesut, the most opinionated of all the Turks in the novel, whom he perceives to be an Oxford-educated son of Persian landed gentry (*Selim* 170). However, in his search for a model Turk, he did turn to Selim, the genius of narration: "Strangely my model for 'Self-representation' was Selim, never Mesut. I believed in Selim, the genius of narration, the lie to discover, studied in him, how one gives oneself the character of stealing time from others, in order to be loved by them for that. A misunderstanding" (171).

This consistent display of vulnerability by the cultural interlocutor/the host/the narrator, further makes room in the novel for the subaltern, native informant Other with varying degrees of success. Alexander struggles with his writing and with his perceptions of Selim. These complications and vulnerabilities expressed in the diary entries push the narrative to vistas from which the guest worker is partially visible, his voice partially audible, and his (oral) narration partially legible. The path to these vistas is laden with stereotypes. Nadolny's novel is replete with stereotypes of Germans and Germany, Turks and Turkey, and as I will reveal in the section on Ayşe, about intellectuals. These stereotypes appear mostly as appropriating speculations (as in the case of Mesut) or as, to cite Rey Chow again, "effective, realistic, political weapons" (*Protestant Ethnic* 59) that grant the object of stereotyping a contextual specificity—not fixity—because they render both the source and the object of stereotyping available to critical probe. Cultural stereotypes appear in Nadolny's novel as manifestations of preformulated ideas that remain largely unchanged even after a direct experience with another culture.[12] However, instead of fixed, formalized, and standardized ideas or beliefs, they appear as self-consciously partisan observations, and—to use Tzvetan Todorov's expression—"transmit, despite these prejudices, something of the societies observed."[13] These stereotypes, as I will show in the following section, prevent the narrator from idealizing himself through his omniscience, and they obstruct the idealization of the guest worker by exposing his manipulative powers. These cultural stereotypes thus further make the narrative self-critical of its own desire to dominate the voice of the Other.

Alexander's fascination with Selim, as pointed out earlier, starts with an almost absolute enthusiasm for Selim's gift for oral narration. After years of conscientious meditations on the science of rhetoric, Alexander's ideas are challenged by the art of communication unraveled by Selim. The confident wrestler from Turkey narrates without inhibitions; he is the master of storytelling. Unlike Alexander, who evaluates the communicative content of his speech before uttering a word, Selim easily makes acquaintance with others through his stories. He exhibits not only a flair for complementing his monologues with anecdotes, but he can also very well recycle an old anecdote as part of a new story. Even if the stories Selim tells are sometimes hard to believe, his major concern is not to convince the people of the actual occurrence of the event. This provides him with the freedom to present various versions of various stories.

According to von Dirke, Nadolny presents Selim as the wise orator from the East and contributes to the stereotypical exoticization of a non-Western character.[14] This is another example of the simplification of the cultural complexities of an area situated in what we geographically understand as the East but having a history intertwined with what is culturally understood as the West. The city of Mugla, Selim's hometown near the Aegean coast, has over the centuries been a site of Greek, Byzantine, Selçuk, and Ottoman cultures. Mugla is a town not far from Izmir, the city of Homer. It is not far from Ephesus, one of the most important cities in Byzantium, as was Selçuk, the capital city of the Selçuk dynasty and center of Islamic culture in pre-Ottoman Turkey. It was around A.D. 1300 that Mugla became part of the Ottoman Empire. Mugla as a city today is a postrevolution construct, an administrative unit. Mugla and the surrounding area are part of the Turkish cotton belt, comprising a conspicuous farming community of Greek ethnicity already early in the twentieth century. Overlooking aspects of various cultures that have formed this city, reducing them to an Eastern-Islamic entity in the present time, would be tantamount to disenfranchising it of its multiethnic/multireligious history and would lead one to believe that hybridity is largely a late-twentieth-century phenomenon and not a formative feature of what we understand as national cultures today.[15]

It is appropriate to briefly mention a related issue, the cryptic history of Greco-Roman wrestling. In her essay "Opposing Opposition," Adelson points out that the privileged Turk in Nadolny's narrative is not a religious Muslim like Mesut but the "westernized" Greco-Roman wrestler Selim.[16] To presume again that Greco-Roman wrestling owes its development to the styles and techniques developed in the geographical West would be to discount its historical development (along with free-style and oil wrestling) in Turkey during and after the Ottoman Empire.[17] It would be very similar to constructing the history of cricket without including the styles and techniques developed in South Asia, South Africa, and the West Indies.[18] Tracing the mechanisms of Othering in this fashion leads to the loss of a number of other exciting associations and affiliations that the narrative solicits, which facilitate the reader's access to the historical networks from ancient Greece to present-day Germany.

In any case, Alexander's friendship with Selim cannot be reduced to his fascination with Selim's oratory or wrestling skills. In the beginning, Alexander accepts that it is not the Turks in whom he is interested, but through Selim, Alexander becomes politically involved with a community. His predicament is his relationship with Selim, despite their various ideological differences, including those on tolerance of homosexuality. Instead of silencing the voice of the guest worker, as von Dirke frames it, Nadolny's novel brings out the voice and the concerns of the guest worker, sometimes through the first-person narrator and at other times through the guest worker.

Nadolny's Turkish characters become the basis of the critique of the German nation's self-image of a tolerant multicultural nation. Nadolny's Turkish characters participate in the "multikulti" discourse of the 1980s by articulating their very distance from this discourse throughout the novel. Upon his arrival in Berlin, Selim does not foresee the difficulties that the new cultural space will force on him. But he gradually learns how to overcome his handicaps. His gradual acquisition of a functional knowledge of German further assists him in resisting victimization by his employers. The Turks' stereotypes about Germany play a significant role in demonstrating this change. The second beginning of this novel, which takes place in a train on the way to Germany, brings these stereotypes to the fore. From the small bridge in the provincial town of Rosenheim, the opening scene of the second beginning is shifted to Munich, where a number of German soldiers—Alexander being one of them—board a train. The car in which Alexander finds himself has a number of young Turkish workers on their way to Kiel to become guest workers. Turkish guest workers, on their way to Germany, exchange their impressions of Germans. For them the Germans are always right (*immer korrekt*), they constantly learn (*lernten ja ständig*), and are busy with work, heating, and shoveling snow. They are also a people who rarely speak, are extremely blond, and when they have time, they read (*Selim* 45). The Turks perceive Germans as disciplined, punctual, and prescriptive people (*Selim* 69) who, despite these differences, are the only people who bear a similarity to themselves (*Selim* 68). However, after a few years of working in Germany, their perceptions change, and the Germans they work under reveal themselves as *Türkenhasser* (Turk-haters), who consider the Turks a barbaric folk: "Überhaupt hielt man die Türken mehr oder weniger für Barbaren, versicherte aber stets, daß man dagegen nichts einzuwenden hätte. Es gab auch einen Türkenhasser" (*Selim* 166). While working for a shipping company, Ismet, one of the workers on the ship, meets a *Türkenhasser* who does not want to share the sink with an oriental man. Nadolny's Turkish guest workers are aware of the insults to which they are subjected, but they neither expect nor appreciate a mere humanist recuperation. Mesut's observations illustrate this thought aptly:

> "You have to understand what they say," Mesut said as he looked away at the sea. "I know, insults. 'Beneath us are the Turks,' said the director. Imagine, we are supposed to be beneath them. Or they say, 'schließlich' he is a human being. I know that much German. 'Schließlich.' It means in the end. For them we are the last ones." (*Selim* 111)

Well aware of these problems, Selim reacts to the "culinary-racism" of Germans with his caustic humor: "For German noses, Turkish garlic stinks really badly, while French garlic smells divine" (*Selim* 180). Selim uses the power of satire and parody to combat stereotypes. He entertains his German acquaintances' preconceived notions of and prejudices against the Turks and reacts to this sanctioned ignorance with ironic confirmation of stereotypes about Turks. He does not restrain himself from telling a German colleague in a pub that the women in Turkey are sold by the kilo, so one has to pay a huge bridal price to marry a well-endowed woman. He is not shy of holding a knife between his teeth in a bar to show another colleague how people walk in Turkey. This ironic self-representation past truth-claims continues in Selim's interactions with intellectuals. During a conversation with a student of the Freie Universität Berlin, Selim tells her that there are harems in Turkey and camels are still the main mode of transportation. Nadolny's Turkish characters, with their unique style of coming to terms with their present, are very capable of reflection on their identities:

> We are not normal Turks, thought Selim.
> There are no normal Turks. You mean "average."
> None to be displayed, not poster-citizen Turks!
> In any case we have higher demands! (*Selim* 112)

Precisely this heightened sense of self-awareness gives Selim the power to criticize Mesut, who is embraced by students participating in the student movement as their diversity token. Selim chastises Mesut for agreeing to play the "exotic monkey" (*exotischer Affe*). This critical awareness inculcates in Selim the skepticism he needs against the so-called German friends of Turks who treat the Turks as anthropological subjects. The novel contains an elaborate critique of enthusiasts of multiculturalism, ready to rescue a suffering Turk or any other minority subject. This critique corresponds to Alexander's articulation of his own anxiety about being the cultural interlocutor. Thus, by juxtaposing Turkish stereotypes about Germans with German stereotypes about Turks, and the Turkish reinforcement of the latter, Nadolny's narrative allows the *Gastarbeiter* to speak through and against stereotypes. The idea of the representation of Turks, fraught from the very beginning, finds extension through the uncertainty of narraphasia, on the one hand, and the certainty of a stereotypical discourse, on the other. Representation is often inlaid with a conscious self-deprecation by the native informant.

The critique of a victimized narrative of the Other, truth-claims about identity, and multicultural pacifism reaches its climax in Nadolny's *Selim* through the figure of Ayşe, a second-generation Turkish immigrant. Ayşe, the daughter of guest-worker parents, moves to Germany from Turkey after her parents die in a car accident. Despite being a bright student in school, she is often ridiculed by students and teachers alike. As a young adult she develops an acute awareness of her position as a cultural outsider. Sentiments that range from the alleged over-population of Turks in Germany ("Viele Türken hier, nicht?") to superfluous proclamations of tolerance toward Turks ("Wieso, ich habe nichts gegen Türken") (*Selim* 372) often occupy her thoughts. In her early twenties, Ayşe faces discrimination in the job market. Although she is qualified, she is often denied jobs because of her Turkish accent.

Ayşe's concerns find expression in a number of literary representations of first- and second-generation immigrants. However, the uniqueness of Nadolny's narrative manifests itself in the complication of discriminatory binaries. With the story of Ayşe, Nadolny not only tries to unveil the discrimination faced by Turks but also presents the other side of the picture: instances of self-victimization by the Turks in order to misappropriate immigration laws. Ayşe's work at a nonprofit organization for Turkish immigrants teaches her about the deep-seated victim mentality among the Turks (*Selim* 371f.). Ayşe acknowledges the discrimination against Turks but is troubled by the indifference and lack of understanding on both sides. Her role model, therefore, is Selim, whose success depends largely on his ability to adjust rather than succumb to the new demands placed upon him as a foreigner in Germany. Working at the nonprofit organization, she also learns about the under-the-table deals and about cheating and lying among the Turks as they twist immigration laws to their benefit. In addition, the complete refusal of some Turks to learn German disturbs Ayşe, for she realizes the importance of linguistic competence for confronting exploitation. Through Ayşe one also witnesses complex repercussions of racial discrimination against Turks: some of her younger Turkish acquaintances try to pass as Italians, thinking the Germans have something specifically against the Turks (363–73).

After her husband's death, Ayşe visits Selim in jail; he shares with her his experience with the German state and inspires her to go back to working for the immigrants. At this instance in the novel, Nadolny supplies Ayşe with the most poignant description of the position of foreigners in Germany: "Germany is tolerant of foreigners, as long as they do not mean to need a home—or as long as they believe that they had one in Turkey. . . . The Germans do not approach the Turks because they think that it is not worth it: they belong to Turkish, not German history" (*Selim* 380). Ayşe tries to break both the fatalistic attitude and apathy among the Turks and the indifference and hatred among the Germans. In the wake of the complicated immigration laws that prevent the reunion of Turkish families in Germany, she tries to inform the Turks of the few rights that they have as immigrants and how they should exercise them. Despite her activism and high-profile political career, Ayşe refuses to be a token Turk (*Vorzeige-, Presse- oder Fernsehtürkin* [*Selim* 382]). She seeks a way out from the circuitous trajectories of the stories of her fellow Turks, as well as from the German condescension that permeates the sophisticated vocabularies of tolerance and acceptance. Eager to let her ideas become public through the media, Ayşe decides to accept an invitation to take part in a panel discussion on *Überfremdung* (overforeignization). She plans to address the indifference of both the German government and German society. She aims to publicly object to the simplified conflation of xenophobia against the Turks with anti-Semitism. Her work with immigrants makes her realize that this is a cause of great angst amongst the Turkish community. She seeks action and not a mere demonstration of problematic historical parallels. She desires to address the indifference she sees within the Turkish community. She wants the Turks to come out of the ghetto and participate in society rather than lead an existence as economic refugees.

Ayşe's idealism fails; she has a very disappointing experience at the panel discussion. For her, the discussion remains lodged in abstractions like "our Turks are an enrichment for us" or in bureaucratic vocabulary like "Ausländerteil" and "Überfremdung" (*Selim* 385). Ayşe tries in vain to explain the importance of negotiation on the part of the Germans as well as the Turks. But her footage is largely edited. When her efforts to secure a second chance to voice her reaction to the "Heidelberger Manifesto" are rejected, she decides to claim media time through the use of violence. She sends letters to the Turkish channels as well as to some other organizations, stating that she wants to make her voice heard or else she will kill herself. Ayşe goes to the roof of a high-rise, but the state and media apparatus that tries to save her and even telecasts her attempted rescue live does not give her five minutes for making her statement (*Selim* 392f.). Ayşe jumps off the high-rise and dies. Albeit not a terrorist or a bomber, Ayşe becomes a "cultural suicider" who commits suicide to claim her right to free speech.

Ayşe's death gives rise to a number of predictable reactions. Nadolny presents these reactions as a stringent critique of intellectuals. Certain German intellectuals see Ayşe's suicide as a statement against the plight of the guest workers, and they blame the Turkish government for it. The Turkish side shoots back questions about the state of human rights in Germany. A German feminist universalizes Ayşe's misery, calling it a misery of all women. In the pub where Ayşe worked for some time, some customers analyze the treatment of her death in the media. A factory newsletter blames Ayşe's unemployment as the cause of her death. The most significant reaction comes from certain sociologists and other intellectuals, who blame her death on the larger cultural alienation of Turks in Germany (*Selim* 395f.). Since Ayşe's suicide in the novel is directly linked to the "Heidelberger Manifesto," it is necessary to make a short detour to the document itself. This detour will also clarify the accentuation of cultural difference as a limit of multicultural politics that Nadolny criticizes.

The manifesto, a public statement on multiculturalism and the politics of difference, was a pamphlet composed by eleven professors from all over Germany, who conferred in Heidelberg in order to bring to public attention the overforeignization (*Überfremdung*) of Germany.[19] The signatories included scholars of medicine, law, theology, literature, and other disciplines. The manifesto centralizes the issue of the growing number of foreigners, the majority of them being Turks, and the declining number of Germans in Germany. This alleged overforeignization is depicted in the document as the principal source of alienation of native/ethnic Germans in the workplace. However, the document is rather sympathetic to the alienation of guest workers: the two kinds of alienation are presented as comparable. The eleven signatories of the manifesto raise the issue of conflicts arising due to Germany's increasingly heterogeneous composition, but they assert that their presentation of these problems should not be "mistaken" for "fascist designs." Hence they invoke the preamble to the German constitution, which promises a reunification of the German citizenry. They pronounce their fear that ethnic diversification of Germany might obstruct the fulfillment of this promise. They remind the German president and the chancellor of their commitment to the German people. They demand the establishment of a workers' union without any connections to the political parties, in order to resolve the problems of the guest workers and those of Germany as a host country, or *Gastland* (Picardi-Montesardo 111–15).

However, Germany's societal problems are not presented only as economic but also as cultural. The manifesto presents the foreign threat to the language and culture of Germany and seeks to raise the issue of protecting German cultural rights in Germany. In order to protect themselves from being labeled conservative, the signatories stress the hermeneutic interpretation of the word *Erhaltung*. They assert respect for other people's right to preserve their own cultural heritage in their place of residence (*Wohngebiet*). They emphasize that they do not demand the loss of minority cultures through their Germanization (*Germanisierung*). The document then quickly shifts from Germany to the larger idea of

Europe, which is portrayed as a lively community of peoples and nations that, through their culture and history, build a totality of a higher kind (Picardi-Montesardo 112). Once these scholars have insinuated the incommensurability of the community of foreigners who do not contribute to the higher totality that formed Europe, they raise the issue of the literacy of the present generation, which they believe is being hindered by the presence of hundreds of thousands of people illiterate in their own mother tongue, as well as in German. Before these messiahs of cultural difference end their plea for the preservation of a German cultural heritage, they suggest a more appropriate use of technology in order to level the economic disparity between developed countries and underdeveloped countries. They believe that machines should be brought to the people and not vice versa. Western nations should help with the technological progress of the underdeveloped nations as part of the outreach program. Only this, they believe, can help overindustrialized countries to get rid of their burden of environmental pollution (Picardi-Montesardo 112f.).

These pundits of cultural difference—with an immense respect for the people's right to education—conclude the manifesto by stating the nature of their profession, which inspires them to discuss contemporary problems in the public sphere. Not unlike Peachum and Co. in Bertolt Brecht's *Three-Penny Opera*, they promise to provide meaningful and purposeful education to needy and dependent people, albeit those from foreign countries, especially the Third World.

Ayşe's reflections on the politics of the coexistence of multiethnic people are precisely against the kind of representation of the subaltern in the "Heidelberger Manifesto." She resists her persistent marginalization; she is frustrated with an abusive accentuation of cultural difference and cultural alienation; and she, thus, plans to cross the limits to make her voice heard. In the everyday political reality of the world, she is silenced. In giving space to her silence, Nadolny presents an unsurpassed critique of himself as an author, of his narrator as a cultural interlocutor, and of the project of segregational multiculturalism.

The end of Ayşe's story marks the end of the story of Turkish guest workers in Germany. The last two chapters take place in Turkey. I want to use this first ending to pause and revisit Spivak's question "Can the Subaltern Speak?" After spelling out the dubiousness of Foucault and Deleuze's insistence on an "immediate" and "substantive" political engagement, Spivak demonstrates the arduous predicament of the subaltern historians who look for "permission to narrate" the histories of the peasants and working classes in India beyond both the (preindependence) nationalist and the (postindependence) neonationalist accounts by Indian and British elites. Spivak asks again if the oppressed and the subaltern forever remain inaccessible to the writing subject, and following that, if the task of the intellectual should be to refrain from representation. In the light of the representationalist critiques that I mentioned earlier in this chapter and the debates surrounding Nadolny's *Selim*, I ask, can the Turkish guest worker speak; can Ayşe speak; or are both of them silenced again in a German author's account? Before I spell out my verdict, I want to cite the story of Bhuvaneswari Bhaduri, whom Spivak discusses as an example of "objects of discourse analysis for the non–self-abdicating intellectual, (who) . . . can illuminate a section of the social text":

> A young woman of sixteen or seventeen, Bhuvaneswari Bhaduri, hanged herself in her father's modest apartment in North Calcutta in 1926. The suicide was a puzzle since, as Bhuvaneswari was menstruating at the time, it was clearly not a case of illicit pregnancy. Nearly a decade later, it was discovered that she was a member of one of the many groups involved in the armed struggle for Indian independence. She had finally been entrusted with a political assassination. Unable to confront the task and yet aware of the practical need for trust, she killed herself. (Spivak, "Subaltern" 307)

I do not seek to draw a crude parallel between two politically active women, Bhuvaneswari and Ayşe, both of whom commit suicide for a political cause. I want to point out the uncanny coincidence that marks the end of the narratives of two very different cultural workers who attempt to reflect on the representation of the subaltern at two very different times, in two very different cultural milieus. One reacts against the epistemic and political violence of a colonial power, the other against that of a financially and politically influential majority. Thus Spivak and Nadolny qua Alexander, while claming limited access to the subject of their writings, do not abandon the predicament of representing. Nadolny's careful construction of the *Gastarbeiter* and his conscious struggle with representation and narration assist him in recognizing and understanding the desire of the narrative to gain power over the subaltern, the foreigner, the ethnic Other. Nadolny thus defies a simplistic critique of representation based only on his own ethnicity. Nadolny affirms that even textual hospitality cannot be simply extended to the guest worker, for it involves the danger of the guest's losing his own voice. The track of ideology that Spivak criticizes turns into a fault line; Alexander's narraphasia positions itself at the epicenter of the narrative, shaking, moving, upsetting the harmonious plates of multiculturalism or a simplified intercultural dialogue. Nadolny intervenes in the programmatic segregation of the Turkish community propounded by the intellectuals in the novel. The question *of* the foreigner finally starts to emerge as the question posed *by* the foreigner.

Nadolny problematizes Selim's deportation on the basis of a "crime" committed in the country of residence, as the (German) pimp-nexus in Hamburg remains unchallenged. Ayşe, the Turkish-German woman, witnesses the Turkish people's harassment at the foreign directorate, whereas Geneviéve, a Swiss woman, manages to live in Germany without any legal problems, even after her passport gets stolen and is used by a German woman, Gisela. Despite being of different nationalities, Gisela and Geneviéve have one passport for some time, even while it is impossible for Turkish parents to get permission to visit their children. Nadolny's project, through its presentation of the Turkish characters and the problems faced by the Turkish community within the larger political scheme of the West German political reality, can be read as a unique treatment of themes central to what came to be known as *Gastarbeiterliteratur*. Nadolny's Turkish workers live and participate in a Germany where the generation that witnessed the rise and fall of the Third Reich is still, perhaps, trying to come to terms with modes of associations with foreigners. During the student protests in 1968, the Turkish guest workers, along with some of their German acquaintances, hurriedly climb the stairs of the Thielplatz subway station, running over to the "Kritische Universität" in order to devise strategies to rescue the world at the Henry Ford Building. This student generation later manifests the concerns of the generation of the 1970s by exploring German history through such new means as films on the relationship of a young woman to the Middle Ages, to those on the German subjunctive as a way of coming to terms with the past. From the train journey to Berlin to the final reunion in Mugla, Nadolny's Turkish characters bear witness to the long march of the 68ers from Adenauer's stress on the work-ethic—via a short-lived legacy of Herbert Marcuse—to an internalization of Habermasian communication theory. Out of this ideological march, *Selim* emerges as a novel about a guest worker in which the Turkish characters will not be restricted to the assembly line. They stake their claims at the center of the German nation and not at its periphery.

In his book *Politics of Friendship*, Jacques Derrida reflects on the paradoxical nature of friendship. Meditating on the oft-cited quotation, "O my friend, there is no friend!" Derrida traces the unusual genealogies of friendships, consanguinities, relations (political/social/familial), and animosities. For Derrida, the European tradition of philosophical reflections on friendship becomes a site to disclose the "inverse hierarchies" and "inverse dissymmetries" of the nature of friendship, which is "to love before being loved." Friendship displaces the hitherto prevalent connotations of the subject and the object. While reflecting on the *Eudemian Ethics*, Derrida writes,

> Philia . . . is first accessible on the side of its subject, who thinks and loves it, and not on the side of its object, who can be loved or lovable without in any way being assigned to a sentiment of which, precisely, he remains the object. And if we do say, "think and love" . . . life, breath and soul are always and necessarily found on the side of the lover or of the loving, while the being-loved of the lovable can be lifeless; it can belong to the reign of the non-loving, the non-psychic, or the "soulless." One cannot love without living and without loving, but one can still love the deceased or the inanimate who then know nothing of it. It is indeed the possibility of loving the deceased that the decision in favor of a certain lovence comes into being. (*Politics of Friendship* 7)

It is indeed this paradoxical nature of friendship that makes friendship for Cicero a site of "epitaph or oration, citation of the dead person, the renown of a name after the death of what it names, all at the same time" (*Politics of Friendship* 5). Friendship is a funeral eulogy, waiting too eagerly sometimes to be signed in advance. Alexander's account of his friendship with Selim is a eulogy, albeit a critical one.

At the end of the novel, Alexander makes a trip to Turkey. All the characters in the novel are in Mugla for a big reunion party. Selim dies in a car accident. On the flight back to Germany, technical problems seem to jeopardize the plane's safe landing. Alexander tries to calm his fellow passengers, but no one listens to him. Following Selim's strategy, Alexander fabricates a story. Alexander's unusual "eulogy" for his friend Selim thus takes place neither in the rococo theater in Degenhardt nor in a Greek amphitheater as he dreamed but on an airplane, somewhere between Istanbul and Berlin.

The drama in the novel thus gets completed not on the land, marked with borderlines, but in the space between nations. The geographical and historical complexities of the protagonist Selim's places of birth and of residence successfully palliate the Orient–Occident divide. These complexities accentuate not only the transnational heritages of cities mentioned in the novel, which exist in the atlas, but also of those that through their fictitious nature promote a reading beyond national borders. What then follows is a long discourse on narrative and cultural challenges, a personal and collective insertion into a history that Alexander wants to access and into a present to which he has very limited access. Between Degenhardt and Mugla, between Berlin and Istanbul, there exists an "Other"—cosmopolitanism, which becomes the engine for the novel. Through the narrator's willingness to engage with the cultural Other, through his reversal of the guest–host relationships at the end, through the narraphasia experienced by the narrator and by Selim and Ayşe, all against the backdrop of a friendship, Nadolny succeeds in telling a story about Turkish guest workers beyond Orientalism and ethnic *ressentiment*.

Nadolny's *Selim* registers cosmopolitan aspirations not just because the plot traverses various German and Turkish cities and includes Turks and Germans who interact with each other. While these features exhibit facilitations of and impediments to the willingness to engage the Other, Selim's cosmopolitanism is what Ulrich Beck describes in his essay "Cosmopolitan Perspective" (Vertovec and Cohen 61–85) as a "reflexive cosmopolitanism," "a learning process" whose "aim ... is to test how in one's life, in a world without distance, ways of relating to the otherness of others can be learned" (ibid. 83). Through these reflections, Nadolny upsets several ontologies, the most important being those of the "identity" of the author and the "authenticity" of the subject of narration. In a published series of lectures entitled *Das Erzählen und die guten Ideen*,[20] Nadolny reflects on the process of narration: "The narrator cares, more or less consciously for a specific perspective. It is never automatically 'his' personal [perspective] in the sense of an identity.... Narration narrates itself.... I think ... that there are doctrinaires here, who cling to a mistaken imagination of an 'authentic' narration, and through that they actually sever the freedom of narration" (*Erzählen* 105). Nadolny thus defies any "good" intentions of an author as part of a set of irritating professional predicaments (*Erzählen* 97). With Nadolny's metareflections on narration, I bring the reader now to the end of this chapter. Nadolny's *Selim* offers a respite from the preoccupation with the always-already-flawed literary representation of a minority character or culture by an author hailing from a majority culture. Through my reading of the novel I have sought to present an intricate and entangled interpretation of the politics of representation and difference, which Nadolny narrates through the friendship between Alexander and Selim and through the suicide of Ayşe. One aspect of criticism of the novel, and of Nadolny, that I have categorically tried to avoid in my reading is the issue of authentication and stereotyping. Instead of listing and criticizing stereotypes, and therefore declaring Nadolny's narrative incompetent—like Sabine von Dirke has done—I have chosen a different strategy: to present stereotyping as a critically enabling feature that can be utilized optimally by an author while narrating the cultural Other. Similarly, I have presented narraphasia as a narrative conundrum but also as a heuristic device, as a kind of legible, narrative chaos, a cacophony of doubt about narration itself, an expression of uncertainty about the native informant and the cultural interlocutor, a state of epistemic inaccessibility, from which is rendered audible the voice of the subaltern, the marginalized Other. In calling Nadolny a successful operator of this device, my urge has been to reformulate the question of authority of representation. While my incessant attempt has been to question the essentialization of cultures and identities, I have not succumbed to a complete relativization of identity.

Thus, my reading has benefited from Satya P. Mohanty's persuasive "post-positivist realist" intervention "Epistemic Status of Cultural Identity" (29–66), albeit only partially.[21] Instead of once again raising Mohanty's foundational question ("who can be trusted to represent the real interests of the group without fear of betrayal or misrepresentation?" [Moya and Hames-Garcia 29]), I have questioned the very ideas of betrayal and misrepresentation and the fear of the two. Indeed in placing Nadolny within and then beyond the literary movement known as *Gastarbeiterliteratur*, I have, on the one hand, emphasized the value of experience with the cultural Other. On the other hand, by not placing undue emphasis on the authenticity of this experience or the critique of this experience as Gökberk successfully demonstrated in her essay "Cultural Studies," I have attempted to upset the very idea of fear, a fear of losing epistemic privilege, which informs and fuels orthodox multiculturalism. For it is this fear that prevents practitioners of orthodox (mosaic) multiculturalism from questioning the arrogance of their own claims of epistemic privilege, self-proclaimed and reclaimed because of their (marginalized) race, ethnicity, sexual orientation, or as Mohanty has correctly pointed out, the commonality of experience (Moya and Hames-Garcia 30). It is this fear that makes multiculturalist critics incapable of thinking through new paradigms for reading multicultural literature in the contemporary period of globalization. It is this fear that makes them first present, and then immediately reject, majority interventions in minority cultures as gestures maleficent to the cause of multiculturalism.

Sten Nadolny emancipates himself from this fear by accepting that he is epistemologically underprivileged with regard to the subject of his narration, and he thus presents his cosmopolitical claims. In *Selim*, he does this through the inclusion of diary entries, in which he constantly questions narrating itself. In his writings on narration and his work as a narrator, he achieves this fearlessness and eventual emancipation from an essentialized identity by expressing his fraught and fragile relationship with language. Nadolny is thus able to stand above essentialist approaches to reclaiming identity, largely due to his fraught relationship with language. He sees language as a stubborn means of transportation (*Erzählen* 136) and concedes that the language loves him but never does what he says (ibid.). Selim perhaps knows, and Nadolny—through the interlocutor Alexander—translates Selim's knowledge into language, which he constantly questions, knowing very well that the guest/foreigner is fully capable of manipulating language, information, representation, and indeed narration.

TWO

Slouching Histories, Lurking Memories
Emine Sevgi Özdamar's *Seltsame Sterne Starren zur Erde*

"GDR border-patrol, your travel-documents, please."
"Are we in East Germany already?"
"In the German Democratic Republic," said the young policeman.
"I love Brecht." He didn't say anything.

EMINE SEVGI ÖZDAMAR, *SELTSAME STERNE*

These lines from Emine Sevgi Özdamar's novel *Seltsame Sterne Starren zur Erde* (Strange Stars Stare toward the Earth) reconstruct the (Turkish) first-person narrator's reentry into Germany through the former GDR. The *re-*, as it prefixes the words *construct* and *entry*, denotes an event that has been experienced in the past and is now being rehearsed to invoke the memory of that past event. The awkward exchange between the narrative *I* and the border-patrol officer immediately leads to a moment in German history that has been subordinated. Refracted through the Turkish narrator, this moment does not invoke immediate nostalgia. The sternness of the border-patrol officer, when retold, offers little recuperation. The exchange takes the reader out of the comfort zone of easy identification. There is no description of history here; the allusion offered by the reconstructive narrative of memory offers a certain discomfiture. What is the nature of this discomfiture? What kind of memory work insinuates this discomfiture? This chapter is an attempt to comprehend the work and political claims of memory when considered through cosmopolitan conjectures that do not strive for universalism, objectivity, and authenticity but acknowledge difference. Through my discussion of Özdamar's *Seltsame Sterne*, I try to understand claims of minoritarian cosmopolitanism and memory when the story of migration is, as Ulrich Beck writes, less about origins and destinations than about somewhere in between.

In "Acting Bits/Identity Talk," Gayatri Chakravorty Spivak reminds us that "what we call experience is a staging of experience" ("Acting Bits"

158). This staging appears for Spivak in the tenacity of the word *origin*—national, ethnic—a word that becomes "the strongest account of the agency or mechanics of the staging of experience-in-identity" (ibid.). Having cited the "pernicious" formulation of this interpretation of origin—"you cannot help acting this way because your origin stages you so"—Spivak moves to re-cite herself and revise her own previously authored statement: "history lurks in it [origin] somewhere" is rewritten as "history slouches in it, ready to comfort *and* kill" (ibid., original emphasis). Through this moment of re-citation and revision, Spivak argues for an understanding of origins through a reexamination of institutions and inscriptions in order to then "surmise the mechanics by which such institutions and inscriptions can stage such a particular style of performance" (ibid.). While Spivak duly acknowledges that this mode of examination of origins "secures the minority voice in Anglo cultures," she does not resist alerting readers to the possibility that this mode "also reveals the manipulation of the very same minorities into superpower identification in the violent management of global cultural politics" (ibid.). Thus, the very possibility of assertion of agency by a minority artist through protest conveys the impossibility of agency, the staging of the "experience of history," of "origin." The danger of pursuing a fixated, limited politics of identity lies in the perception that the terrain of intercultural translation occurs almost automatically through the assertion of cultural difference by the cultural Other through self-representation. Spivak admonishes that this illusion of a harmless and easy translation carries the potential of becoming absolute, cemented, and that this very "absolute interculturalism" quickly results in the cooptation of the artist by "imperialist malevolence" ("Acting Bits" 159).

Spivak offers these remarks to bridge two important moments in her essay: the first moment signifies her self-identification as a Bengali, whereby she discusses her deconstructive reading strategies in Bengali (her mother-tongue) in her home state of West Bengal in India.[1] The second moment—more important for our discussion here—is one of enforced, almost immediate betrayal of self-identification, a disidentification, a detachment, a sudden distancing from the origin, instigated by videographic art of the Lebanese-Canadian artist Jamelie Hassan. Not only does Hassan's installation *Midnight's Children*—her treatment of Salman Rushdie's famous novel of the same name—remove the novel from its direct historical and cultural context of the partition of India; for the critical viewer Spivak,[2] it challenges any easy transcoding of identity as a person of Indian origin born in pre-Independence India who witnessed or experienced the political reality of the partition of India. Spivak concedes that Hassan's work takes away her privilege of absolute identification with the experiences of the generation born at the cusp of the decolonization of India. Spivak thus stands in front of the installation, "stripped, precisely, of my 'identity'" ("Acting Bits" 162). The staging of the history as origin, the "experience-in-identity," the coding, recoding, transcoding, and decoding of cultural difference through a superficially beneficial economy of intercultural translation, all collapse into a moment of identitarian discomfiture. The concordance that might be derived from affiliation to any one experience, be it gendered, ethnic, or national, quickly transforms into a disaffiliational discordance from all three markers of belonging. By deterritorializing Rushdie's novel, Hassan's installation deterritorializes Spivak. History—Indian or Lebanese— slouches in the origin once again to comfort and to kill.

But what exactly does the lurking or slouching of history in the origin mean? How does it assist in surmising the mechanics of institutions and inscriptions that force a particular kind of performance in securing the voice of the minorities? What are the modes of disidentification, and how do they challenge and belie easy translation through "absolute interculturalism"? As I ask these questions in the context of cosmopolitics, I anticipate the reader's recognition of a conceit: this chapter discusses a woman writer who happens to be an ethnic minority in Germany, and therefore, the chief organizing principle of my reading is identity—in assertion or negation. That is not my intention; my reading of the first part of an essay by Spivak is guided by my genuine curiosity to trace approaches to answer these questions. But instead of looking for answers in Spivak's text or immediately in Özdamar's novel, I want to move toward these questions in a circumspect fashion. I want to briefly retrace salient points of two discussions on history, memory, experience, and pasts that underscore the thematic relevance of these terms in specific contexts of, and minorities and diasporas in, contemporary understanding.

In his essay "Minority Histories, Subaltern Pasts" (*Provincializing Europe* 97–113), Dipesh Chakrabarty deliberates on the responsibility and ambition of democratizing the discipline of history through an inclusion of "minority histories," an expression, he writes, "which has come to represent all those pasts on whose behalf democratically minded historians have fought the exclusions and omissions of mainstream narratives of the nation" (ibid. 97). Defining history as a "subject primarily concerned with the crafting of narratives," Chakrabarty raises two important questions: "Can the story be told/crafted? And does it deploy for a rationally defensible point or position from which to tell the story?" (ibid. 98). Chakrabarty's definition of minor intersects with, but does not entirely overlap, that of Deleuze and Guattari: "Just as minor in literature implies 'a critique of narratives of identity... the 'minor' in my use similarly functions to cast doubt on the major" (ibid. 101). Minority history "leads ... to the 'minority' of some particular pasts" (ibid. 100). Chakrabarty calls such subordinated relations to the past "subaltern pasts" (ibid. 101). In addition, outlining the distinction between "historians' history and other reconstructions of the past," Chakrabarty lists practices such as "fictionalizing the past... studying memory rather than just history, playing around with forms of writing, and other similar means" (ibid. 106). Having made these distinctions, Chakrabarty raises another crucial question, "Are there any experiences of the past that cannot be captured by the methods of the discipline, or which at least show limits of the discipline?" (ibid. 107). I do not wish to rehearse Chakrabarty's illustrations of minority histories through subaltern studies in India in its entirety. Two observations, however, need to be pronounced. First and foremost, "minority history" is not be confused with the history of a minority. Chakrabarty categorically frames his question in the contexts of "'minority' of some particular pasts" (ibid. 100). This may include the history of a minority. Second, by presenting Chakrabarty's distinctions between history and memory, and history and past, my concern is not to comment on the discipline of history but on the context of considerations of those narratives (of memory or of history) that are not "official" or "officially blessed" (ibid. 97), that is, majoritarian, dominant, and therefore, hegemonic.

While Chakrabarty illustrates these differences with a specific example from Indian history, his thoughts resonate in a discussion on diasporic and national memory in the German context by Andreas Huyssen. In his essay "Diaspora and Nation: Migration into Other Pasts" Huyssen asks "how the diasporic immigrant can relate to the memory of the host nation" ("Diaspora" 154). Huyssen begins by acknowledging his puzzlement about "globalization of traumatic memory discourses" (ibid. 147) as a means of thinking through registers of memory of the Holocaust in Zafer Şenocak's novel *Gefährliche Verwandschaft*.[3] "National memory presents itself as natural, authentic, coherent, and homogenous," Huyssen states. "Diasporic memory is in its traditional sense cut off, hybrid, displaced, split" (ibid. 152). So the temporal difference between "the act of remembrance" and the "content of that which is remembered" through diasporic memory is, Huyssen argues, "an act of *recherché* rather than recuperation" (ibid. 152, original emphasis). Although traumatic memory discourses are not the focus of my discussion here, Huyssen's insights on the relationship between migrants' imaginations and (German) national memory merit attention:

> Home, Heimat, is no longer what it once used to be, either for the nation or for the diaspora. Clearly, national memory today, in an age of ever more transnational institutions, migrations, and networks, is being colored ever more by nostalgia and an imagined memory. But so is diasporic memory at a time when pasts and presents of migrant populations lose the traditional coherence of diasporic community as a result of multiple travels and relocations back and forth. Traditional diaspora separated a diasporic present existentially from a past which thus could become ever more imaginary and mythic. Today's hyphenated and migratory cultures develop different structures of experience which may make the traditional understanding of diaspora as linked to roots, soil, and kinship indeed highly questionable. (ibid. 151)

Chakrabarty's and Huyssen's commentaries, when considered in juxtaposition, illuminate significant conjectures of diasporic and migrant (ethnic) minorities' interventions in the national history and memory of the host nation. They assist in distinguishing between personal or collective experiences that take place in a temporality that is framed by the bygone—a past. A subaltern past is determined dimensionally; this past is subaltern because it can be identified as having been subordinated in relation to the ordinate—regulated, moderated, ordered, or even ordained—versions of a past. The narration of these pasts in the discipline of history is thus minority history. Minority history does not declare a past minor; its predicament is to lead to a past that has been hitherto subordinated by "official" or "officially blessed" histories or even to determine what are normative or mainstream interests in accounts of history. The task of minority histories is not only a recollection and narration of the subordinated pasts but also an accounting for the difference between such pasts and those that have been ordinate and ordained for reasons that could range from doctrinaire ideology, to epistemological interests of the historians themselves, to perhaps even methodological constraints that impede access to those pasts in order to then be able to narrate them. A democratic inclination to include what has been hitherto excluded has a recuperative (i.e., a corrective, restorative, if not necessarily always a medicinally healing) ambition. This ambition can realize itself through *recherché* (quest, search), but also through desire to quest and search. Minority histories, as they lead to and facilitate our access to subaltern pasts, have a double responsibility of—borrowing from Huyssen—recherché *and* recuperation.

Huyssen, it must be noted, does not use or invoke the words *subaltern* or *minority*. His reflections pertain directly to memory and not to what Chakrabarty refers to as a "historian's history." Nonetheless, it is worthwhile to follow the distinction he makes between a "national memory"—marked by naturalness, authenticity, and coherence—and a "diasporic memory"—"cut off, hybrid, displaced, split" (ibid. 152). I cite Huyssen's descriptors of diasporic memory twice to emphasize his categorical restraint from presenting artificiality, inauthenticity, and incoherence as attributes of diasporic memory. Diasporic memories of a nation do, however, as Huyssen states, reflect degrees of severance, amalgamation, displacement, and rupture from national memories. If this interpretation is valid, there might be some intersections between Chakrabarty's theorization of the task of minority histories and Huyssen's formulation of diasporic memory. Diasporic memory also accords narrative structures to a past that has yet not been narrated as such, even though it might not always be a past lived or witnessed or experienced by the member of the diaspora in the host nation. Due to the lack of a direct, given, natural, easily cognizable, and therefore, coherently perceivable connection to national memory, narratives of diasporic memory lead to what has hitherto been subordinated in relationship to national memory.

The contexts in which minority history and diasporic memory are conceptualized by Chakrabarty and Huyssen obviously do not permit easy conflation. Huyssen's main focus is the significance of interventions of diasporic memory in a past of the host nation; Chakrabarty situates his theories of minority history without singling out immigration as one of the contexts. Yet the functions of minority history and diasporic memory as delineated by these two scholars provide valuable insights into normative standardizations that ordinate and regulate imaginations of national histories and memories and into the modes through which minority histories and diasporic memories differentiate themselves from those norms. Extending this interpretation, I want to point out that to assume that diasporic memory's relationship to the past of the nation of birth—origin—will be necessarily natural, authentic, or coherent would be a mistake. I stand in agreement with Huyssen's proposition that the shuttling back and forth in the age of accelerated mobility increases access to the nation of birth and, therefore, absolves a gross idealization of the links to "roots, soil, and kinship." Therefore, diasporic memory's relationship to the national memory of the nation of birth is equally "cut-off, hybrid, split." In other words, if minority history leads us to subaltern, subordinated pasts, diasporic memory also leads us to pasts that have been subordinated in the respective host nation but also in the nation of birth. Increased mobility and multiple relocations might facilitate access, but do not necessarily guarantee easy access, to these pasts. To express it with a reference to Seyla Benhabib, if the *demos* of the host nation does not simply overlap with the *ethnos* of the host nation, the *ethnos* of the nation of birth, when in diaspora, acquires a disjunctive relationship with the *demos* of the nation of birth. It is perhaps safe to conclude that the narration of these pasts is a matter of recherché *and* recuperation.[4]

In other words, narratives of minority history and diasporic memory bring forth subordinate pasts but do not necessarily ordinate them; that is, turn these pasts into narratives that might be official or officially blessed. Minority history and diasporic memory define themselves with and through the modes of their subordination and their supplementarity. By virtue of their amalgamated, severed, and disjunctive relationship with their nation of birth, the diasporic, migrant *demos* cease to nurture a simplistic and idealized nostalgia for the nation of birth. The ordinate and ordained, natural and authentic history and memory of the nation of birth itself undergoes subordination when filtered through the experience of diaspora. Once subaltern pasts have been identified as subordinated, there is no easy identification available with the *ethnos* of the nation of birth through mythologized nostalgia. Narratives of minority history or diasporic memory can at best register the discomfiture, and not comfortable identification, with the nation of birth and its history. If easy identification with nations and cultures of birth is the basis for interculturalism, identitarian discomfiture prevents and resists any easy translation through "absolute interculturalism." Moments of identitarian discomfiture with the nation of birth inscribe the subaltern, subordinated moments of origins. Once that identitarian discomfiture has been recognized and registered, the prowling, loitering, creeping, lurking national history or memory of the nation of birth in origins immediately stoops, sprawls, slumps, and slouches in origins, to comfort, and to kill.

I indulge in this long discussion of subaltern pasts and minority history not only to illuminate the conceptual framework within which I shall situate my reading but also because history, memory, and intentional subordination of ethnicity and gender through performance have acquired centrality in recent discussions of Özdamar's works. To understand the relevance and innovation of these discussions—which I shall present in a subsequent section of this chapter—it will be beneficial to glance at Özdamar's intellectual biography and situate it in the larger context of women authors whose works register multiple languages, cultures, histories, and ethnicities.

Emine Sevgi Özdamar is one of the most well-known and celebrated "Turkish-German woman authors."[5] I present the descriptors of Özdamar's identification here in quotation marks due to the identitarian value they have accrued over the past decade and a half. Since the publication of her first collection of short stores, *Mutterzunge*, Özdamar has been praised and condemned for a variety of reasons. In the German press, as well as among literary scholars, she has been applauded for her creative courage, first and foremost for transforming and deterritorializing the German language through an abundant inclusion of Turkish phrases, idioms, and proverbs. While writing as an immigrant author in Germany, Özdamar's struggle with her "Mutterzunge" and "Großvaterzunge" (grandfather tongue) made her well-known for her critique of the programmatic modernization of Turkey. Her first novel, *Das Leben ist eine Karawanserei* (1992),[6] which won her the prestigious Ingeborg Bachmann Prize the year of its publication, was widely read as her exploration of the bifurcated cultural legacy of Turkey through the eyes of a young girl. In her insightful reading of this novel, Azade Seyhan states that the "major focus of Özdamar's work is language as rite, ritual, mode of survival and a zone of comfort in an inhospitable environment" (*Writing Outside* 143). These rites and rituals of language continue in Özdamar's second novel, *Die Brücke vom goldenen Horn*, in which the young girl from *Karawanserei* arrives in Berlin as a female guest worker and mayhem ensues. The first-person narrator of this novel witnesses and comments on the tumultuous events in Berlin and Paris in the late 1960s both as a guest worker and a *Dolmetcherin* (simultaneous interpreter), her residence in Berlin shaped and informed by experiences in the radio-lamp factory, the women's hostel, and the streets and pubs. While in Turkey, she reports on the split between Brechtian and Stanislawskian methodological camps in the Department of Drama at the Istanbul University. Then, as a failed harbinger of a Marxist revolution in the Kurdish village of Hakkari at the border of Turkey and Iraq, she ridicules her inability to reconcile theory and praxis. The novel ends with the narrator's magical realist account of the revival of political conservatism in Turkey in the late 1960s. As books by Marx and Engels float in the Marmara Sea and pages torn from these books litter the streets of Istanbul, the narrator returns to

Germany with hopes of becoming an actress. Much like *Karawanserei*, *Goldenen Horn* documents experiences of Turkish immigrants in Germany while simultaneously rendering the German language porous, permeable, and perceptive to those experiences. Writing, indeed, becomes rite, ritual, mode of survival. Özdamar's modes of survival through writing acquire complex manifestations through expressions of her difficult affiliations with guest workers in Berlin, with theater artists in Istanbul, and with the hegemony of unified national cultures in Turkey and in Germany. The novel thus emerges as a brilliant commentary on intellectual subscriptions to political ideologies of race, gender, class, and nation.

These very reasons for Özdamar's applause have also emerged as grounds for her condemnation. The controversy surrounding her winning the Bachmann Prize was interpreted by conservative critics as a literary institution's succumbing to pressures of multiculturalism and the politics of recognition and as a crude celebration of the exotic.[7] Arno Widmann, in his article in *The European*, held Özdamar's "grammarless flow of Oriental images" responsible for the inaccessibility of her work to German readers (12). On his television show *Das Literarische Quartett*, Marcel Reich-Reinicki, the Bill O'Reilly of German literary criticism, reduced Özdamar to an Oriental spinner of fairy tales. In a more sincere engagement with Turkish-German women authors, Deniz Göktürk has performed a nuanced consideration of aspects of Özdamar's writings that could amount to her self-promotion as an exotic Other. Göktürk does so by demystifying Özdamar's language and by criticizing the celebration of Turkish idioms in German by scholars illiterate in the Turkish language ("Kennzeichen" 529–30).

Özdamar's critical reception alludes to an itinerary that has established itself as orthodoxy within literature by minorities, especially women authors who write at cultural and linguistic intersections. Their narratives are often confined to being occasions of self-discovery, self-fulfillment, and self-realization of—to state it facetiously—the "souls" of minority women authors. The authors either turn into authentic subjects with experiences of patriarchal subjugation, native informants who "finally" (and rather simplistically) claim their own stories in their own voices by writing (graphing) their selves (auto). Or they are aptly criticized for self-exoticization and self-promotion, in that they confirm and reinforce prejudgments, stereotypes about their cultures—often perceived as part of the abstract oriental monolith—or their status as women: subjugated, colonized, eternal victims of oriental patriarchal malevolence with no agency for resistance. Especially in scholarship on literary works by women authors whose origins are identifiable as the geo-cultural non-West, the author's ethnicity or national origin acquires the tenacious perniciousness of which Spivak reminds us: you must write this because you are this way! As the verb *writing* collapses into being, critical deliberations turn into reductive readings, and the literary works are made to fit one (or more) of the following bills: 1) Third-World literature (as a political allegory of the country of birth) if the literary work explicitly engages with the country of birth, experiences of patriarchy, and struggles against patriarchy[8]; 2) migrant-women's literature, expressions of a gendered social discrimination and resulting isolation in the country of residence; 3) hyphenated (hybrid) literature, articulations of biculturality, being in-between cultures, negotiation of one or more ethnic/national/sexual identities by the author or the narrator.

While research on women's writings within the realm of minority literature has undoubtedly expanded and enriched the body of knowledge about these authors and their works, the reductionism discussed above has invariably led to a restricted understanding of the other literary claims of the authors. This mode of reductive reception of these authors' works by scholars and popular media, on the one hand, reifies the binaries between East and West, often expressed in terms of regression and progression, repression and emancipation; on the other hand, in all its complexity, it propagates the idea that victimized identities can indeed be searched for (and then found) in and around the cultural hyphen. I state this bluntly, not in order to discount the fact that patriarchal structures—both in the countries of birth and in the countries of immigration—subject women to multiple forms of discrimination. As has been documented by many sociologists and cultural anthropologists, immigrant women who primarily work at home experience the sudden loss of social networks that they enjoyed in their countries of birth, thus experiencing heightened alienation and isolation in their countries of residence.[9] In addition, due to their financial dependence on male members of their families, immigrant women who work as mothers and primary caregivers experience extensive imbalances in domestic equations of power. Unsurprisingly, the pathos of a forced existence at the margins, the discrimination faced outside the place of work, cultural differences, alienation due to lack of cultural adaptation, and a transportation of existing patriarchal structures into the countries of residence become some of the central themes of narratives of immigrant women. The critics, however, in the search, perhaps, for objective experiential evidence of non-Western women, ascribe to these authors what the feminist critic Sara Suleri aptly diagnoses as a "racially encoded privilege, an iconicity" that turns them into native informants (Suleri 134–35). The native informant woman author, once established as both a weapon and a soldier of identitarian politics, feeds the hungry multiculturalist critic with objective truths about the culture of the Other. Criticizing such an unreflective investment in the autobiography of the Other (woman) turned into a native informant, Gayatri Chakravorty Spivak comments:

> If one looks at the history of post-Enlightenment theory, the major problem has been the problem of autobiography: how subjective structures can, in fact, give objective truth. During the same centuries, the Native Informant ... was unquestioningly treated as the objective evidence for the founding of the so-called sciences like ethnography, ethno-linguistics, comparative religion, and so on. So that, once again, the theoretical problems only relate to the person who knows. The person who *knows* has all the problems of selfhood. The person who is *known*, somehow, seems not to have a problematic self. (*Postcolonial Critic* 66, original emphasis)

Although Spivak situates her comment in the context of theoretical writings, her insight poses an important question for our analyses of fictional writings of immigrant authors in the second half of the twentieth century. In the past thirty years, as is well known, members of ethnic minorities in the United States and Western Europe have given expression to diverse themes like cultural conflicts, social discrimination, exploitation at work, and the pressure of assimilation. In their well-intended endeavor to recognize these immigrant narratives as contributions to the diversified social text of the West, cultural critics have inclined toward considering works by minority authors as sources of objective truths about minority communities. In their attempts to understand the struggles of collectivities through these largely autobiographical individual narratives, as stated earlier, these authors are turned into undisputed representatives of their communities, native informants, who provide the coveted authentic voice to the trials and tribulations of ethnic minorities.[10] However, it would be a mistake to hold scholars of multiculturalism and feminism singlehandedly responsible for this reification and fetishization of the native informant's authenticity. A number of immigrant writers/artists and their (minority) readers have sought refuge from the everyday conflicts in a perpetual nostalgia for an idealized homeland.[11] Some immigrant authors of first or subsequent generations have celebrated their position between cultures by comparing milieus of the Western metropolis where they were resident aliens with those of little villages and towns in Asia or Africa where they were nonresident aliens. Immigrant narratives have gradually become projects of proving one's contact with grass roots, sometimes invoking as many local gods and goddesses and religious and social customs as possible, thus indulging in self-exoticism.[12] The literature of identity politics thus reads as a commitment to the ethnology of idiosyncrasies and the aesthetics of poverty of the home-culture.[13] For publishers and readers, as well as critics, the poorer the immigrant, the more authentic he or she is. Real Asian and African women come from small villages; those from towns or urban locales with exposure to Western education or lifestyles who do not quite experience an intense culture shock as immigrants to the West are either papier-mâché figurines or dangerous, unreliable, not-quite native informants.

Manifestations of these trends can be easily found within writings of Turkish-German women authors, where both literary production and scholarship have demonstrated an affinity for a native informant as the authentic ethnic for about two decades. Even as a few women authors were being hailed as the voices of the communities by literary scholars on both sides of the Atlantic, they themselves never questioned if their projects were conveying the same homogenous, monolithic idea of the non-Western woman that had been part of the Western imagination for centuries. Adalet Agaoğlu's *Die zarte Rose meiner Sehnsucht*; Ayşel Özakin's *Die Leidenschaft der Anderen* and *Soll ich hier alt werden?*; Saliha Scheinhardt's *Drei Zypressen* and *Frauen, die sterben, ohne dass sie gelebt hätten* are a few examples of literary works that gave expression to themes in a genre that was gradually being recognized as *MigrantInnenliteratur* (migrants' literature). These authors' representations of Turkish women's helplessness and despair resulted in confirming the stereotype of the eternally repressed non-Western woman. Ayşel Özakin, despite her public denial of her categorization as a Turkish-German woman author, has insisted on her authentic accounts of the plight of Turkish-German women. Similarly Saliha Scheinhardt has publicly asserted "what I narrate, really happened; all of my figures are authentic" (Scheinhardt, interview 7). Against such authentications, Sigrid Weigel suggests an awareness of the limitations of self-representation by immigrant women writers. Although her statement is specifically a reaction to Saliha Scheinhardt's writings, it holds currency for works of other authors as well: "In her [Scheinhardt's] representation of a Turkish woman's everyday life between discrimination, isolation, and fettering through traditional role models and moral ideas, the first-person narrators appear as completely discouraged victims, and their life-stories as examples of social and sexual exploitation. Streams of light from this darkness exist only in idealist looking back at the Anatolian homeland and in looking forward to an 'emancipation' oriented toward western models" (Weigel 223). Leslie Adelson shares Weigel's perspective in her succinct remark that Turkish-German women authors have established themselves as "doubly othered," invoking not compassion but pity. Adelson imputed this to a tendency to see Turkish-German literature "through a lens that reflects a double othering: [where] the otherness of Turkish experience is 'added' to that of female gender" ("Price of Feminism" 307).[14]

I stand in agreement with the observations of these two scholars. The cultural heritage of Turkish-German women has been too quickly decried as backward, patriarchal, and chauvinistic. Most of the discussions on the writings of these women have been centered either around the authenticity of their accounts of oppression *or* around their potential to purge the oppressor in his own language. The binary opposites of the affluent Western and the economically backward non-Western dominated the vocabulary of critique, resulting in a neglect of the intricate contours of cultural conflicts based on class and social status that existed *within* the cultures these women supposedly represent.[15] To borrow from Spivak again, in surmising the institutions and inscriptions that condition the staging of identity, the institutions and inscriptions acquired in the country of residence are usually neglected, once again disenfranchising the woman author/narrator of the right to intervene in the political discourse of the country of residence. In a bid to distance themselves from a larger Eurocentric agenda, scholars and artists—as they ruminate on the differences between the indigenous and the foreign—disregard, or at times dismiss, the presence of Western cultures and their appropriation and indigenization by non-Western cultures. The Turkish context is one such example, where the debate between traditional and modern is almost always equated with the debate between religion and secularism. This has perturbed, disconcerted, and thereby enriched Turkish feminism in the twentieth century.[16] The top-down secularization and modernization of the country in 1923 instated an ambiguity in the position of Turkish women vis-à-vis modernity. Turkey's state-sponsored feminism, like many others, modeled its emancipation on the West yet, by way of insisting on an indigenous model, laid emphasis on the feminism in pre-Islamic Turkey and on the regressive nature of Islam. Kemalism, the ideology that continues to influence Turkish society today, introduced modernism and secularism as its two most important tenets. The official program toward a realization of these principles involved the transition from a multiethnic (Islamic) Ottoman Empire to a secular, republican nation-state (1923), the abolition of the caliphate (1924), the abolition of the Islamic law Sharia and the adoption of the Swiss civil code (1926), and the abandonment of Arabic script, replacing it with the Latin alphabet (1928). As Nilüfer Göle aptly observes in her book *The Forbidden Modern*, women became the touchstone of modernism in Turkey during the course of these changes. They were propagated as the "bearers of Westernization and carriers of secularism" (Göle 14).[17] This project, as other scholars have demonstrated, did not bring about the optimal social equality it had proposed.[18] Women's backwardness was all too quickly blamed on Islam, and the headscarf for women and the fez for men were banned to symbolize this historical fissure.

A detailed analysis of the intricacies of Turkish feminism is beyond the scope of this chapter or my area of expertise. However, in order to situate my own interests in exploring subordinated pasts through rehearsals and recitations, I want to outline two recent theoretical and conceptual frameworks through which scholars have destabilized Özdamar's status as a native informant on Turkey or Turkish migrants in Germany. Such destabilizations have occurred due to a close scrutiny of the very autobiographical nature of Özdamar's texts. These analytical frameworks can be tentatively divided in two: while one accords signification to performance, referencing thereby intentional abnegations of gender and ethnicity to affect unsettling identities, the other discusses the significance of referencing history and memory in Özdamar's writings.

I have already mentioned Deniz Göktürk's critique of Özdamar's reliance on Turkish vocabulary and structures, whereby she identifies a self-promotion of exoticism through the performance of such narrative strategies in Özdamar's works. In *Ethnic Drag*, Katrin Sieg discusses the political potential of travesty through Özdamar's *Kelgolan in Alamania*, whereby Özdamar "rewrites the story of the tragic Oriental embodied by Madame Butterfly, subverts its pathos, and envisions a much needed political coalition around the spectators' disidentification with a mode of perception that reads appearances as racial truths" (Sieg 223). Sieg locates her discussion of Özdamar in her larger study of "ethnic drag," which reveals the "continuities, permutations, and contradictions of racial feelings in West German culture" (ibid. 2). Referencing Homi Bhabha's mimic man, she presents the protagonist Kelgolan as an example of what Bhabha terms the "not quite/not white" (ibid. 248). In her article "Meine Herren, spielt in meinem Gesicht ein Affe?" Claudia Breger deploys

Bhabha's conceptualization of mimicry and the mimic man. Breger's comparative analysis of Emine Sevgi Özdamar's and Yoko Tawada's works decodes the function of naïveté in Özdamar's *Mutterzunge* and *Karawanserei*. Kader Konuk extends Sieg's concept of "ethnic drag" as a point of departure in her essay, "Identitätssuche ist ein [sic] private archäologische Graberei." Konuk's reading exposes the complex forms that "ethnomasquerade" acquires in Özdamar's *Karawanserei* in order to explain the playfully emancipatory (*spielerisch befreiende*) potential of Özdamar's language (Konuk 67).

Performance through language finds extension but receives a different treatment in Azade Seyhan's reading of Özdamar in *Writing Outside the Nation*. Seyhan situates Özdamar's works in the contextual specificity of Turkish migration to Germany while simultaneously identifying the archives that inform Özdamar's narration of specific subordinated pasts of the Turkish republic with exactitude. Seyhan discusses Özdamar's insertions of Turkish into her German-language novels to illuminate the exigencies of survival and sustenance in a language (German) that belies naturalness and, therefore, must be naturalized (my term). As Özdamar naturalizes herself in German, Seyhan demonstrates how she (Özdamar) changes the very imaginary structure of German.[19] Seyhan reads in these linguistic transformations the resistance to monocultural and monolingual norms in the host nation. Reading Özdamar's tales through the Chicana author Ana Castillo, Seyhan explains "the words in flight, that is, the shifting, mixing, and dancing codes are often linked to themes of flight from the real to the fantastic, from one realm of experience and its expression to the other" (*Writing Outside* 110). Refuting the critique of exoticism associated with the success of *Karawanserei*, Seyhan presents the "linguistic novelty" of Özdamar's writings as a "semiotic puzzle" (ibid. 142). Especially "in the context of the history of the young Turkish republic, where private and public ordeals and generational terms intersect," Seyhan explains, Özdamar's narrator, through her use of "proverbs, fairy tales, children's games, rumor, superstition, ritual, rites of passage, and folklore remedies for individual and collective mental imbalance ... tells a magical history to ease the pains inflicted by modern times" (ibid. 143). Seyhan's analysis of elements of autobiography in Özdamar is based in "recuperation." Seyhan interprets autobiographies as "unrecorded histories" (ibid. 67), "reflexivity of human story telling" (ibid. 68), "reimagination of genealogies and geographies" through "testimonial, confessional, and biographical dimensions of exilic writing" (ibid. 69). She accrues centrality to the "dialogic and self-reflexive tone of exilic writing" (ibid. 93), whereby the "irony towards memory and nostalgia provides the space of self-reflexivity" (ibid. 94). Memory becomes a healing agent, a "potent medicine" that brings back to life "names, identities and histories that expired along with passports and visas" (ibid. 121).

Adelson situates her readings of three of Özdamar's texts into two different contexts. Framed in—albeit not presented as an illustration of—Arjun Appadurai's *Modernity at Large*, Adelson's reading of the short story "Der Hof im Spiegel" investigates the "social labor of imagination," "production of locality," the "here and now" in the story (*Turkish Turn* 42). In her discussion of the stories "Mutterzunge" and "Großvaterzunge," she challenges Seyhan's claims of loss and recuperation through autobiographical narratives. Proposing an intensification in the "entanglement" (ibid. 150) of "Turkish and German remembrances" (ibid. 149), "in the wake of the geopolitical upheaval in 1989," Adelson proposes, "even here, we are mistaken, if we imagine that acts of recollection in the literature of migration are always or only about the past" (ibid. 150). She prefaces her discussion of "Mutterzunge" and "Großvaterzunge" to claim that such "re-collections also labor to imagine a post-ethnic future shared by Germans and Turks among them" (ibid.). The work of diasporic memory, according to this proposition, ceases to be merely recuperative. It takes on the arduous task of *recherché*.

We have returned to the question of division between recuperation and *recherché* as predicaments of diasporic memory. An attention to this division, which I have rehearsed in great detail, frames my reading of *Seltsame Sterne*. What kind of unrecorded histories does the novel record? Does the past only appear as the lost object of nostalgia, guaranteeing identification through "reimagination of genealogies and geographies," or does it warrant identitarian discomfitures to interrupt and impede any easy access to that lost object or to anything else that evokes affiliation with that lost object? Does the novel lead us to subordinated/subaltern pasts through the memory work of recuperation, or does it sever itself from pasts and origins altogether to engage in *recherché*?

Seltsame Sterne forms the third part of the trilogy that started with Özdamar's *Karawanserei*. To recap briefly, the first-person narrator of *Karawansarei*, growing up in Turkey in the 1950s and 1960s, receives her formal training in the theater arts in Istanbul and then moves to Berlin in *Goldenen Horn*. She reappears in *Seltsame Sterne* as a resident of a left-liberal *Wohngemeinschaft* (shared residence) in the working-class West

Berlin neighborhood of Wedding and as an actress and a *Hospitantin* (intern) at the Volksbühne in East Berlin. On the surface, *Seltsame Sterne* stands closest to the genre of autobiography or memoir. The narrator's experiences in the two Berlins are described in chronological order throughout the text. The narration acquires temporal exactitude in the second part: events and thoughts are documented with precise ascription of dates. The second part consists of fragments from the narrator's diaries, reconstructed in a linear chronology. In the interstices of these diary entries are notes from rehearsals of the theater productions with which the narrator is involved at the moment of recording that entry.[20] Unlike the first two parts of the trilogy, *Seltsame Sterne* is neither particularly infused with innovations of language—that is, Turkish structures into German—nor does it centrally reference Turkey or Turkish migrants. While the first-person narrator's move from Istanbul to East Berlin via West Berlin bears upon the plot of this novel, the narrator's reflections, losses, and gains of languages, histories, cultures, and origins are accorded fewer mentions than in her other works from the 1990s. In addition, the pace of the first two parts of the trilogy decelerates in this novel. In short, there are few, if any, spectacles in this novel characteristic of the first two parts of the trilogy. The first-person narrator transforms herself into a spectator, even if this spectatorship does not register West Berlin as the site of experiencing and discovering novelties. The narrator seems interested, but not excited; disengaged and studiedly detached, but not aloof.

Seltsame Sterne begins in the author's *Wohngemeinschaft* in West Berlin with a dog barking in the courtyard. A collection of poems by the German-Jewish poet Else Lasker-Schüler sits on a pillow next to the narrator's head. The sleepless narrator tries to suppress the sound of the dog in her head by reciting lines from a poem by Lasker-Schüler, "Else," as she calls her by her first name:

> Strange stars stare towards the Earth
> Iron-colored with desire-trains
> Looking for love with burning arms ... (9)

Strange stars that stare toward the earth provide a preview of the disengagement of the narrator from her own experiences throughout the narrative. A strong desire to observe and a yearning to perform both on- and off-stage escort the narrator during her journeys between West Berlin and East Berlin. As the desire turns into language, it either interrupts itself or is shortened—a thought seems to be left in the middle as the narrator describes the colors, textures, and sounds of a divided city. By borrowing lines from Lasker-Schüler—who established herself through her estranging, distancing, and deferring visions of nature but also later through her political vocalizations against the Holocaust— Özdamar's narrator alludes to a lost fragment of post–Second World War German history. However, the lines are accompanied by a citation from a commentary from the jacket of the collection of poems. The only commentary that the Turkish-German writer offers the reader on her narrator's alliance with the German-Jewish poetess originates from the prescriptive, conditioning biography of the jacket-text: "This was the greatest poetess that Germany ever had. Her themes were multiplicatively Jewish, her fantasy oriental, but her language was German, a luxuriant, magnificent, tender German" (*Seltsame Sterne* 15). With this abrupt invocation of the standardized description of the poet on the book-jacket, Özdamar places and then instantly displaces Lasker-Schüler for her reader. The register of this entire passage is very factual, parataxical, functionary, staccato, almost austere. The "Else" of Else Lasker-Schüler might affect a migration to a temporal (Holocaust) or geographical (Turkey) "elsewhere."[21] However, the passage neither feigns nor promotes this easy movement. A moment from German history reveals a past that is now subordinated. It is alluded to, but the effort to allude to that moment is quickly aborted by the narrator. Despite the allegedly oriental fantasies that might embark affiliation between Lasker-Schüler and the narrator, there is, and will be, no simple transcoding available from one (minority) woman author to the next—just uneasy insertions and co-optations. Lasker-Schüler's book reappears in the middle of the novel, as the narrator's lover, Peter, reads another poem to her (*Seltsame Sterne* 58). He prefaces the reading with further descriptive notes: Lasker-Schüler lived in Berlin, was part of expressionism, died in Jerusalem in 1945; she had to flee from the Nazis (ibid. 58). Immediately following Peter's reading are the narrator's thoughts on Shen-Te in Brecht's *The Good Person of Sichuan*. Immediately following these thoughts is the narrator's reinvocation of her mother's thoughts on prostitutes. "They protect us from hungry men—they are our saints" (59). This sentence appears in the *Karawanserei* novel as well. Two disconnected thoughts from two different frameworks in two different languages are registered in one passage. The *recherché* combines itself with recuperative thinking.

As the reader of the novel discovers later, in her reconstruction of her experiences as an aspiring actress the narrator will rehearse works of German playwrights from Johann Wolfgang von Goethe to Bertolt Brecht to

Heiner Müller. Yet these rehearsals, too, will not present themselves as occasions for hasty allegorical readings of her self through the works of these authors. The inclusion of Lasker-Schüler at the very beginning of the narration, in conjunction with the narrator's specific elaboration on the poetess, signals the idea central to the narrator's reconstruction of her experiences in both East and West Berlin in the mid-1970s: allusions to political or cultural history of Germany will only invoke inaccessibility and semiaffiliations. While subordinated pasts will be alluded to, there will be no easy historical narrative available to be identified with. National history or national literary history will only slouch in lurking memories as allusions to the history of the host nation or the nation of birth are placed before the reader and then instantly displaced.

This slouching of history and the accompanying placement and displacement of origins and heritages becomes manifest in the narrator's commentaries on both East and West Berlin. The ideological tensions between the two Berlins are experienced and staged by the narrator at home in the *Wohngemeinschaft* (in West Berlin) that she shares with seven young Germans who represent the generation of the student movements, outside on the streets, and at the checkpoints between the two cities. In the very first section of the book, before she embarks upon her journeys between West Berlin and East Berlin, the narrator provides a vivid account of her residence, which sits above a workshop for seamstresses. She reflects on the political legacy of the residence, formerly an AA-commune. She reconstructs the members' visit to Austria to attend a seminar on self-experience and self-discovery (*Selbsterfahrungsseminar*) offered by the thinker and cult figure Otto Mühl and their return having at least superficially replaced the ideas of the self and the private with that of the collective. The members of the former commune stay convinced and committed to the abolition of all differences—"alle Unterschiede müssen abgeschafft werden" (*Seltsame Sterne* 10)—to the elimination of private property, and to the eradication of language. Believing that language itself creates and constructs class differences, the members of the commune resort to the use of the primal scream (*Urschrei*) as a means of self-expression. By recreating her residence's history through an engagement with Otto Mühl's *Aktionsanalytische Organization* (action-analytic, as opposed to psychoanalytic)—a utopian movement that centralized the problem of self-representation through a crossover from Freud to Marx[22]—Özdamar's narrator rehearses her own mode of self-representation. Although she reinvokes the AA-commune through satire and irony, it is difficult to immediately read this as a critique of prescriptive political ideologies. The AA-commune signals the forthcoming of a series of moments of estrangement and displacement for the narrator. By the end of this sleepless night, which is composed of recitations of Lasker-Schüler's poem and reconstruction of the history of the *Wohngemeinschaft*, all against the backdrop of the barking of the dog in the courtyard, the narrator decides to go to East Berlin. At the immigration point, when interrogated about her reasons for crossing the border, she promptly responds with the dog's bark: "*Hundegebell!*" (*Seltsame Sterne* 18)—a faint satirical allusion to Otto Mühl's *Urschrei*.

The narrator's entry (and her later reentries) into East Berlin, she confesses, bears marks of instant amnesia of the western half of the city. She expresses her inability to think of the two halves of the city together; the overwhelming presence of the ideological divide makes her forget that the two halves could ever be considered as a unit. The possibility of their coexistence seems as unimaginably remote to the narrator as that of seeing Mozart and Freddy Quinn on a single vinyl disc (ibid. 18). Due to her continued residence in West Berlin, people in East Berlin initially appear as shadows from old and yellowed paintings (ibid.). At this moment, the narrator also registers her role as a spectator, but one of a special kind: a participant observer. She accepts that she looks into faces as if she were viewing Rembrandt's self-portrait in order to imagine what he were thinking at that time, to understand the secret of his face. This viewing of a self-portrait—a painting (or a photograph) resulting from the painter/photographer's viewing of him- or herself—registers in the narrator's own vigilant yet distanced self-representation throughout the narrative, as well as in the viewing of her experiences within the everyday realities of the two Berlins.

The narrator's initial impressions of East Berlin do not bear specific marks of her origins in Turkey; unlike the first two parts of the novel, Istanbul ceases to be a consistent point of reference. Instead, years of residence in West Berlin condition her first perceptions of East Berlin, expressed explicitly in her observations on material culture. The narrator comments on the calming effect of the fewer objects in the stores in East Berlin. The smaller tubs (*Waschwannen*), the rear-view mirror for a bicycle (*Fahrradspiegel*), and many other consumer products simultaneously alienate and integrate her into the East German culture. The minimalist and functional packaging of beans, coffee, or salt gives her the impression that children had crafted the packaging out of used paper and cardboard (ibid. 19). She notices that the names of consumer products describe the exact nature and function of the products: ice-cream preparer (*Stieleisbereiter*), salt full of spices (*Speisevollsalz*). She remarks as if the text on the consumer product were deemed more important than the packaging itself (ibid.). The unpretentious humility of the East-German Trabant has a more powerful appeal for the narrator than the overwhelming presence of a West-German Mercedes, where the car, she remarks, not the driver, seems to be in charge.

Superficially, these initial impressions of East Germany exhibit *Ostalgie*, a peculiar nostalgia that has recently become part of the museumization of products from the former East Germany, celebrated extensively, for example, in Jana Hensel's *Zonenkinder*, in Thomas Brussig's famous novel *Am kürzeren Ende der Sonnenallee* and its film version, or in Wolfgang Becker's internationally successful film *Goodbye, Lenin!* What prevent the narrator's observations from nurturing this nostalgia are her austere, detached, and at times cursory observations. While her thoughts recreate fragments of East Berlin, they affect a sense of distance from nostalgia that accompanies postunification writings. Her impressions of East Berlin verge neither on the idealized nor the burlesque.

While the texts and text fragments from austerely packaged products become central to her view of East Berlin, West Berlin as a "text" presents itself as graffiti in the bathrooms of cafés and bars. As in *Goldenen Horn*, headlines from newspapers continue to form part of her text. Through the news of Franco's death, the civil war in Angola (*Seltsame Sterne* 14), and the earthquake in Turkey in 1976 (ibid. 218), the narrator provides glimpses of global politics in the mid-1970s. However, these headlines are now juxtaposed with something more intimate to the city. Özdamar's narrator absorbs the social text of West Berlin through graffiti in women's bathrooms. This intimate engagement with the city lays bare both the cultural and sexual politics of West Berlin. The slogans she reads range from "Frauen wehrt euch" (Women protect yourself), "Männer? Nein Danke" (Men? No thanks), "Atomkraft nein Danke" (Atomic Energy? No thanks) to "Schlappschwanz? Nein Danke" (Limp dick? No thanks) (ibid. 64). The graffiti sometimes contains messages from men, with telephone numbers and accompanying depictions of humungous penises. The narrator's friend and roommate, Susanne, explains Berlin as a "großes Zelt" (a huge tent) where people move around like prisoners in jail and only find an outlet by smearing the walls with their repressed emotions (ibid.).

The inscriptions on the walls of the toilets are further juxtaposed with the writing on the west side of the Berlin Wall. As the narrator recalls the absence of graffiti on the east side, she quotes from the graffiti on the west side in its abundance:

> NO FUTURE, LET US LIVE, OUR LIFE IS REALLY NO LIFE AT ALL, WARDANCE, BERLIN BURNS, BECOME HUMAN, AM I ALONE, HARALD JUNKE FOR PRESIDENT, GDR: GERMAN FILTH, STRAUSS GET OUT!, BULLY-WEST, LET US TEAR THE WALL, WORLD WAR I: 5% CIVILIANS DEAD—WORLD WAR II: 48% CIVILIANS DEAD—KOREAN WAR 84% CIVILIANS DEAD—VIETNAM WAR 92% CIVILIANS DEAD—WORLD WAR III WILL BE 100%, ALL COMMIES IN THE GAS CHAMBER, IS WEST BERLIN THE CLITORIS OF THE GDR? (65)

For the narrator, the entirety of West Berlin seems to be in a state of a war of words; words seem to come out of every hole, with little effect on social change. The narrator compares West Berlin to a shooting gallery, with everyone using their words as ammunition. She learns more about the presence of war in Berlin through her roommates. West Berlin looks like a city of widows, with dogs having replaced the men who are dead. In the midst of these liberal wars of words, the narrator occasionally overhears anti-Semitic conversations. She reconstructs a conversation between two older women that she overhears in a park. One of the women quotes Goebbels, who reportedly said that Jews are also humans, as much as lice are also animals, but really a nuisance (ibid. 66). In the midst of left-liberal ideology, fascist and military inscriptions of history reappear, to discomfort, and to kill.

The narrator's readings of Germany's political reality, literature, and history occur parallel to her references to her origins and her reflections on her status as an immigrant. The inscriptions of the origins of the narrator serve as an intermediary, connecting and disconnecting the texts of East-German packaging and West-German graffiti to the dramatic texts from German literature. These inscriptions of moments from another past and from another nation (Turkey) frame the narrator's documentation of her present in East or West Berlin; however, these associations do not necessarily guarantee recuperation.

As mentioned earlier, unlike in the first two parts of the trilogy, Turkey and Turks in Germany do not form a continuous discussion in *Seltsame Sterne*. The narrator's origins, her remembrance of her grandmother, her observations on Turkish immigrants in Germany, all appear sporadically, abruptly, incidentally, coincidentally—as afterthoughts, as insertions in the narrative. This oblique and occasional character of the discussion on

Turkey and its fragmented and fractured rhetoric reveals the uneasy, insecure, and always insufficient transportability of the import of experience. It is as disjunctured and disjointed as her invocations of German (national) memory.

The narrator's first description of Turkey is addressed to her Swiss friend Joseph, who later facilitates her meeting with the director Benno Besson. Playing on the word *Morgenland* (Orient), she describes the Turkey of the 1970s as a nation where the morning does not seem like a morning anymore, where humans do not feel connected to fellow humans, "ein Land wo der Morgen kein Morgen zu sein scheint" (*Seltsame Sterne* 25). The national framework invoked here is one of despair. Two words: *Militärputsch* (army coup, 24) and *Folter* (torture, 25) provide clues to the tragedy of General Cemal Gürsel's military coup of 1960, which reappeared as a farce during the civil unrest in Turkey following Süleyman Demiral's election as president in 1969. However, there are no political figures named in these passages, no headlines to familiarize and orient the reader with crash courses in Turkish history.[23] The reader is just given hints of the culture of torture following the military putsch that casts its shadow on public memory. The state has propagated in the public a fear of youth: every young person is suspected to be an anarchist, guilty of plotting against the state, a danger, until proven innocent and safe through the institution of heterosexual marriage: the narrator legitimizes her relationship with her boyfriend through the acquisition of a marriage license (*Trauschein*) in order to be able to rent a place together and to avoid getting arrested. *Lodos*, she describes, the wind that blows in Istanbul from the Marmara Sea, feels like "ein Brief der Getöteten," a letter from those who were killed through state-sponsored violence (*Seltsame Sterne* 26). In this political culture of torture, human beings disappear suddenly and turn into photographs (wurden zu Fotos, 26). Parents walk around with these photos, asking others if they know the whereabouts of their disappeared children. In these times of a brutal display of legitimized state violence, the narrator finds respite in reciting poems by Brecht (27).

History as tragedy and farce weighs like a nightmare and finds expression in tired, decrepit, and diseased words. The narrator registers: "I am unhappy in my language. For years we have only been saying sentences such as: They will hang them. Where were the heads? One does not know where their grave is. The police did not release the dead body! The words are sick. Like sick mussels, my words need a sanatorium" (23). This is one of the most important passages in the novel. The recollection of lost images and scripts through a reconnection with Turkish—which accrued centrality in "Mutterzunge," "Großvaterzunge," *Karawanserei*, and *Goldenen Horn*—is no more recuperative. The mother tongue itself is in need of recuperation. The healing will come from elsewhere. The sanatorium for mussels, recounts the narrator, is the name for a place in the Aegean Sea where three currents meet. Fishermen from Istanbul and Izmir, but also Italy, bring the sick mussels from their catch to be healed in these waters; therefore, this part of the sea is called the mussel sanatorium. With her words wounded and hurt by the repression of thought and critique in Turkey, the narrator seeks a place where words can be rejuvenated. Much as in Özdamar's previous works, the narrator recites the common knowledge that a mother tongue is lost in foreign countries. However, with her words paralyzed and stunned through state-orchestrated censorship, her mother tongue is lost in the motherland itself, and with her friend's recommendation letter, she decides to leave for Berlin.

With her sense of affiliation with the Turkish nation traumatized by her experiences in an authoritarian Turkey, the narrator's connection to fellow Turks in Berlin is limited. While the narrator of *Goldenen Horn* builds a community with other immigrants from Turkey soon after her arrival in West Berlin, the narrator in *Seltsame Sterne* observes fellow Turkish immigrants from a distance. In Alextreff, a restaurant in East Berlin, she notices Turkish *Gastarbeiter* desperately seeking East-German women for sexual relations (*Seltsame Sterne* 43). Their promise of sexual exoticism to the East-German women makes the narrator hesitant about getting acquainted with them. In fact, any insistence on ethnic difference only accentuates her growing disenchantment. She recounts her meeting with a young Kurdish man who works for Amnesty International. He starts his conversation by identifying her as a fellow Kurd. When she registers her irritation by offering the possibility of her being an Armenian or a Greek, he crassly responds: "You cannot be Armenian. Armenian women have moustaches" (41). His next attack comes in the form of homophobia: "I am happy that there are so many homosexuals in Germany. I only hope that there would be more, so there are more German women left for us to fuck" (41). If fellow immigrants from Turkey do not appear as self-righteous champions of the politics of ethnicity or interpreters of cryptic advantages of homosexuality among German men, they take the form of small businessmen whose goal in life is to buy a Mercedes. Her acquaintance Murat, a waiter, states the exchange-rate economy of gender rather explicitly. He wishes to have a girlfriend in East Berlin because "there the Turk is considered a *Westler* [West German]. West-German money is the ideal money in East Germany" (71). These comments from her fellow Turks contribute to the increased gap between them and the narrator. There are no easy communities available for identification. The mother tongue and motherland cease to be a source of comfort; the inscriptions of home, belonging, community are only uneasily legible.

This uneasiness with the script of the country of birth results in her constant reminiscing about her grandmother, an illiterate woman in whose imagination everyone who is literate is a doctor of medicine, a healer. Özdamar's narrative return to the figure of the grandmother after *Karawanserei* is significant. As the narrator engages the two Berlins through texts—packaging, graffiti, drama, production-notes—memories of her illiterate grandmother emerge as her exclusive connection to Turkey. However, the grandmother does not provide any idealized, peaceful, pastoral escape from the demands of the narrator's metropolitan location. The anecdotal glimpses of the grandmother that the narrator provides establish her neither as a dependent subject of oriental patriarchy nor as an oriental matriarch. She is not the easily available, traditional binary opposite to her modernized granddaughter (the narrator). The grandmother represents a complex matrix of belief systems and practices that are too independent to be tamed as traditional or modern. The grandmother believes that she can assure a place in paradise by converting a non-Muslim into a Muslim (*Seltsame Sterne* 22). However, she cannot decide which of the three dead husbands she would live with once she is in paradise:

> We often asked her: "With which one of your husbands will you live in paradise, grandmother?" She answered: "What do I know? The first one had a beautiful voice, the second was a good man, the third went to Istanbul to look for a job. There he went to the whores, they taught him that a woman can sit on top. That is why from then on he wanted that I sit on his stomach. When we made love, a fire went through my whole body." Then I said, "He is the one, with whom you will meet in paradise. Isn't that true, grandmother?" (50)

The grandmother claps when the narrator's brother in Istanbul makes love to his girlfriend: she stands at the door and tells her grandson, "Kiss her once for me" (51). The narrator tells these anecdotes to her roommates during her very first conversation with them at the *Wohngemeinschaft* and remarks, "It is not as if I, but my grandmother was supposed to live here" (50). Through the prominence of sexual pleasure in these anecdotes—recounted in the *Wohngemeinschaft*, which, as the narrator observes and is told, embodies the polyamorous sexual culture of the late

1960s—the grandmother ceases to be a comfort zone of innocent motherly love. Instead, she turns into the narrator's accomplice in contesting the allegedly emancipated rhetoric of gendered politics and sexual practices that the narrator encounters in the two Berlins.

This rhetoric of gendered politics is presented to the narrator by Susanne and Barbara, her roommates at the *Wohngemeinschaft*, as they explain their strategies of intellectual and physical assertion. Susanne and Barbara proactively resist the presence of men in their lives. Susanne believes that men should become softer (*weicher*) and more conscious (*bewußter*). They cannot give birth and, therefore, have politics, science, and power as substitutes (54). With pride, Barbara relates to the narrator Susanne's method of preventing herself from becoming dependent on a man: when approached by a man, Susanne starts farting very loudly! Özdamar's narrator does not provide her rejoinders to these and other statements and situations until toward the end of the book. During an evening with Heiner Müller and Monika Maron, the narrator's East-German friend Gabi relates the story of a West-German woman who spoke on television about learning how to belly-dance while simultaneously criticizing all oriental women for their submissiveness. Gabi comments, "When a German woman performs a belly-dance, it is her possibility of personal erotic expression. When a Turkish woman performs a belly-dance, she shows her submission to a man in a patriarchal society. The Turkish woman is explained through the system, while the German has her own, special biography. That is racism" (201f.). The passionate critique of a populist feminist criticism of oriental submission comes not from the narrator but from her East-German/Western ally. As for the narrator's own reaction, she claims that during conversations between Müller, Maron, and Gabi, she feels as if she were in a foreign-language class (*Fremdsprachenkurs*, 202). Özdamar's narrator does not, and will not, provide detailed explanations of the intricacies of her feminist agenda. She strategically detaches herself from the offered position of a native informant feminist. She will claim her "own special" biography by choosing to remain silent when she so wishes. The native informant has now established herself as a participant observer of both East and West Berlin, and she sustains this position in her role as an actress and an intern at the Volksbühne. The participant observer's self-insertion into the history of the GDR will be relayed through her notes on rehearsals of theater productions, to which I now turn.

Seltsame Sterne could, perhaps, be read as an *Erziehungsroman*, a novel of education. The *Gastarbeiterin* in the West Berlin of the *Goldenen Horn* now transforms into a *Kulturarbeiterin*, a cultural worker, a *Hospitantin* (intern). The narrator's professional assignments range from translating director's notes from German into Turkish for her friends in Turkey and playing small roles in plays to sketching stills from rehearsals. The second half of the work is replete with visual representations of rehearsals: actual sketches made by Özdamar during her year of apprenticeship at the Volksbühne. During this internship as a cultural worker, the narrator documents three kinds of challenges: as a politically committed actress, she struggles to reconcile the gap between theory and praxis; as an immigrant, she constantly struggles to maintain her legal status in East Berlin; and as a Turkish woman, she observes her exoticization as the Other with a studied distance.

The narrator embarks upon her engagement with the Volksbühne as a translator of rehearsal notes for Besson's 1969 production of Brecht's *Der gute Mensch von Sezuan* (The Good Person of Sichuan).[24] The narrator cites selected passages from these notes. Besson's interpretation of the play centers around the idea of not being able to cope (*Nicht-fertig-Werdens*, 38), which he wants to emphasize in his production. Beyond simple binaries that superficially distinguish the socialism of a good Shen Te from the capitalism of an evil Shui Ta, Besson wants to highlight the complexities that Brecht himself brings forth in his reconstruction of a war of values in an imaginary village in China. This understanding of the play finds extension in Besson's conceptual vision of the stage itself, which he also sees as a space marred by conflict. An actor either succeeds in exerting him- or herself to get up on one's feet (*hochkommen*) or tumbles (*runterpurzeln*) and then has to be attentive to the extent to which he or she falls (68). For Besson, in a society in and beyond Sichuan, capitalism reconstructs itself in most disparate codifications (*höchst unterschiedlichen Chiffrierungen*, 68). The narrator's citations of Besson's rehearsal notes serve two significant functions. They appear as fragments of a larger conversation on theater and its role in representing capitalism and its critique through theater, thus becoming a part of the narrator's recounting of her experiences in East Berlin. Simultaneously, these citations also carry the import of notes inscribed at the margins of Besson's text by its reader, the narrator. Preceding the narrator's own rehearsal notes, citations from Besson's notes become foundational to the narrator's understanding of theater in East Berlin, not just through Besson, but later through Fritz Marquardt and Heiner Müller. Emerging from the margins of a so-called marginal text, they present and represent the disparate codifications of the narrator's self-understanding of her location as an actress, as a woman, as a Turkish-born woman in East Berlin.

These codifications appear as abrupt, incomplete, unprocessed, but also as repetitive, reiterative, reconstructive moments in the narrator's diaries, which form the second part of the book. At the end of Part I, the narrator is offered an internship with Fritz Marquardt's production of Heiner Müller's play *Die Bauern* (The Farmers). For the narrator, this signals a journey back into the history of the GDR. With her notebook and pencil, the narrator sits in a corner, makes notes, and sketches the scenes, and as she imagines inserting herself in the history of the GDR through Müller's play, she begins her own archives of the history of some of the most famous theater productions of East Berlin. These archives form part of the narrator's diary entries. The performance of everyday life is interrupted by reflections on preparations for performance on stage. Beginning with Marquardt's production of *Die Bauern*, the narrator's archives continue to Matthias Langhoff's production of Goethe's burlesque *Der Bürgergeneral* and end with Benno Besson's production of Shakespeare's *Hamlet*.[25] The recording and staging of history as experience occurs simultaneous to the experience of staging history, captured in the narrator's notes on rehearsals.

The narrator's rehearsal notes are italicized in the text, much like citations from Else Lasker-Schüler, Konstantin Kavafis, and Benno Besson. These notes, accompanied by sketches, are extremely detailed observations on theater productions as works-in-progress. In them, the narrator registers blocking, lighting, costume, expression, and various other details of theatrical production. These details are accompanied by brief but astute comments on ideological conflicts that she considers central to particular plays, scenes, or rehearsals. While registering a scene from *Die Bauern*, the narrator remarks on the GDR as an emergent socialist state, even as a very recent fascist past poses both logistical and ideological challenges. She examines the connections between party-work (*Parteiarbeit*), agitation (*Agitation*), and consciousness-raising (*Bewußtseinsarbeit*), which are often laid out as mutually contesting technologies in Müller's play (*Seltsame Sterne* 82). She documents tedious, engaging, but also conflicted moments of the rehearsals. Marquardt demands from his actors a comprehensive understanding of the play's historical time, only to declare that theater itself is no substitute for history (88). This demand for distancing and displacement from the play's historical time reflects upon the narrator's own engagement with the GDR of the 1970s. Her conversation with the critic Rudolf Bahro deepens the narrator's understanding of the distance between theory and praxis in the GDR. Bahro's reflections amplify the narrator's own moments of distance and displacement from the political culture of the GDR. Bahro registers the schism between the bureaucracy and citizenry as the problem central to the conflict between the theory and the practice of a socialist state. He declares the idea of the GDR as a classless society intellectually bankrupt, blames the bureaucracy for the stunting of ideology through the suppression of critique, and considers the theater in East Germany as the only space where critique and imagination (*Phantasie*) continue to exist and enrich the hope of socialism (91).

The narrator's encounters with bureaucracy in Turkey render Bahro's thoughts on the suppression of critique and imagination all too familiar. This momentary identification surfaces in her rehearsal notes on Goethe's *Der Bürgergeneral*. *Der Bürgergeneral*, with its satire on the direct import of revolutionary ideas from France to Germany (*Seltsame Sterne* 142), treats ideology as false consciousness, much like Müller's *Die Bauern*. However, the moments of angst, curiosity, desire, and excitement (*Angst, Neugier, Lust, Aufregung*) of the political radicalism of the bourgeoisie, as embodied by Schnaps, the main character, bring about an immediate, if indirect, association with Turkey. The site of Schnaps's speech, the male public sphere of a barbershop, brings the narrator back to Turkey (ibid. 171). The barbershops of Istanbul surface as spaces where people, as they let themselves be shaved, let go of their ideas about politics, morals, and economics in front of mirrors. The viewing of one's own self, of the portraiture of self-portraits, returns in the rehearsals. The rehearsal note ends with the sentence fragment: "Goethe in Istanbul!" (ibid.).

The narrator's desire to hold the mirror to her Turkish self manifests itself in her idea to write a play, *Hamlet-Ahmet*. As she documents her preparations for Besson's production of *Hamlet*, the narrator reads and cites passages on *Hamlet* by Heinrich Heine, Bertolt Brecht, and the theorist Ekkard Schwarz. Schwarz's interpretation of *Hamlet* as the play about the "uncanny insecurity in the state" (*unheimliche Unsicherheit im Staat*), delivered with a suppression of death (*Verdrängen des Todes*) and bad conscience (*schlechtes Gewissen*, 190) bring alive the desire to adapt *Hamlet* for the Turkish stage. The money from *Der Bürgergeneral* would finance the typewriter to write this play. The narrator characterizes her *Hamlet-Ahmet* as a story from a village in Turkey (*eine türkische Dorfgeschichte*). The allegory of immigration, technology, and economy in *Hamlet-Ahmet* unfolds as follows:

> Hamlet is a Turkish farmer; his father was a wealthy landowner and was poisoned by his own brother, so that he could inherit the land and

property of his brother. Alongside that, he marries the wife of his brother, Hamlet's mother. There have always been such incidents in Turkey. When a man dies, his brother marries his wife. My play is called *Hamlet-Ahmet*. His dead father appears to the shepherds as a spirit, the herdsmen consult the village teacher. The teacher claims that the spirit has appeared to the shepherds because there are no tractors in the village. The farmers in the neighboring villages own tractors from Germany, which they brought with them from there. As Ahmet speaks with the spirit of his father and finds out that his uncle has killed him, he [Ahmet] swears to seek revenge. When he [Ahmet] begins to utter nonsensical monologues, his uncle sends him to Germany as a worker. From there, he brings a tractor back with him, and at the end of the play he is the owner of an apple orchard and lets his uncle, his mother, and his wife Ophelia work there. The spirit of the father stands as a scarecrow in the field. (195)

The origins come into play again, however not as tenacious entities but as malleable allusions to subordinate pasts. They return, inspiring the narrator to stage her own historical experiences from a distance as she experiences the staging of various aspects of European history, from Shakespeare's *Hamlet* to Goethe's *Der Bürgergeneral* to Müller's *Die Bauern*. While Marquardt, Langhoff, and Besson lead the narrator to subordinated pasts, the narrator's *recherché* posits her as an interlocutor of select pasts in European (cultural) history. This transformation happens with and through rehearsals, which—to borrow from Richard Schechner—bring about the "jerky," "disjointed," and "incoherent" aspects of performance (Schechner 206). She feels partially fulfilled in her role as an intern at the Volksbühne. But specters of the political suppression of theater in Turkey during the late 1960s and early 1970s continue to haunt her. Her artistic work offers her glimpses of the "lies, disguises, double plots and ironies" (Schechner 207) applicable to the larger political drama of East Berlin, as well as Turkey. The notes on rehearsals thus become testimonies to aesthetic and political issues that beleaguer a politically committed theater of East Germany, with the problem of both artistic and political representation—*Darstellen* and *Vertreten*—at the center. Rescue will not come in the form of Otto Mühl's primal scream (*Urschrei*) but through language: some of it her own, some borrowed, and some constructed. The narrator's notes and sketches on rehearsals thus rescue themselves from becoming an eclectic commentary on random plays and turn into rites of viewing more than rituals of experiences. Throughout these rites and rituals, various subordinated pasts of two different national frameworks render themselves visible through narration—at times through identification, at other times through identitarian discomfiture and disaffiliation.

I introduced this chapter with an elaboration on an essay by Gayatri Chakravorty Spivak in an effort to understand the slouching of history. In conclusion I want to offer a few comments on the work of diasporic memory in leading us to subordinated pasts. For this I want to return to Andreas Huyssen's essay, which argues against propositions of "one global memory" or a "cosmopolitan memory" (Huyssen 148).[26] As I have discussed in the introduction, Huyssen conceives cosmopolitanism as a legal and political project of international human rights and universal claims. Memory discourses, he suggests, "remain tied to the specific memories of social groups in time and place" (ibid.). The work of diasporic memory in our times, as Huyssen rightly elaborates, cannot be reduced to nostalgia and recuperation. It involves *recherché*, to reflect upon the "act of remembrance" and the "content of that which is remembered" (ibid. 152). I agree with Huyssen on the difficulty of imagining "one global memory"; nonetheless, as I have tried to demonstrate in my discussion of Özdamar's *Seltsame Sterne*, the focus of narration in this work is neither the legend of the country of origin nor the lore of the country of residence but unevenly jointed bits of both. Özdamar's relationship to Turkish or German national memory, as she reveals certain subaltern pasts, is split and cut off. Allusions to these pasts from national histories of Germany and Turkey, albeit with a studied distance and detachment give us clues to distinguish one global memory from a cosmopolitan memory that remains anchored in multiple national frameworks without a complete identification with and investment in any one of them. This memory work is marked by severance and dislocation from both nations. Political claims of cosmopolitan memory do not privilege recuperation over *recherché*. The vulnerability of the narrative itself leads us to subordinated/ subaltern pasts without ordaining these pasts with authenticity. Such narratives of pasts cannot be performed; they can only be rehearsed. Like the rehearsals, the narrative remains fractured, fragmented, and disjointed. Origins do not disappear, but they occasionally fade in order to reappear. History slouches, memory lurks.

THREE

Authentic Hybrid? Feridun Zaimoğlu's *Abschaum*
Die wahre Geschichte von Ertan Ongun

> [N]ow I sit here and try to shock our intellectuals, I try to shock our assimilated ones, to fascinate certain people here: fascination through the criminal subject, fascination through the wild other, fascination for those who come from down below, and if I am happy about it, I do not know, fascination pain. For you this might be a fascination, but for me it is only shit, all of it is shit. Trust me man, there are only two kinds of things in Germany: one is dirt, the other the 0815 society. And you know what, I shit on the society. There in dirt, I was at least something there, there I was scum, you know, and now I go down.
>
> FERIDUN ZAIMOĞLU, ABSCHAUM

Feridun Zaimoğlu's *Abschaum. Die wahre Geschichte von Ertan Ongun* (Scum: The True Story of Ertan Ongun) begins with "Die Beerdigungs-Story" (The Burial Story 7–11),[1] the first of the thirty-six stories that make up the "true" story of the protagonist Ertan Ongun. The story is about the last rites of Farouk, a Syrian friend of Ongun, whose corpse has been rotting for about a month. The exact conditions of Farouk's death are not described, but the descriptions of the corpse are detailed and graphic—it is wrapped in a "*Scheiß-Folie*" (shitty-foil), gives out a "*Scheiß-Gestank*" (shitty-smell), and causes a "*Scheiß-Gefühl*" (shitty-feeling, 8). Through these and many other words prefixed with shit or shitty, the reader is oriented to a linguistic register of the stories. Farouk's funeral is managed and organized by his brother and a couple of friends including Ongun. The presence of the *Hodscha* (the Muslim priest) does not deter the young men's disgust; even less so does it decontaminate the language of its fecal content. The body is washed per Muslim rituals and buried, and as Ongun describes, Farouk lies in the hole after leading a "*Scheiß-Leben*" (shitty life), perhaps a midstation to his final destination of "paradise or hell or some such shit" (11). The stench of the corpse—intensified by repeated references to feces—drifts into the rest of the stories that follow. The true story of Ertan Ongun has begun.

This chapter denotes my last entry in this log book of cosmopolitical claims of narratives of Turkish immigrants in Germany. So far I have discussed the issues surrounding the subaltern signification of a Turkish guest worker in a novel by a German author, followed by the unraveling of subaltern/subordinated pasts through self-representation in a literary work by a Turkish-German (woman) author. This chapter convolutes this distinction. While discussing *Abschaum*, I engage with a narrative process where both Ertan Ongun, the source of Zaimoğlu's stories, the native-informant narrator, and Zaimoğlu, his cultural interlocutor, centralize definitive markers of cultural, ethnic, class-based, and linguistic Otherness. In the process of narrating this Otherness, they create their own racial and gendered Others. This chapter follows the slippery trail of an author who documents—much like Nadolny's Alexander—stories of disgust, despair, desperation, disparity, and discrimination in the life of an outlawed Turkish resident of Germany. However, unlike Nadolny's *Selim*, the stories in *Abschaum* are neither reconstructed in High German nor interrupted by the author's reflections on the problems of narrating. Zaimoğlu reproduces Ertan Ongun's stories in the extreme and brutal vernacular of the hybrid Turkish-German street slang in which they are narrated. As Zaimoğlu asserts at the end of the novel, the stories are neither mediated nor ameliorated but, rather, retold in the "authentic" language. In these stories and in the process of their telling, Ertan Ongun, the first-person narrator of Turkish origin—a drug dealer and a junkie who feels ostracized due to his class and ethnicity—registers his resistance through convoluted assertions of his ethnicity on the one hand and his heterosexual masculinity on the other. In short, the protagonist's assertions of masculinity as a protest against his exclusion—at times inflicted by society, at other times self-inflicted—occur through an exclusionary protomasculine interlanguage. Through these linguistic registers, I argue, a particularly aggressive assertion of conflicted political claims becomes legible.

What is the nature of the conflict of these claims? What kinds of critical approaches assist in evaluating the "authentic" and purportedly "hybrid" structures of these claims in the context of cosmopolitics? What are the registers of assertion of ethnicity in the novel? How are they inscribed and reinforced? How do these registers bear upon our critical evaluation of hybridity? How and why does the ethnic similarity between the author and the narrator, indeed between the interlocutor and his native informant, privilege such claims? Does the aggressive assertion of self-representation of minorities validate these claims? Does the subaltern finally "speak" when the interlocutor is a self-proclaimed practitioner of cultural hybridity?

These are some of the questions central to my reading of *Abschaum*. As I embark upon answering these questions, I offer one admonition: my aim is neither to valorize nor to condemn the aggressive nature of the protagonist's assertions. Instead, in order to successfully evaluate the effect of the affect, I desire to acquire a critical distance from the aggression of the linguistic spectacle that Zaimoğlu offers in *Abschaum* and also from the spectacle that is Zaimoğlu, whose journalistic reception in Germany has turned him into a superstar author, performer, and media personality. Since the publication of his work *Kanak Sprak. 24 Mißtöne vom Rande der Gesellschaft*—a collection of protocols of marginalized Turkish youth—Zaimoğlu has emerged as the most widely read, discussed, and visible Turkish-German author in Germany today. His establishment as a favorite of the publishing company and media can safely be attributed to his prolific creativity. He is the coauthor of the film script of *Kanak Attack*, which was based on *Abschaum*. In addition, he performs hip-hop texts, regularly writes columns for and is interviewed by major German newspapers such as *Die Zeit, Frankfurter Allgemeine Zeitung*, and *Berliner Tageszeitung*, and is a popular guest on talk shows. His status as a maverick and an *enfant terrible* of the contemporary German literary scene can be accredited to his scathing and inexhaustible critique of *Multikulti*, institutionalized German multiculturalism. Zaimoğlu's defiance of institutions notwithstanding, he is extremely well received and rewarded by institutions. In 1997, he received the Civis Prize for Radio and Television for his work *Deutschland im Winter—Kanakistan, eine Rap-Reportage*. In 2004, he served as the Samuel Fischer Guest Professor of Comparative Literature at the Freie Universität Berlin, a position previously held by scholars of literature and philosophy such as Valentin Y. Mudimbe (1999), translators and poets such as Robert Haas (2002), and fiction writers such as Alberto Manguel (2003).[2] In 2005 he received (and gladly accepted) the Adalbert von Chamisso Prize, whose former recipients such as Aras Ören and Yüksel Pazarkaya have been benevolently criticized and, if I may add, publicly insulted by him.[3]

Zaimoğlu thrives on a paradox that makes him a "fascinating author," although, to repeat, the aim of this chapter is not to amplify the fascination. The journalistic/public fascination with Zaimoğlu, therefore, needs to be critically contextualized in the public sphere where he has acquired his fame as a public intellectual. In other words, a productive reading of *Abschaum* will emerge when the work is read adjacent to, but not under the shadow of, Zaimoğlu. It is, therefore, necessary to examine the problematic symbiosis between the author and the public/media personality.

Abschaum demands a sincere and rigorous consideration, not merely because it was authored by Zaimoğlu, the superstar, but because it brings forth a number of highly pertinent embattlements of authorial interlocution and narrative authenticity in a hybrid vernacular. In the thirty-six stories, which contribute to the true story of Ertan Ongun, truth-claims of a marginalized existence and their authentic reconstruction inform and condition the narrative. A highly charged and conflicted force field is created by the author, summarized and offered to the readers in a cryptic algebraic equation of difference. Ethnicity and class become transient coefficients in this equation. Heterosexual masculinity emerges as the only constant, and ethnic Otherness is registered parallel to misogyny and homophobia.

It is indeed this cryptic equation that I desire to decode in my reading of the novel. In order to deliver the import of this statement in the context of *Abschaum*, my reading of the novel will be preceded by three critical maneuvers. First, I reconstruct some scholarly positions on hybridity, in order to think through the position of connections between hybridity, cosmopolitanism, and subaltern significations through claims of authenticity. Following this, I move to an investigation of the journalistic enthusiasm for Zaimoğlu. This will assist in evaluating the peculiarity of simultaneous invocations of ethnicity, hybridity, and authenticity through which Zaimoğlu's image as a protesting author is created and reinforced. Lastly, I report on the resonance of these ideas in some recent scholarly commentaries on Zaimoğlu's first and most famous work, *Kanak Sprak*, which paves the way for my reading of *Abschaum*.

Since the publication of Homi Bhabha's *Location of Culture* in 1994, cultural hybridity as a concept and phenomenon has become crucial to understanding forms of aesthetic expressions, which consciously fuse and diffuse linguistic and cultural idioms and at times genres and media, to convey the mixing and matching of cultures in the contemporary contexts of mass migration. Since Bhabha's work marks the beginning of systematic considerations of hybridity, it might be useful to cast a glance at the varied—though not mutually contesting—formulations of hybridity in Bhabha's essays. In the *Location of Culture*, the word *hybridity* premiers in the introduction as Bhabha discusses the "possibility of cultural hybridity" in an "interstitial passage between fixed identifications" (4). In Bhabha's discussion of Frantz Fanon in "Interrogating Identity" (*Location of Culture* 40–65), hybridity appears as an "identity," bearers of which are—"for Fanon"—the "liberatory people who initiate the productive instability of revolutionary cultural change" (ibid. 38). In "Articulating the Archaic" (ibid. 123–38), hybridity is "the uncertainty of culture's in-between," "neither 'one' nor 'other,'" attributed to the narrative of the "epistemological visibility [that] disavows the metonymy of the colonial moment" (ibid. 127). Central to the discussion of agency in "The Postcolonial and the Postmodern," hybridity appears in a historical moment "as camouflage, as a contesting, antagonistic agency functioning in the time lag of sign/symbol" (ibid. 193). As part of his brilliant reconstruction of aspects of the Indian Revolt of 1857 in "By Bread Alone" (ibid. 198–211), Bhabha explains hybridity in terms of its "margin . . . where cultural differences 'conditionally' and 'conflictually' touch" (ibid. 207). In addition, Bhabha situates hybridity in "cultural enunciations," "in the process of translating and transvaluing cultural difference" (ibid. 252). As an aesthetic "invention" and "intervention," Bhabha attributes hybridity to a "'newness' that is not part of the continuum of past and present" (ibid. 7). Thus, in his discussion of Salman Rushdie's *Satanic Verses* in the essay "How Newness Enters the World" (ibid. 212–35), hybridity becomes "heresy," an attribute of a "borderline culture. . . that articulates its problems of identification and its diasporic aesthetic in an uncanny, disjunctive temporality that is, at once, the *time* of cultural displacement, and the *space* of the untranslatable" (ibid. 225, original emphasis).

The first and the last three definitions of hybridity—as an interstitial space between fixed identifications, as cultural enunciation in a new world, as intervention through invention, and as an aesthetic attribute of borderline cultures and diasporas—have been heavily discussed and debated in the specific contexts of immigrant cultures and their aesthetic expressions. Hybridity denotes on the one hand a coming-together of various cultural and linguistic genealogies, on the other hand a movement away from these genealogies toward newer, fresher, hitherto unseen, unread, or unexperienced manifestations of complex cultural experiences, primarily at the metropolitan centers of immigrant populations in the West. In the prevalent understandings of cultural hybridity, urban spaces in the geographical non-West are considered equally fertile for such new and innovative modes of expression—largely due to their exposure to the West either through colonialism or, more recently, the proliferation of technology. Hybridity denotes more than a sum of two or more cultural parts: its force and appeal rest on its capability to inaugurate transformation, transgression, translocation, indeed, translocution. When cultures and languages of countries of birth and countries of residence come together, when past and present collide, when inheritance and acquisition pose a productive challenge in the everyday lives of immigrants, aesthetic expressions arrest and release the dockets of cultural predicaments by appropriating and reconfiguring many ways of locution, interlocution, articulation. Salman Rushdie's creative deployment of Hindi and Urdu in *Satanic Verses*, Gloria Anzaldúa's juxtaposition of Spanish and English in *Borderlands/La Frontera*, Rachid Boudjedra's interspersing of Arabic in his French novel *La Repudiation* are now well-known examples of what Bhabha has termed the "newness" that we encounter in our world (*Location of Culture* 6, 38).

This very idea of newness—caused by transgressions of ethnic, religious, national, and/or gendered boundaries, realized and registered in vocabularies of linguistic transgression, and understood as a function and a consequence of cultural hybridity—has invited sincere and rigorous contestation. Its singular, almost hegemonic validity as a critical strategy to understand diasporic and immigrant cultures and their artistic expressions has been challenged by a number of scholars. Aijaz Ahmad draws attention to the ephemeral, contingent nature of hybridity and questions the sustainability of hybridity's commitment to long-term political changes.[4] While examining the "Dialectics of Cultural Hybridity," Pnina Werbner considers hybridity no more than "a theoretical meta-construction of social order" (Werbner 1) and poses the daring question, "What if cultural mixings and crossovers become routine in the context of globalising trends?" (ibid.). Werbner expresses his unease with the allegedly shocking and disturbing quality of hybrid aesthetic forms and doubts the propagation of "heighten[ed] reflexivity" and "double consciousness" through a form that is simultaneously capable of conveying the "uniqueness" of cultural identities (ibid. 21). Jonathan Friedman casts his scathing critique of hybridity in terms of a questionable overcoming of essentialism (Friedman 78). In his insightful and stimulating critique, Friedman questions the emancipatory potential of hybridity, presenting it as an elite pursuit of individuals in "international politics, academia, the media, and the arts" (ibid. 84).

In these and many other critical positions on hybridity, the central tension can be easily identified as one between location and dislocation. Cultural hybridity situates itself in movement; it locates itself in the act of dislocation; it abandons the hitherto inhabited in order to strive toward newness. All these elements make the idea of hybridity extremely useful—after all, it offers itself as the most dynamic, fluid, and motional modality and therefore promises high degrees of freedom, emancipation, and perhaps even creative autonomy. It is, therefore, not too difficult to understand hybridity's appeal for otherwise marginalized, subjugated, neither-here-nor-there, dislocated, and displaced immigrant communities and their artists. However, the *awareness* of displacement and dislocation are very important to the idea of hybridity, and the intentionality of this awareness is highly significant for the execution of cultural hybridity in artistic forms that can be labeled as new. Since hybridity offers itself as a self-conscious mode of freeing oneself from the fetters of one or the other form of imposed cultural identities, its practice is a privilege of the class of immigrants for whom displacement itself is a matter of choice, an alternative, not a political contingency. In an age of increased mobility through globalization, hybridity also offers a semblance of being an inevitability, unmoored from any national or cultural framework.

Such semblance and inevitability of hybridity theory is subjected to sustained scrutiny by Pheng Cheah in his essay "Given Culture" (Cheah and Robbins 290–328). Cheah's essay is specifically directed against what Cheah recognizes as a "foreclosure" of "material dynamics of nationalism in neocolonial globalization" (ibid. 292). Cheah singles out James Clifford and Homi Bhabha as "hybridity theorists [who] subscribe to the same concept of normative cultures as the old-style philosophical cosmopolitanism they reject: the understanding of culture as the realm of humanity's freedom from the given" (ibid.). In Clifford's and Bhabha's conceptions of culture, Cheah diagnoses "aporetic cases of nationalism as given culture in a cosmopolitical force field" and suggests that "these cases of given culture . . . require us to reconceptualize the relation between culture and political-economic forces in terms of our responsibility to the given rather than our freedom from the given" (ibid.). While an elaborate discussion of Cheah's critique of postcolonial nationalism is beyond the scope of this chapter, his criticism of "hybridity as a more enabling theory of cultural resistance in postcolonial globality" (ibid. 293) is worthy of a brief recitation. The focus of Cheah's critique of hybridity theory is directed against the subversive, oppositional, emancipatory potential accorded to hybridity by Bhabha and Clifford. In presenting cultures and identities as "processes or production in language," in viewing culture only as "constructed by discourse or signification" (ibid.), hybridity theories present culture as "the site of permanent contestation" (ibid. 292). This makes hybridity theories' relationship with cosmopolitanism significantly problematic, Cheah suggests. Hybridity theory, he proposes, assumes "that new radical cosmopolitanisms already exist." He diagnoses in Bhabha and Clifford a reductionism of all global mobility to "cultural hybridization" (ibid. 297), and therefore, transnational migrant cultures become examples of "already existing radical cosmopolitanism" that subvert national culture (Bhabha) or localism (Clifford). Hybridity thus becomes a form of "closet idealism" and remains the privilege of migrants for whom dislocation, displacement, immigration, and mobility, were alternatives (ibid. 302).

Beyond the critique of hybridity as a privilege of choice and awareness, Cheah's argument also reveals the unspecific implications of cultural hybridity, its ambition of freedom through its self-pronounced predicament to detach itself from any given framework. While Cheah focuses mainly on national and cultural frameworks, his argument receives a comparable treatment in Rey Chow's *Protestant Ethnic*. Chow aligns herself with Cheah in thinking through the inadequacies of hybridity in the specific context of ethnicity.[5] She critiques the valorization and idealization of all that is "different, mobile, contingent, indeterminable" (*Protestant Ethnic* 134) to diagnose what she terms "a refusal of reference" (ibid. 130). Especially in the case of autobiographical writings, Chow postulates the resurgence of a "compulsive self-referentiality" in "ethnic narratives," which instead of becoming a source of "existential freedom, often painfully unveils the abject reality of a thwarted collective narcissism" (ibid. 127). Chow situates her argument in the specific genre of autobiographical writings to explain "compulsive self-referentiality" as a reaction to the "coercive mimeticism": "a complicated process in which incessant, ubiquitous interpellations and internalizations . . . confession, self-display and conscious mimicry of ethnicity as object inform the politics of [cross-ethnic] representation" (ibid. 126). Extending Julia Kristeva's[6] reflections on the "abject"—"a jettisoned object," "something rejected from which one does not part"—Chow presents "ethnic hybridity itself as a form of abjection" (ibid. 148). Instead of being a freedom from the given, for "ethnically marked writers," "hybridity . . . as the cultural given, becomes . . . a form of existential entrapment" (ibid. 146).

When hybridity postures as an always already revivalist agency of a culture that is always already being reinvented and rejuvenated, textually produced, and determined, as an alternative to one or two "Given Cultures"—to reinvoke Cheah's phrase—its specificity does not result from rendering two or more cultures unspecific. On the contrary, in order to achieve this movement, hybridity's dependence on the specificities of these cultures becomes far more pronounced. In other words, what makes hybridity dubious is its complete dependence on location and affiliation—be it ethnic, national, religious, gendered, or even linguistic—in order to dislocate and disaffiliate. Thus in the very moment and movement of de-essentialization, hybridity essentializes itself. Unsurprisingly, cultural hybridity strives toward idealism precisely due to the practitioners' and critics' subconscious acceptance of cultural specificities through the very denial of these specificities. Thus the closet idealism secretly denies, indeed repudiates, the presence of specificities in the favor of the allegedly unspecific nature of cultural hybridity, while it clandestinely depends on and highlights those very specificities to declare an artist or a work of art culturally hybrid. In the context of an ethnic minority author, the aspect of cultural specificity that undergoes direct denial is indeed ethnicity itself. On the one hand, ethnicity is inscribed within the narrative by the author him- or herself, and through his or her autobiography, his or her self-referentiality, which in turn surfaces in the form of references to his or her biography by critical readers. On the other hand, in positioning the ethnic minority author as the hybrid native informant, the author's references to the ethnic self are subjected to a closeted admiration. In the process of situating and celebrating an author as a practitioner of hybridity, there exists thus what Chow aptly terms the "refusal of reference" (*Protestant Ethnic* 130). Ethnicity becomes the refused, denied, repudiated, indeed the "abject" specificity, one that is excluded but cannot be entirely parted with.

Precisely through this kind of abjection, I propose along with Chow, through the simultaneity of denial and acceptance of specificities, the ethnic hybrid artist emerges as the "authentic." In other words, the mixed, adulterated, bastardized, messy, and therefore, the most forceful harbingers and propagators of transgression, translation, and translocution become the singular, pure, unadulterated, genuine, and therefore, the most situated, located, reliable authorities on the multiethnic and multicultural experience. Elitist privileges and aspirations of hybridity notwithstanding, cultural nativity and naturalization of the hybrid artist/author become the chief evaluating criteria for establishing his or her authenticity as the authentic hybrid—old models of evaluating authenticity through religious, ethnic, linguistic, and national affiliations exercise influence over the validation of hybridity. Bi- (or multi-)culturality, biraciality, biethnicity, binationality, all evaporate into thin air; transgression of boundaries suddenly becomes definitive, normative, prescriptive, and regressive. The authentic hybrid native informant is born, his or her ethnicity purloined in the act of declaring him or her the authentic hybrid. The hybrid then emerges as the most assimilated Other, one who retains his or her Otherness and his or her authenticity by purloining his or her own ethnicity.

These are some of the tensions between hybridity, ethnicity, and authenticity that motivate my reading of Zaimoğlu's self-creation and reception in the following section. The journalistic discourse I am about to discuss emphasizes, circulates, and thrives upon the authenticity of the author as the hybrid, as the new model minority. In this section, journalistic writings on Zaimoğlu are juxtaposed with two articles from a series on Turks in Germany published in *Die Zeit* in 2003 in order to lay bare the categories against which Zaimoğlu's newness is defined. As I demonstrate, a consistent signification of hybridity is deducible in these journalistic writings, one which simultaneously shuns and validates ethnicity. Through these problematic maneuvers, Zaimoğlu is established and accepted as the authentic voice of the second and third generation of Turks in Germany.

The journalistic portrait of Zaimoğlu as a young author establishes him on the one hand as an assimilated Other who can communicate and can be comprehended in the language of the majority, indeed, in the vocabularies of assimilation, and on the other hand as the Other who protects and sustains his Otherness through a persistent defiance of assimilation. Central to this defiance is Zaimoğlu's powerful reclamation of the pejorative German term *Kanake* in his book *Kanak Sprak*. Shortly, I will discuss the definition of the term *Kanake*. Right now it suffices to state that through this reclamation of a historically derogatory category, Zaimoğlu aggressively asserts the permanent presence of Turkish immigrants and the following generations in Germany—a move that makes him and the aggressive/assertive *Kanaken* of his ilk not just acceptable, but also welcome in the journalistic discourse. This resurgence of the *Kanake* finds numerous and repetitive references in writings about Zaimoğlu. However, the assertion and the following celebration of the *Kanake* cannot be fully grasped without understanding the categories against which it defines itself. It is, therefore, productive to glance at the first two articles of the series "Türken in Deutschland" (Turks in Germany), published in 2003 in *Die Zeit*. These articles effectively illustrate the value of social assimilation of immigrants as a measure of their success.

The inaugural article of the series promises a departure from the image of the guest worker, who is the lowest of the low in the social chain. Titled "Nie mehr Migrations-Ali" (No more Migration-Ali), the article focuses on "Die neue türkischstämmige Mittelschicht" (the new middle class of Turkish origin). The author, Susanne Gaschke, seeks to present the "unbekannte Erfolgsstory"[7] (the unknown success story) of Turks in Germany. The article includes interviews with four "successful" Turks. The new faces of success include two men—the young and hip author Feridun Zaimoğlu and the old and wise professor of hydrogeology Asaf Pekdeger—as well as two young women—Dilek Kolat, the SPD spokesperson for economics and technology, and Hacer Yüksel, a young architect and bureaucrat for the city of Hamburg. Zaimoğlu, Kolat, and Yüksel belong to the second generation of Turks in Germany. They are children of Turkish immigrants, albeit not necessarily from a working-class background. The article provides the readers with a guided tour of the history of the educations and achievements of these individuals. With the exception of Prof. Pekdeger—who hails from an elite family in Istanbul and came to Germany as a student—the stories of the other three successful Turks include descriptions of social isolation, difficulties in schools, language problems, and so forth. Of the four successful Turks, Zaimoğlu, distinguished by his appearance and his otherwise critical attitude toward Germans, comes across as the most integrated Turk. He is presented as a warrior who wages a constant war against the victim-narratives of Turks in his works and seems to exhibit little sympathy for immigrants who do not attempt to secure a social space for themselves in their country of residence.[8]

Zaimoğlu is thus a warrior integrated into the German society through education. The statistical parataxis titled "Integration Heute" (Integration Today) accompanying the narrative of successful Turks further highlights the efficacy of integration. Education implies integration; so does departure from Islam and a movement toward Western-style clothing. Toward the end of the article, Gaschke supplies the reader with a description of Yüksel's five-year-old daughter, who wears an outfit that is *bauchfrei* (with bare midriff). "Kein Erziehungskonflikt" (not a conflict of upbringing) is Yüksel's response to Gaschke's observation; she proceeds to explain, "I am a Muslim, but I think that one can believe in Allah without following each and every of the day-to-day rules of Islam." Moderate Islam, perhaps embodied in the bare midriff of a five-year-old girl, becomes the uncontested and universally valid sign for emancipation, cultural assimilation, and social integration.

The second article in the series registers the failure stories of nonintegrated, isolated, "loser" Turks living in the Turkish neighborhood Kartenberg in the city of Essen. The nameless women photographed for this article wear long skirts and blouses with headscarves, have children sitting in their laps, and thus stand in stark contrast to the successful Kolat and

Yüksel with their business suits and dyed and styled hair showcased in the previous piece. The author, Jochen Bittner, picks up where Gaschke left off: this article moves from the integrated bare midriff to the disintegrated covered head, as captured by the title, "Ghetto im Kopf" (Ghetto in the Head). The Turkish men interviewed for this article include a thirty-one-year-old roofer, Mehmed Tufan, and his friends Mustafa and Ismail. The author carefully lists their serving of Turkish tea in *Fincans*, their conservative views about marriage and women, and their differences with the German lifestyle and customs, without reflecting for once on the reasons why the people in this story might not have the same opinions as those in the previous one. In listing the statistics for this neighborhood—46 percent of the residents live off welfare—Bittner stops short of reporting the reasons for the lack of upward mobility among these residents. As he calls the neighborhood a *Problemviertel* (problem-quarter) and declares the process of integration "gescheitert" (collapsed), he turns to the German social worker Thomas Rüth, apparently a natural authority on failed integration. But Rüth also lists only the shortcomings of the community, and Bittner reaches the conclusion, "Integration? *Sie ist hier ein fernes Ziel*" (Integration? Here it is a distant destination). Once again, a journalist, the quintessential field-worker, in search of truth in another culture, establishes the native informant as the vessel of regression and epistemic lack. The social worker, the interlocutor, takes the position of authority; the subaltern is simply shut up forever. In the second half of the article, Bittner returns to the women, who assemble once a week at the local Ayasofya mosque to discuss the education of their children. Bittner declares the women incapable of improving the problems of their children because of their own lack of competence in German. The reason given for this linguistic isolation is the presence of Turkish-speaking doctors and lawyers and grocers and café staff. Citing the Center fur Turkish Studies in Essen, Bittner names this phenomenon *ethnishce Koloniebildung* (formation of ethnic colonies). The hero of the story is Halit Pisnek, the Imam of the Ayasofya mosque, because he inspires women to partially shed the patriarchal shackles of Islam and embrace evangelical German emancipation masquerading as secular integration. The article ends with another anecdote by Mehmed Tufan. Tufan narrates the story of a German woman who sold off her husband's assets and changed the locks while he was away. "So was . . . passiert mir nicht" (This does not happen to me). Whereas in the first article moderate Islam and upward mobility become the keys to Turkish success, conservative Islam and retention of patriarchal hegemony are, in the second one, declared the most important obstacles in the path to the integration of minorities, in what should be understood as an otherwise liberal, emancipated, classless utopia that is Germany.

Against these recently reinforced categories that continue to dominate the public image of the Turks forty years after the first wave of Turkish immigration to Germany, Zaimoğlu's assertion of difference in the assimilatory equation and the reasons for his journalistic fascination are not difficult to understand. Detlef Grumbach's citation of Zaimoğlu in an article in the *Süddeutsche Zeitung*[9] provides a further clue. In Zaimoğlu's own words, "The assimilated caraway seed is the most miserable trip since the arrival of the *Kanaken*.... The assimilated caraway seed is one who is properly trimmed and made up, the noble immigrant who squats in his niche like the ever same non-Turk and the ever same fresh-off-the-boat arrival and only serves to uphold the image of the friendly reception of migrants."

Grumbach locates Zaimoğlu's *Kanake* against the Turk who has undergone the process of assimilation and adjustment (*Anpassung*), which has forced him to give up and compromise on the notion of his self (*Selbstaufgabe*). However, the *Kanake* is not just the binary opposite of the assimilated Turk. As Grumbach further reports, the *Kanake* secures his or her place beyond another binary oppositional model, inhabited on the one hand by the completely assimilated Turk bereft of his or her sense of self and on the other hand by the nationalistic and religious bigot, characterized by *türkischem Stolz* (Turkish pride) and *Reislamisierung* (re-Islamization). The clear opposition between Turkish and German identities is thus resolved and absolved in the figure of the *Kanake*, of which Zaimoğlu, the "educated Kanakster," is the sole representative. As the title and the subtitle of this article promise, Zaimoğlu plays as the captain and the coach of the league of the damned and the wretched (*Liga der Verdammten*) as he comes from a generation that is beyond its origins and confers a voice to those who find no listeners.

Thus with one broad journalistic stroke, a number of old—and as we just saw in the series in *Die Zeit*, still extant—social anxieties about the immigrants in Germany become transparent. First, against the assimilated, integrated, adjusted members of the middle class, the unassimilated Turks are qualified by their affinity to the Turkish nation and/or to traditional Islam. Furthermore, the unassimilated Turks appear as curiously autonomous agents who condition, control, and are therefore responsible for their undesirability and unacceptability in the social fabric of Germany. Beyond the two, Zaimoğlu, part of the wretched—but not quite—offers himself as a more attractive alternative to, and perhaps an easy recourse from, the prevalent modalities of a discriminated Turk. By mentioning that Zaimoğlu confers a voice upon those who do not have a listener, Grumbach does not necessarily make a case for listening to the wretched or the often suppressed or contained nature of their lament. That necessity is eliminated by the sheer presence of Zaimoğlu and by the consolation that he writes in a language that, despite its being a form of German, could be the language of the lament of the wretched. In establishing Zaimoğlu as the most brilliant ventriloquist of the voice of the wretched, Grumbach's article privileges Zaimoğlu's authenticity through his biographic uniqueness. Zaimoğlu's education, his somewhat erotic relationship with the German language, and—perhaps most importantly—his understanding of his father's anger at the discrimination he faced as an immigrant, all amount to his empowerment and his articulation of a systematic rejection of multiculturalism as mere "folkloristic enrichment."

Grumbach's article is just one example of an entire spate of journalistic writings whereby the authors centralize connections between Zaimoğlu's uniqueness and authenticity. Petra Ahne of the *Berliner Tageszeitung* highlights Zaimoğlu's racial and class-based difference in an elitist milieu in Sylt.[10] Stephan Theil, the German correspondent for *Newsweek*, declares Zaimoğlu part of the generation that refreshes the sedated cultural establishment of Europe.[11] Andrea Gerk of the *Frankfurter Rundschau* identifies claims of uniqueness and authenticity in Zaimoğlu's capability to capture the "voice from the street [that] harasses bourgeois consciousness."[12] In these and other articles, authenticity and uniqueness maintain a circuitous relationship. They are promoted and propagated by the authors in their reception of Zaimoğlu and his works; Zaimoğlu, in turn, propagates and promotes them through compulsive self-referentiality.

These self-referential claims become most pronounced in Zaimoğlu's interviews, which can be read as annotations to his works. They are replete with his ideas on literature and his passionate views on a number of political issues, mostly related to the status of Turkish immigrants and minorities. His disregard for *Multikulti* and his rejection of an entire traditional literature of immigrants written and published before him manifests itself often in variants of the following statement: "Literature of the emigrants has been here for 35 years, effusions from field researchers, who send it hastily to the ghetto. Or there are representatives of the *Multikulti-*industry. All these different posts of the Turkish records department have one thing in common, to upset the situation of the *Kanaken*. What I do is really a kind of public work" (Zaimoğlu, interview with Edith Kresta).

Despite his continued celebration in the German press, Zaimoğlu describes and valorizes his victimization by his critics. Zaimoğlu positions his literary work beyond what he claims were lachrymose documentations of a myth: the myth of anxieties caused by a bicultural existence. He reduces the work of other Turkish-German authors to mere folkloric antiquity, declaring the superiority of his literary work and his work as a public intellectual. In another interview, he defines this public work as a process of empowerment of minorities and the reclaiming of cultural hegemony.[13]

My own inaccessibility to his claims to cultural hegemony notwithstanding, a clear pattern can be deduced in Zaimoğlu's interviews. Throughout his self-righteous defense of his mode of thinking against the modes of others, his rejection of institutionalized multiculturalism, and his pedantic interpretations of his literary works, a peculiar tension is notable. The tension resurfaces over and over again in his reiterations of his uniqueness and authenticity, which are reinforced through his self-referentiality. On the one hand, Zaimoğlu perceives his literary work as authentic not only due to his own claim that he collects his materials and documents them as they are—without make-up (*ungeschminkt*)—but also because his works do not centralize the bicultural anxieties of other Turkish-German authors. In other words, Zaimoğlu's claims of authenticity in his interviews, which are then reproduced in articles, therefore rest on a definition of authentic as original, genuine, unadulterated, unmixed. Zaimoğlu persistently resists his categorization as a hyphenated "nicht-Deutsche" author—he rightly stakes claims in the corpus of German literature. However, his claims for his rightful place in German literature do not get transmitted without undulating references to ethnic difference. Zaimoğlu concedes the importance of ethnicity; he asserts that his writings are about the *Lumpenethnics*. Therefore, his uniqueness rests precisely in his difference, his ethnicity, his biculturality—all the elements that he criticizes in the literature written by other Turkish-German authors. Indeed, his self-promotion, his originality, his authenticity, rest on a language and identity that is urbane, mixed, adulterated, hybridized—indeed, bastardized. The word *hybrid* tends to become the main descriptor of Zaimoğlu's language and identity. In his retelling of an interview with Zaimoğlu for the cultural organization LAKS, Michael Rappe locates Zaimoğlu between Goethe and Kanake, and, therefore, "im Haus und represented."[14] Rappe accredits Zaimoğlu's representative claims in the house of German literature to his ability to give voice to the *Gastarbeiterkinder* of the second and third generations. The mixture of

(High) German, Turkish, and the "Slang Stakkato" of the streets enables Zaimoğlu to distill a "literary report, a shrill, anarchist canon of mistones from the cosmos Kanakistan." Zaimoğlu represents a movement away from the tamed and "pretty guest-worker literature" (*brave Gastarbeiterliteratur*) and strives toward his own show-place of difference (*zur-Schau-Stellung der Differenz*), a defiant celebration of the Other. Having qualified Zaimoğlu as such, for Rappe, the defiant celebration of Otherness curiously becomes a function of ambivalence in Zaimoğlu's works. As Rappe reports, Zaimoğlu is able to present the "real face of Immigration" through an "unleashing of his hybrid existence." The article ends with references to the "American cultural theorist" Homi Bhabha's *Location of Culture*, and Rappe presents Zaimoğlu as a member of the club of postcolonial authors who, paraphrasing Bhabha, conceptualize an international culture that does not rest upon the exoticism of multiculturalism or the diversity of cultures but on the registering and articulation of the hybridity of cultures.

These are just a few examples isolated from scores of interviews, book reviews, and articles that discuss Zaimoğlu and his works. In almost all of Zaimoğlu's press coverage, an anxious reference to ethnicity and the ethnic-self renders itself legible.[15] Zaimoğlu's Otherness is defined by his ethnicity, and yet in the constant "defiant celebration of Otherness," to borrow again from Rappe, references to ethnic difference turn into effete reminders of exoticism, of a spectacle of multiculturalism and diversity only capable of reproducing the allegedly exhausted discourse of *Gastarbeiterliteratur*. Zaimoğlu offers himself, and is offered by others in turn, as the alternative to this exhaustion. The ethnic Other reinvents himself as a hybrid subject. Ethnicity is selectively and programmatically purloined and at once reclaimed.

More specifically, ethnicity itself, purloined from Zaimoğlu's media personality, reinserts itself in his literary works, sometimes as mimicry of Zaimoğlu's narrative subjects—whom he meets during his *Szenenforschung* in his literary works—other times in his performances and readings through mimicry of the perceived emancipatory, hybrid vocabularies of hip-hop and rap. Most importantly, this purloined ethnicity appears as self-mimicry and self-referentiality in all of his creative work and becomes the source of his obscurantist representational claims over an entire (third) generation of Turkish immigrants. If these arguments hold currency, the revolutionary, novel, unique, and authentic character of Zaimoğlu's writings is, indeed, debatable. As the ethnic author becomes a hybrid interlocutor, Zaimoğlu's native informants—outlawed outsiders ready to claim their takeover of the hegemonic German majority culture—are simultaneously validated and suppressed under the misleading aegis of authentic self-representation. To recapitulate, Zaimoğlu's claims of authenticity rest on his rejection of a bicultural angst, even while he and his characters cannot distance themselves from the struggles of a bicultural existence and the predicament of an ethnic Otherness, which he articulates in a language that can be, and has been, qualified as hybrid.

It is important to highlight the emphasis on Zaimoğlu's reputation as a practitioner of cultural hybridity and as a symbol of newness for a number of reasons. The concept of hybridity forms and conditions his journalistic reception and his self-creation in the media. Even if the process of journalistic formation and conditioning is carried out in a telegraphic, short-handed, and relatively less self-reflective fashion, it guarantees Zaimoğlu a place beyond the binaries of the immigrant and the citizen, a kind of cultural assimilation-in-difference. Moreover, in registering claims of authenticity and uniqueness, a peculiar sort of hybridity bereft of reference to, independent of, indeed, emancipated from, ethnicity establishes itself as the dominant paradigm of understanding Zaimoğlu.

This exercise is not limited to journalistic writings. Scholars such as Sandra Hestermann locate Zaimoğlu in the "third space" of what "Homi Bhabha has termed as the 'interstitial passage' where cultures meet and merge" (Hestermann 330). Hestermann discusses Zafer Şenocak's *Gefährliche Verwandtschaft* (Perilous Kinship)[16] and Zaimoğlu's *Kanak Sprak* to illustrate "how the German multicultural environment has produced new forms of diasporic existence in which German and Turkish identities have becomes hybridized in an emergent diasporic Kanakster identity" (ibid. 368). She assigns this hybridized identity to a biracial/bireligious character such as Şenocak's narrator Sasha (ibid. 352–58) and, with equal benevolence, to the many narrators of Zaimoğlu's *Kanak Sprak*. The hybrid *Kanake* or *Kanakster* are "Turkish migrants who have not managed full integration into Germany, where they are despised and stigmatized as Kanake" (ibid. 359); they are culturally alienated "from their parents and grandparents" (ibid. 360), who are "fossilized and backward looking" (ibid. 362); the Kanakster do not consider Turkey their "homeland (which most of them have only visited during their annual summer vacation)" (ibid. 360); they are "neither the friendly assimilated Turkish neighbor of the 'Ali-Type' nor the intellectual, highly educated academic," and they are "disillusioned with the German society" (ibid. 361); they are "neither German nor Turkish" and "set out to construct an alternative self-image that emancipates itself from both German and

Turkish stereotypes, prejudices, and clichés" (ibid. 367). And yet they are the "living conscience of the nation" (ibid. 366), a "confident voice from the diasporic Turkish-German community, which has made itself at home in Germany" (ibid. 367). Through such chaotic and mutually self-negating characteristics of the *Kanake/Kanakster* and a Turkish-Germanness that are neither German nor Turkish, Hestermann succeeds in establishing hybridity as a phenomenon devoid of any references to ethnicity.

Unlike Hestermann, Tom Cheeseman exhibits extreme caution in his highly nuanced study of Zaimoğlu's antiracist movement *Kanak-Attack*. Cheeseman analyzes "Kanak-Chic": the "media's 'discovery' of bright, young, non-white, hybrid Germans" (Cheeseman 180), and connects this with the German critics' hopes "that the magic of hybridisation, working on the ferment of migration, might yet produce a world-class writer from Germany" (ibid. 182). Cheeseman neither promotes nor negates this hope, nor does he indulge in a rampant celebration of Zaimoğlu's hybridity. In fact, Cheeseman falsifies the claims of the originality of *Kanak Sprak* by revealing that it was modeled on Dursun Akçam's *Alaman ocağı: Türkler Almanları anlatiyor = Deutsches Heim—Glück allein. Wie Türken Deutsche sehen* (ibid. 183), a fact Zaimoğlu would not own up to. More important for our discussion here is a productive discrepancy in Cheeseman's engagement with Zaimoğlu. While the abstract of the article attributes elements of Zaimoğlu's work to the media's discovery of "hybrid Germans" (ibid. 180), Cheeseman comments later in the article, "The mainstream discourse of multiculturalism—talk of the 'Other,' 'cultural difference,' 'identity,' and 'hybridity'—come under vehement attack in Zaimoğlu's work because of its use in deflecting attention from plain social and political injustice" (ibid. 186).

Zaimoğlu's attack on institutionalized multiculturalism and his self-promotion as the champion of social and political injustice are uncontestable. However, as Cheeseman's own pronouncements convey, by proposing *Kanak* as "a parody identity," even if to "make visible the artificiality and rigidity of the conventionally ascribed identities" through highlighting the cultural difference of the "ethnographic informants" (ibid. 187), the Others, to register his disillusionment with multiculturalism and assimilation in a "mixture [crossing] of Turkish and German into a highly original literary German" (ibid. 184), Zaimoğlu reutilizes the very terms that dominate the mainstream discourse of multiculturalism, even as he claims distinction and distance from those terms.

There are other analytical frameworks through which Zaimoğlu's *Kanak Sprak* has been evaluated. In *Rewriting Germany from the Margins*,

Petra Fachinger positions Zaimoğlu's *Kanak Sprak* against Günter Wallraff's *Ganz Unten*. "Ali"—the stereotypical Turkish guest worker—explains Fachinger, gets a "more playful and satirical" treatment in *Kanak Sprak* (*Rewriting Germany* 100). Fachinger views Zaimoğlu's figure of the Kanake in opposition to the victimized Turk in Wallraff's *Ganz Unten*, attributing the power of opposition to Zaimoğlu's use of "a language that is based on underground vocabulary and its own rhythm" (ibid. 101).[17] The Kanake thus "draws his identity from the insider language, a German of his own creation," writes Fachinger (ibid.). Emphasizing the resistant dimension of Zaimoğlu's work, she presents his characters as "caricatures who embody the stereotypes associated with Turks" (ibid. 102). She reads Zaimoğlu's use of gangster-rap as a "transnational consciousness comparable to that cultivated by the Black power movement" (ibid. 101). Leslie Adelson identifies Zaimoğlu's Kanaken as illustrations of "the protestant ethnics as Chow defines them" (*Turkish Turn* 134), but in her reading of *Kanak Sprak* she exercises restraint in the celebration of the protesting potential of *Kanak Sprak*. Commenting on the limited reliability of the protocols as "ethnographic transcriptions," Adelson understands "the text as consistently bespeaking a creative product made in Germany by Zaimoğlu" (ibid. 97). She asks if Zaimoğlu's Turkish figures offer a counterpoint from the "failed powers of speech" of Homi Bhabha's Turkish guest worker, not so much to affirm the latter, but to highlight that "Zaimoğlu regards the incoherence of Kanak speak as powerful rather than powerless" (ibid. 98).[18]

Zaimoğlu thus presents a particular problematic of subaltern signification. His writings, as well as the journalistic and (select) scholarly discussions of him and his works, mobilize "hybridity" as a definitive marker. However, as Cheeseman and Adelson demonstrate, the revolutionary potential of this hybridity requires a sober look away from the sensationalism and excitement that his speech creates. It is, therefore, necessary to subject Zaimoğlu's purposeful creation of stereotypes—or his caricatures, as Fachinger suggests—to careful scrutiny. Zaimoğlu's writings are caught between assertions of cultural/ethnic hybridity *as* authenticity. Claims of political and cultural citizenship in Germany are registered without a rejection of Turkish Otherness. However, in registering these claims, the Turkish aspect of Otherness, overwhelmed by underclass realities, becomes abject. Ethnicity is thus presented and immediately purloined as authenticity, documented through hybrid language. *Abschaum* is not an autobiographical work but a biography of the Turkish underclass Zaimoğlu creates "authentically" from the accounts of his informant that are replete with the "consistent self-referentiality" of the narrator on the one hand and a secret refusal of reference to ethnicity on the other. Amid this tug and pull of referentiality and the refusal thereof, hypermasculinity assumes a normative position. What is the validity of such self-referential claims? What is at stake in the politics of ethnicity and cultural hybridity promoted and propagated by the self-referentiality of an ethnic minority author? What kind of cosmopolitical claims can be identified in this charged force field of ethnicity and class? These are some of the questions that guide my reading of Zaimoğlu's second novel, *Abschaum*.

Abschaum contains thirty-six stories narrated to the author Zaimoğlu by Ertan Ongun, his (ethnographic) native informant. These stories are entitled, at times, after the action central to the story, like "Die Beerdigungs-Story" (The Burial Story 7–11); after the place central to the action of the story, like "Die Steakhaus-Überfall-Story" (The Steak-House-Robbery Story 84–88); or after the character central to the action at the time of the action, like "Die Story von der türkischen Nutte" (The Story of the Turkish Whore 32–39) and "Die Albaner-Story" (The Albanian Story 129–36). The stories are narrated in the first person by the protagonist Ertan Ongun; only in the Nachwort (Afterword 183–84) does the reader learn that the stories were narrated to Zaimoğlu and reproduced by him.

All of these stories center around events in the life of Ertan Ongun, whose reaction against discrimination, whose resistance to assimilation, and whose consistent assertion of sexual prowess grant him the status of the angry young man, the tough guy, the antihero, whose illegal deliberations are incessantly valorized by him, as well as by his interlocutor Zaimoğlu. Ongun's antiheroism situates itself in recurring themes such as cultural and religious differences between Germans and Turks, class differences within the Turkish communities, differences of values and principles between the first and second or third generations of Turks, discrimination against Turks by Germans, especially by the German police. All of these themes have been part of the *Gastarbeiterliteratur* that Zaimoğlu particularly detests. What distinguishes Zaimoğlu's reconstruction of Ongun's stories is the aggressive assertion of these themes, his clear delineation of good and evil, the selective celebration of a specific variety of evil—Ongun's illegal actions—and most importantly, the excessive references to Ongun's difference from all the Germans, some Turks, and most German residents of other national and ethnic minorities. Moreover, the language of these stories, apart from being explicitly heterosexual, homo-assaulting (not just homophobic), misogynist, and at times racist, is abundantly interspersed with Turkish sentences, or Turkish-German code-switching phrases. Statements made in Turkish are only approximately translated into German or not translated at all. The language itself bears its own distinct marks of hybridity and gives contour to the bicultural and bilingual aspects of Ongun, even while Turkish ethnicity and cultural difference are asserted through masculine aggression.

"Die Skinhead-Story," which follows the first story about Farouk, is an apt example of the above-stated observations. While "The Burial Story" presents Ongun as a dedicated friend willing to wash the rotten corpse of his deceased friend and ready to organize his funeral, "The Skinhead Story" lays all the cards on the table. Hanging about at the *Flohmarkt* (flea market), where Ongun and his friends are almost permanent fixtures, Ongun hears about an assault on a Turkish woman by Skinheads. His reaction immediately reinforces loyalty toward his ethnicity and community and hatred toward the Skinheads or any other Germans who might consider the Turks weak, and he exhibits chivalry and a sense of protection for the Turkish woman who has been assaulted: "What, how? Turkish woman? Who has the courage to mishandle a Turkish woman? Everyone knows that we stick together" (12). Turkish solidarity finds expression in a counterassault on the Skinheads that Ongun plans and executes with a dozen or so of his Turkish friends. The woman in question is lost from the narrative immediately, almost instantly replaced by the spirit of revenge for her assault. After breaking glass and smashing windows and display counters, Ongun tries to escape the crime scene. Having established his image as the daring protector of women's honor, as an antiracist activist, Ongun delineates his distinction from an allegedly conformist variety of Turks that he labels as high-schoolers (*Abitur-Türken*) and strivers (*Strebertürken*, 15). As opposed to these apparently passive Turks, Zaimoğlu's Ongun is a *Hardcore-Türke* (16) who considers officials such as the police chief, the judge, and the social pedagogue to be "wankers from the uppermost class" (*Wichser vonner alleroversten Klasse*, 17). Ongun leads the band that can take apart the entire city of Kiel if a Turkish woman is assaulted because, as he tells a female journalist, "today any [Turkish] woman, tomorrow my mother" (17).

This momentary alliance with Turkish women, posing as antiracist chivalry, stops just there. The unknown Turkish woman and Ongun's mother are the only two who belong to an allegedly honorable space that must be protected at all times and avenged in the case of intrusion. The rest of the women in the stories are barred from this privileged domestic honor. They work in strip clubs or at their residences as prostitutes or get drunk in bars and become part of Ongun's sexual encounters. Ongun's unflinching adulation of his masculinity continues through the rest of the stories, but it is particularly emphasized through the superior quality of his sexual performance, described in great detail in the fifth story, "The Story of the Turkish Whore." Ongun's urgent need for sexual satisfaction at first encourages him to publish a classified advertisement in the local newspaper offering his services as a male prostitute (32), but he decides against it and, instead, responds to an advertisement. Yasemin, the prostitute assigned to him, is Turkish; having established that he is a Turk, she initiates the conversation in German by asking where he is from, implying perhaps his hometown in Turkey. When he responds with "Ich bin Kieler" (I am from Kiel, 33), she asks the specifics in Turkish and in German:

> "wo ist deine Heimat inner Türkei, memleketin neresi?" "Dedim Adana," sag ich. "Adanadan adam çıkmaz diyo, aus Adana kommen keine richtigen Kerls," sagt sie.[19] (33f.)

However, her response to the fact that he is from the city of Adana in Turkey does not necessitate an immediate ethnic bond between the two. She does not consider Adana as a city of "real men" (*richtigen Kerls*) and refuses to have sex with him. What follows is an account of Ongun's refutation of her claim through descriptions of his enormous genitalia, his impressive art and science of sexually satisfying a woman, his charm—all of which apparently impress Yasemin so much that she decides to make an exception and kiss him. In addition, Ongun further asserts his hyper-heterosexuality by mocking Yasemin's desire to dominate the sexual interaction and by categorically refusing to be penetrated by a dildo (35–37).

These details need to be mentioned not only to illustrate Ongun's selective ethnic alliances and problematic chivalry. If misogyny is a vital characteristic of a hybridized *Kanaken*-identity—to borrow from Sandra Hestermann again—Zaimoğlu's Ongun has certainly established it. More importantly, by proving his masculinity, the macho resident of Kiel (*der Kieler*) has forever disproved the allegation of a lack of masculinity among men from Adana. Ethnicity gets purloined first through the claim that the hometown is indeed Kiel—and then gets reclaimed through a violent display of masculinity. In the "true" story of Ertan Ongun, sexual details and masculine attributes do not receive an ironic or exaggerated treatment as deployments against stereotypical perceptions of Turkish machismo. If the revolutionary potential of the *Kanaken*-narrative requires misogyny to be overlooked, then by virtue of pornographic realism, the entire narrative can be considered revolutionary. If not—which would be my hope—accounting for such details, along with a discussion of their regressive, oppressive politics, is necessary before Zaimoğlu or any of his works are received as inherently progressive. The oppressive politics of the *Kanake* surface in misogynistic forms later in the text, although this time they are presented as a recourse from potential homosexuality. In "Die Schlampen-Story" (The Slut-Story, 137–39), Ongun meets an on old woman at a bar where he spots potential buyers of heroin. She is described as an "overdone old woman, really acrid, really dirty, big hair, totally dirty clothes, totally fat and short, she stank, the old one, I don't know, not even Robinson would fuck her" (137). Her ugliness initiates Ongun's understanding for gays: "In a moment like this, one understands the men who become gay" (137). This fleeting understanding for the cause of homosexuality becomes fundamentally important for Ongun to initiate a sexual intercourse with her:

> Man, ok, she's disgusting, the old one, she really makes me want to throw up. But imagine young man, you'll be caught with the stuff [heroin], then you'll end up in prison, and then you'll jerk off, there's nothing else. Yeah, ok, you can also become gay, but it's not quite my thing to change sides. Think about it from this point of view, jerk off, jerk off, jerk off, afterwards you'll think, when you lie in your cell and you've ejaculated and you smoke one, after that, man, that day, when the old one was there, you could have just fucked her or have let her blow you. According to this motto I went up to her and said: come with me, I want to fuck you. (137f.)

The woman agrees, and the two have sex in a dingy staircase. Ongun later explains his logic of preventing homosexuality by default to his friends; they understand and agree and condone his act. His masculinity reinforced and heterosexuality reassured, Zaimoğlu's *Kanake* registers—to cite Hestermann again—the "confident voice from the diasporic community."

While misogyny and homophobia emerge as distinct features of Ongun's personality, his Turkish ethnicity remains, for the most part, muted and suppressed. Apart from the few direct references to Turkish ethnicity—in moments when Ongun orchestrates violence to avenge the assaulted honor of a kinswoman, when he distinguishes himself from assimilated Turks, or when he asserts the masculinity of his ancestral city Adana—Turkishness defines itself against and as superior to a number of other ethnicities and nationalities. In the underworld of Kiel, mentions of Ongun's male friends and enemies are usually followed by or qualified by references to their ethnicity. Farouk is the Syrian (7), Zlatko the "Jugo" (19), Haydar, Ongun's friend in Turkey, is called Tabs (sic) because he looks like a "Neger," the African American policeman in the American television show *Miami Vice* (58). In addition, Ongun comes across courageous Albanians ("mutige" Albaner, 129–36), slime-shitting (*Schleimscheißer*) Pakistanis (71), and other "niggers," African American soldiers who come from the Bronx (*aus Bronx herkamen*) and have huge nostrils (*Nasenlöcher*, 64). Apart from the Albanian—whose courage impresses Ongun—all of the others must be defeated, conquered, or impressed with an adequate display of Turkish masculine power. Zaimoğlu's *Kanake* is not necessarily the category that encompasses all the marginalized, oppressed minorities. Even as a "parody" identity—as Cheeseman describes it—the *Kanake*, or *Kanakster*, identity surfaces in *Abschaum* only as exclusionary; its hybrid aspirations, articulated in the Turkish-German street slang, are limited to its assertions of space within the German social text.

These assertions are registered through a specific, brutal critique of the racist practices of German police. Almost all the stories are replete with abundant references to *Bullenhuren* (bull-whores), or German policemen. In the violent life of the heroin addict and dealer Ongun, the German police are a constant presence, a force to be reckoned with. In the "Wir-Kriegen-Euch-Kanaken-Story" (We-Will-Get-You-*Kanake* Story, 52–57), the police in Kiel plan to arrest Ongun's friend Attila, and they use Fevzi, another friend, as a conduit to arrest him in the act of selling cocaine. The deal takes place in the fast-food kiosk of Attila's father. During the police raid, Attila's father has an asthma attack, but the police, convinced that he is pretending, refuse to call emergency health care professionals. Due to lack of immediate medical attention, Attila's father dies. On hearing about the death of Attila's father, Ongun comments, "For the bulls you are always a liar, you are a *Kanake*, you are already presentenced in their eyes; you should only be behind bars and nothing else. When they arrest a German and he says, I need a doctor, I'm screwed, I have some kinda shit, then immediately: What do you have? Then the law kicks in, but in the case of a Turk, they [the Turks] are assholes, they are liars, a primitive pack" (56). As Ongun further elaborates, such incidents are, however, publicized not as the story of a father and a son but of a father and a criminal Turkish son (57). Slowly but surely, Ongun states, the rest of the family members are deported to Turkey, and thus "a Turkish family is dissolved in Germany" (57).

These comments appear to be buried in the larger mess of drugs, women, and violence that make up Ongun's life. But the sections on criminal culture and police encounters are the strongest in the book. Mentions of 5- and 7-millimeter guns appear at least once in every story. Ongun confesses that he gains a sense of identity through criminality (90). Disturbed by police brutality and discrimination, tired of police searches in the disguise of searches for terrorists (103), Ongun declares Germany a police reserve and calls his opponents Nazis (106). Against police oppression, knowledge of the German criminal code provides him a semblance of control (119), but his criminal activities take that control away from him. Accounts of police brutality continue in the last stories. Ongun gets arrested for drug trafficking and is illegally mistreated in the Neuenmünster prison (157). Racial politics dominate the prison, and Ongun experiences many confrontations with the wardens and other officers. His opposition to torture has no effect on the officers. A bitter and disappointed Ongun strips the mask from the German pretense of protecting human rights: "There is no state with rights, I don't believe in this shit. There are no laws, I don't believe in that shit either. There is only power and the powerful and powerlessness and the powerless—that is all. Germany has make-up on its face.... When her face is washed and Germany shows her true colors, then it'll be different" (163).

Ongun's story ends on a pathetic note. He jeopardizes his life and health by drug overdose; the cycle of going in and out of prison continues; he feels useless, hopeless, and defeated, but he sees no advantage in leaving the world of crime. He sees himself as one of the "cocksuckers" (*Schwanzlutcher*), "sons-of-whores" (*Hurensöhne*), "niggers" (*Neger*), and "Arabs" (*Araber*, 179), all the wretched and the downtrodden, and the shitty-country (*Scheißland*) in which they live has little to offer them apart from a miniscule welfare stipend. The true story of Ertan Ongun, which starts with references to stench and fecal matter, ends with stench and fecal matter.

Once Ongun finishes his story, Zaimoğlu appears in the Nachwort and spells out claims of authenticity. It is Ongun's story, Zaimoğlu claims: "he narrated it to me ... in his powerful language" (183). Zaimoğlu lets the readers know that Ongun wanted him to write a book about immigrant children (*Migrantenkinder*) because they have replaced the characters from Christiane F.'s *Wir Kinder vom Bahnhof Zoo* (We, The Children of Train Station Zoo). Zaimoğlu further relays Ongun's message: "We are the *Kanaken*, about whom Germans had always warned you. Now we are here, congruous to your picture and your fears" (183). After reading

Kanak Sprak, Ongun asked Zaimoğlu if he would narrate his story. Zaimoğlu shares with the reader that he has "cautiously constructed" (*behutsam eingerichtet,* 183) Ongun's story.

Zaimoğlu's acknowledgement of Ertan Ongun at the end of his book does not end the debate over Ongun and his stories—indeed it sheds a new light on it; it takes it out of the semblance of innocence. Nowhere in *Abschaum* does Ongun's interest in reading find mention; nowhere is his awareness of his comparability with the punks of *Bahnhof Zoo* legible. One can always debate if Ongun necessarily read Zaimoğlu's *Kanak Sprak,* or if Zaimoğlu wants the readers to consider this book in the literary tradition of *Kanak Sprak*. These debatable facts notwithstanding, one factor is reinforced in the Nachwort—the authenticity of the *Kanaken*. The stories are presented as authentic; the experiences they capture are consequently authentic. They were recorded and reconstructed by a Turkish immigrant author; they are recorded and reconstructed in authentic language; and, hence, they must be superior. The real *Kanake* is now presented to the world to be welcomed and celebrated. However, as I have argued in my reading of *Abschaum*, such claims of authenticity merit careful scrutiny—not in order to prove that they are inauthentic but because the spectacle of authenticity overwhelms and paralyzes the critique of both textual and societal politics. When an author from an ethnic minority presents a work of fiction as authentic, that authenticity becomes doubly amplified. When the ethnic minority author presents the life of an underclass social outcast who is also an ethnic minority, the amplification of authenticity is quadrupled. Authenticity as a narrative device is unreflectively perceived as radical; the radical, then, becomes decisively influential in the evaluation of the author and his or her work of literature; the work of literature is then celebrated as an authentic work due to the authenticity of the author. Moreover, the idea of authenticity deserves to be understood in its complex relationship with ethnicity and hybridity, especially when an author like Zaimoğlu constructs his or her image as a staunch critic of ethnic ghettoization, as a postethnic authentic, and is then perceived by the media and even by his or her critical readers as a practitioner of cultural hybridity. In such instances, cultural hybridity manifests its ineluctable dependence on the two or more constituent components, be they ethnic or linguistic.

Several years ago, while thinking through *Kanak Sprak* for the first time, I juxtaposed it with Aras Ören's *Bitte nix Polizei* (1983). I criticized

Zaimoğlu for replacing commonly prevalent perceptions of the Turk in Germany—"a fanatic Muslim or a wrestler, or in more recent history a garlic-eating, impoverished but good-at-heart guest worker"—with "the gum-chewing, bandana wearing, agile teenager with a penchant for American hip-hop, a teenager who arbitrarily defies elements of Turkish and German cultures" (Mani, "Phantom" 128). I further criticized Zaimoğlu's "belief in the Kanak's having a clear idea of self-assertion" and argued that "Zaimoğlu's project of giving voice to everyone on the margins of the society . . . fails miserably" (ibid.).

With *Abschaum* I have confronted the necessity to review my evaluation of Zaimoğlu's degrees of success. Zaimoğlu has published several new works after *Abschaum*, a few of which have in some ways replicated his belief in the representation of the *Kanake* through unmediated, unameliorated, authentic accounts of a subcultural underclass. *Abschaum* represents a particular station in Zaimoğlu's writings. It does operate on the pretext of authenticity—as I have demonstrated—and purloins ethnicity through conjectures of hybridity. That stated, there exists a deducible dependence on the given and not entirely a freedom from the given in the character of Ertan Ongun. Indeed, Zaimoğlu's characters like Ongun, through their acceptance and denial of ethnicity, through their propagation and containment of Otherness, and through their constant assertion of heterosexual normativity, further highlight the delusional nature of absolute and ultimate emancipation. What is thus fascinating about Zaimoğlu is not the authenticity of his characters, or the authenticity of his aggressive language, or the authenticity of his political and literary aspirations to become the most important representative voice of the second and third generation of Turkish immigrants. Zaimoğlu is fascinating because works such as *Abschaum* and its claims of authenticity reveal the inadequacy of representation, the inefficacy of imagining an absolutely radical immigrant, and the incompleteness of a hybrid immigrant such as the *Kanake*, which is as much a model immigrant as the assimilated Turk Zaimoğlu detests.

In creating Ongun, Zaimoğlu—and here I agree with Adelson—does not present a counterfigure to Homi Bhabha's silent Turkish guest worker. But Ongun is also not the "not-quite, not-white mimic-man" that Bhabha discusses in his essay "Of Mimicry and Man" (*Location of Culture* 85–92). Ongun is not an illustration of what Katrin Sieg calls "ethno-masquerade." He is not a caricature, certainly not a conscious duplication of either of the stereotypical images of a Turk that I mention in my previous reflections on Zaimoğlu. Through his clandestine abjection of ethnicity in the figure of Ongun, which occurs in tandem with a constant positive and negative invocation of the (Turkish) ethnic community, along with the fraternity of heterosexual hypermasculinity, Zaimoğlu forces us to recast a glance at the multifaceted relationship between *demos* and *ethnos* in Germany, one that is based on difference and opposition. Zaimoğlu, therefore, does not "fail miserably." The novel, to some extent, accords referential specificity to the notion of hybridity. Ongun is not the subaltern from a decolonized nation-state. However, Ongun's cosmopolitical claims are by no means postnational or postethnic. The world of Ongun, between the street and the prison, between his home and the bed of his client, between Kiel and Bodrum, cannot be comprehended in the "in-between" interstitiality of these spaces. It is anchored in all of these spaces and articulates itself in a vernacular that forces us to locate such claims in the political reality of Germany, even when Ongun looks beyond. Ongun's cosmopolitanism is not shy of difference. As Ongun comes to terms with the thwarted nature of his *Kanake*-narcissism through drugs and misogyny, Zaimoğlu registers his cosmopolitical claims by simultaneously laying bare the thwarted narcissism of the German *demos*.

FOUR

Turkish-German Reattachments
Orhan Pamuk's *The New Life*

I read a book one day and my whole life was changed.
ORHAN PAMUK, *THE NEW LIFE*

Outside of the immigrant narrative, where else is the "elsewhere" of the national imaginary identifiable? At the end of a book whose title promises an investigation of cosmopolitical claims, this question demands attention beyond the national confines of Germany. The first three novels discussed in this book registered the claims of participation of the isolated, the fringe, and at times the marginalized Turkish figures in the German nation. In the Turkish-German narrative, I have so far tried to elucidate the narrator's acute alertness to the transformations of and within the German nation at the end of the twentieth century. My own itinerary thus far bears the mark of migration, that of coming to Germany from elsewhere, and marking various elsewheres within Germany. This specific tradition of minority literature has hitherto had Germany as the central point of reference; the predicament of the author has been to write him- or herself on, with, or against the German nation. The intricacies of a Turkish-German dialogue and conflict, the various forms of fellowship that I have tried to distill in this study, have had Turkey either as a point of embarking upon a journey or as a point of tentative and temporary disembarking.

With this chapter I move to the other side of the hyphen. Shifting emphasis from the migrant's intervention in the national imaginary of the country of residence—to expose the multifaceted relationships between the *ethnos* and the *demos*—I examine a vagrant's disruption of the national imagination as the only form of fellowship in the country of birth. Orhan Pamuk, the author I will be discussing in this chapter, has himself registered his dissidence of the Turkish national project many times, lately in the form of an interview with the Swiss newspaper *Tagesanzeiger* in February 2005, in which he asserted that the Turkish nation-state should acknowledge the massacre of "a million Armenians and

30,000 Turks." Following the publication of the interview, he was charged with treason under Article 301 of the Turkish constitution.[1] Pamuk's interview and the charges that followed led to a short-lived controversy, whereby Turkey's entry into the European Union seems to have been jeopardized. The charges against Pamuk were dropped in January 2006.[2] Before Pamuk went to trial, he forcefully articulated his reserve in conflating his right to dissent from Turkey's membership into the European Union. In his acceptance speech of the German Peace Prize (2005), Pamuk stated, "I cannot imagine a Turkey that does not dream of Europe, as much as I do not believe in a Europe that defines itself without Turkey."[3]

Regardless of his interventions in the script of the new Europe, an attempt to present Pamuk—a citizen/resident of Turkey whose intellectual production is in Turkish[4]—as a veritable participant in the Turkish-German narrative might appear implausible. What might also appear notoriously remote is the inclusion of his novel *Yeni Hayat* (The New Life) and not the more recent *Kar* (Snow) in this discussion. The connection between Turkey and Germany in the late twentieth century, questions of economic migration to and political refuge in Western Europe, and the debate surrounding headscarves, are admittedly more visible in *Snow* than in *The New Life*. This superficially perceived impalpability of direct interactions between Turkey and Germany becomes the foundation of my interest in, and inclusion of, *The New Life* in this project. This chapter aspires to make certain impalpable connections palpable. In my reading of *The New Life*, as in the three other novels, the line of inquiry focuses once again on registers of political and cultural affiliation and contestations of domicile and belonging. The questions raised in the previous chapters—subaltern significations, functions of history and memory, the dubiousness of hybridity as a freedom from the given—acquire a slightly different dimension in this chapter. This reason for this change of dimension rests upon Pamuk's reception in the print media and scholarly discussions—over the course of past decade—as the author between the East and the West, as the author who transcends the national literary traditions of Turkey, as the author who in person and through his writings presents us with a consistent challenge of understanding the modern Turkish nation-state: in short, the quintessential transnational, cosmopolitan author. I will only list a select few examples from scholarly journals to give a glimpse of Pamuk's enthusiastic reception and the critical conceptualization of his work. In her article "Öst-Westliche Spiegelungen," Erika Greber discusses the figure of the doppelgänger in Pamuk's *White Castle*; in "Beloved Istanbul," Martin Stokes analyzes Pamuk's realistic style to investigate transnational images;

in "Contested Mysteries," Walter G. Andrews discusses the historical content of Pamuk's novels with references to the Ottoman Empire; and in "Reclaiming History," Banu Özel compares Pamuk's conceptualization of history with those of Toni Morrison.

My discussion of Pamuk's *New Life* is not directed toward reaffirming his status as a transnational, cosmopolitan author. Instead, I want to situate Pamuk's novel in an equation that does not insinuate a freedom from the nation to claim cosmopolitanism but, in fact, reveals its critical dependence on the nation in order to then unsettle and challenge its very conceptualization.

I return to Homi Bhabha's essay, "DissemiNation" (*Location of Culture* 139–70). I have discussed this essay in the context of a Turkish guest worker in Chapter 1; here I want to focus on the section before Bhabha discusses the *vox populi* in migrant contexts in the section Foreignness of Languages. Bhabha's essay centers around the imagination of the people in a nation. "It is precisely in reading between these borderlines of the nation-space," Bhabha writes, "that we can see how the concept of the 'people' emerges within a range of discourses as a double narrative moment" (ibid. 145). Proposing an understanding of the people beyond "simply historical events or parts of a patriotic body politic," Bhabha emphasizes the need to reflect on citizenry as a "complex rhetorical strategy of social reference" that "must be thought in a double time." He distinguishes between a "nationalist pedagogy"—that deems people as objects in an authoritative discourse "based on the pre-given or constituted historical origin in the *past*"—and a narrative performance, whereby people "are also the subjects of a process of signification that must erase any prior or originary presence of the nation-people" (ibid.). Having established this dual location of the people, Bhabha arrives at the following observation: "In the production of the nation as narration there is a split between the continuist, accumulative temporality of the pedagogical, and the repetitious, recursive strategy of the performative. It is through the process of splitting that the conceptual ambivalence of modern society becomes the site of *writing the nation*" (145, original emphasis).

This distinction is key to grasping the ambition of Bhabha's essay, especially with regard to its postulations about countermodernity. With Edward Said, he presents the "sensuous particularity as well as historical contingency . . . as the textual object itself" (ibid. 140); with Bakhtin's reading of Goethe, he (Bhabha) highlights the coexistence of realist (creative) and romantic (originary) conceptions of the temporality of a nation (ibid. 142f.). An engagement with Kristeva assists him in reflecting on the nation as a "symbolic denominator" (ibid. 153); in his reading of Freud he lays bare the unease of not feeling at home in the uncanny (*unheimliche*) political reality of the nation (ibid. 143). For Bhabha, the "double-writing" of the nation thus includes both a sensuous particularity *and* a historical contingency. The nation emerges not as an entity woven around a text, a singular metaphor of home, the *heimliche*, but rather, around a series of replaceable metaphors, replaced every day by members of the minority, the immigrants.

Bhabha's design for an elucidation of the national imaginary departs from Benedict Anderson's thesis on *Imagined Communities*. For Bhabha, the quest for narrating the contemporaneity of the belated will not be productive in the pursuit of the "meanwhile," a "form of temporality" that "produces a symbolic structure of the nation as 'imagined community' which, in keeping with the scale and diversity of the modern nation, works like the plot of a realist novel" (*Location of Culture* 158). Bhabha's unease with the notion of a realistic meanwhile can be traced back to the list of novels he presents as metaphors of a nation, a list that includes titles so disparate in their representations of the nation (and in their interpretation of realism) as *Middlemarch*, *Midnight's Children*, and *The Magic Mountain* (ibid. 141). These are metaphors that, as Bhabha explains at the beginning of his essay, "transfer the meaning of home and belonging, across the middle passage, or the central European steppes . . . that span the imagined community of the nation-people" (ibid. 139). "Nations are entitled to metaphors," he states, and elaborating on the list, he later magnifies the doubleness in writing that this metaphoricity requires, the doubleness he then dubs the pedagogical and the performative. Against a homogenizing national conception based on origins of communities, or the much emphasized shared historical experiences, Bhabha attempts to conceive the nation as a text that inherently resists multiple interpretations, stays in conflict with the everyday enunciation of the people, a text that is written and erased by the people as they imagine and claim affiliation to the national collective in discursive countermodernity.

Bhabha's explications of the belonging of the people to a nation or its national culture and his postulations of countermodernity have been subjected to stringent criticism by Pheng Cheah in his essay "Given Culture." I have discussed aspects of Cheah's critique directly related to hybridity in Chapter 3. Cheah's interpretation of Bhabha's conceptualization of the nation extends his (Cheah's) commentary on Bhabha's (and James Clifford's) conceptualization of culture. While culture as a given predicates emancipation from its givenness through hybridity, Cheah explains, for Bhabha the nation, too, becomes an entrapment that is emancipated through contestation ("Given Culture" 297). Parallel to criticizing James Clifford's privileging of physical mobility as the generator of "stasis-disrupting forms of cultural displacement" (ibid.), Cheah takes issue with Bhabha's promotion of migratory and transient cultural practices as the prime initiators and facilitators of transnationality. Cheah accuses Bhabha's formulations of hybridity as a linguistic culturalism (ibid. 299) and his (Bhabha's) imagination of affiliation to the nation through the linguistic sign as a mode of thinking "typical of cultural analyses from literary studies" (ibid. 295). Cheah's harsh criticism of Bhabha's discussion of nation and national affiliation is reflected in the following statement: "he [Bhabha] suggests that if we denaturalize the nation and understand national identity as 'a form of social and textual affiliation' [*Location of Culture* 140], 'an ambivalent signifying system' [ibid. 146], and a narrative process ridden with contestation, then we become more alert to the constitutive ambivalence within the nation that leads to its undermining" ("Given Culture" 297).

I present Bhabha's conceptualization of the nation parallel to its critique for a variety of reasons. Bhabha's attempts to highlight the heterogeneity of a nation—whereby the idea of the people as a historical given, as an object of a nationalistic pedagogy, as an easy overlap of the *demos* with the *ethnos*—cannot be simply relinquished. However, to conceive of the transient, migrant, and itinerant subject as the sole agent of contestation of a national pedagogy invites intervention, a task that Cheah undertakes. While I agree with Cheah on this point—I have already expressed my agreement with Cheah's criticism of hybridity in Chapter 3—I also believe that Bhabha's theoretical reflections on the nation cannot be reduced to cultural analyses typical of literary studies ("Given Culture" 295). Bhabha's investigation of modes of survival of people "living on the borderlines of history and language" (*Location of Culture* 170) instigates the conceptual design of the nation—the pattern that ordains the official text of the nation. It is challenged and contested not just by the migrant but also by the resident, the citizen, who exists not just within but at times also parallel to the nation. This point is especially relevant for discussions on transnationalism and cosmopolitanism, where normative perceptions almost always privilege a sense of transcending the nation—leaving the nation behind, acquiring freedom from the prison house of the nation—

or signal a consistent resistance of the nation as an always already hegemonic agent seeking absolute control over its subjects. No legendary "interstitial passage" of "cultural hybridity" then seems to leave room to account for stratagems and subterfuges that bring forth hegemonic aspirations apart from those of the nation, which might not be organic in constitution but are certainly not ambivalent of constituency. For there are other tensions between the pedagogical and the performative that unfold when not the transitional, the transient, the migrant from elsewhere but the resident/citizen himself or herself intervenes and obscures normative perceptions of affiliation to the here and now of the nation. In these moments, it is not the elsewhere (outside) of the nation but the elsewhere within the nation that is illuminated. This elsewhere does not always present itself in emancipatory registers of a freedom from the nation, even though it is time and again accused of striving toward such freedom. Rather than rendering the *heim* (home) *unheimlich* (uncanny)—as Bhabha proposes—the elsewhere within the nation, anchored in the nation, manifests its transcendence of nationalism by unraveling the *Geheimnis* (secret) of the nation itself. That, and not the routine denial and contestation of the signification of the ambivalence of the nation, becomes the source and the practice of this elsewhere's cosmopolitics. How does it work in Pamuk's novel?

Pamuk's *The New Life* can be best described as a novel that transforms the meaning of home and belonging, of the *memleket* (dominion) and the *millet* (country/nation), of the *Heim* (home) and *Heimat* (homeland) by obscuring the legibility of the arbitrary sign; by distorting its immediate communitarian aspirations; indeed, by rejecting the historicity of the sign by declaring history as "gossip." It is a novel in which the productive tension between the pedagogical and the performative, the original and the endless, and—and to paraphrase Vinay Dharwadker—the embattled relationship between the local/national and the global/cosmopolitan (Dharwadker 3), surfaces through the tragicomedy of a controversial book, first mystified and mythologized and then parodied by the narrator. The metaphoricity of national lives, the doubleness of meanings, and the hope to create and find a community that shares the same imagination—all of these form multiple centers of Pamuk's novel and gain currency through Pamuk's critique of a singular interpretation of nation and community. Fortifying this critique is a long debate between the national "here and elsewhere" and the global "from elsewhere," between "one's own" and "from the outside," a debate that emerges in the novel through ideological wars with appellations such as the Great Conspiracy and the Dealers' Conspiracy. The reading that follows aspires to unfold the novel's uneasiness with the nation and its restlessness with the givenness of an originary national text, not to claim freedom from the nation, but as a series of interventions in and beyond the nation. In addition, apart from the novel, through a discussion of selected texts mentioned and discussed in *The New Life*, my reading tries to locate the novel's cosmopolitical claims beyond the context of Turkish migration into Germany. In the backdrop is my wish to contradict a curiously provincial claim about Pamuk and *The New Life* published in 1999 in *The New York Times*, a purportedly cosmopolitan daily: "as if a carpet weaver had suddenly become color-blind."[5]

In *The New Life*, a slim volume promising a new life becomes the center of a national controversy. The author of the book, as the reader of the novel finds out much later, is (Uncle) Rıfkı Ray, a close friend of the narrator, Osman's, father. Uncle Rıfkı is an avid reader, a regular contributor to *Rail*, "a magazine for railroad buffs," as well as a writer and illustrator of children's comics. The book he writes is inexpensive and published by an obscure press in Istanbul.[6] It provides incomplete sketches of social values, and their ingenuity is highly contested. The book gains acceptance and wide acclaim, albeit only among the young people. It is banned in Turkey within months of its publication, and Rıfkı Ray is killed. Pamuk's novel depicts Osman's journeys in search of other readers of this banned book and the new life that the book promises.

"I read a book one day and my whole life was changed" (*New Life* 3). Pamuk's novel starts with the protagonist's confession of an absolute identification with an untitled book. The first description of the book that the readers of the novel receive is not of the book's content but its effect on its reader. Osman's first reading of the book is at once an experience of enlightenment and revelation. It is a visceral experience: he feels his "body dissociating"; he admits that he feels "its influence not only on my soul but on every aspect of my identity. . . . The light surging from the pages illumined my face; its incandescence dazzled my intellect but also endowed it with brilliant lucidity" (ibid.). With "the new words on each new page," Osman perceives a change (ibid.). He realizes, "for a moment I sensed that if any old object from my old world were to be discovered and scrutinized now, from my new of viewpoint enlightened by the book, it could be transformed into that magical piece children are always looking for" (11). Thus, very similar to the rabbit hole that brings Alice into Wonderland, the phantom tollbooth that becomes Milo's gateway to Dictionopolis, and the reading of the letter delivered by an owl that becomes Harry Potter's passport to the magical world, the book renders Osman's immediate surroundings unfamiliar. The moment he takes his eyes off the book, he feels "as if [he] had been stranded in a country where [he] knew neither the lay of the land nor the language and the customs" (4). The book invokes feelings of stability and guarantee in its promise of newness but also of instability and insecurity caused by a realization of being isolated and severed from everything hitherto familiar. Osman cannot judge if the book is ordinary or extraordinary. As "minutes and pages followed one another" (ibid.) the familiar auditory cityscape made of "the everyday roar of the city, the tinkle of the yogurt vendor's bell in the street" turns into the unfamiliar visual spectacle of "shabby rooms, frenetic buses, bedraggled people, faint letters, lost towns, lost lives, phantoms" (5).

In a carefully inserted observation about the book toward the end of Osman's first reading, Pamuk gives readers of his novel the first clue of the book's content. Osman believes at first that the book is about him: "Someone had already imagined my ideas and put them down" (6). Very soon he is led to the understanding that "the words and their meanings were, of necessity, dissimilar." He is able to see his "way through the murders, accidents, deaths, and missing signs with which the book was filled"—which coincidentally summarizes Pamuk's novel. Although the first reading collapses a distinction between "the world that existed within the book from the book that existed within the world," by the time Osman reaches the final pages he registers the claim that "I too had come up with the same ideas" (ibid.).

It is important to comprehend the gravity of the effect of the book on the protagonist for two reasons. The first is the connection of this passage to the prologue of the novel, a quote from Novalis's *Heinrich von Ofterdingen* (1800), a discussion I will save for later. The second is that a careful reading of the novel clarifies that the passage foregrounds a narrative irony woven into Pamuk's text. This passage is an oblique address to the readers of the novel. Through the glorification of a text and the act of reading, Pamuk forms and informs the narrator's relationship to the author, the co-readers, and the nonreading enemies of the book. Furthermore, as I shall demonstrate in the following pages, he uses this very tactic to parody his own (Pamuk's) readers' relationship to the text before he can create a geographical and cultural divide between the East and the West, only to disintegrate it slowly by the end of the novel. The novel thus urges its readers to examine their existing relationships with texts in general and, through a complicated parallel move, upsets the reified binary of the East and West.

Pamuk mocks the culturally sanctioned ignorance of his readers as they read a novel from the other side of Europe.

Osman's initial interaction with Rıfkı's book gets translated into a search for a congregation of readers. He feels the urgency to identify readers who share his literary experience and new terrain where readership defines citizenry: "Where was the country in which I'd find the dream that spoke to my heart? Where were those who had also read the book? Where?" (11). The book appears to Osman sometimes as a sin and other times as a scripture that links him to the congregation of readers to whom the he can bare his soul. On one of his walks in town after reading the book, Osman realizes that he is incapable of relating with anyone but the readers of the book (10).

Struggling between fascination and anxiety, skeptical about his complete submission to the book, Osman questions his understanding with other reading experiences where the text was almost internalized. He mentions having read about someone who read the *Fundamental Principles of Philosophy* in one night and doubts how "in total agreement with the book . . . he joined the Revolutionary Proletarian Advance Guard the very next day, only to be nabbed three days later robbing a bank" (13). He expresses his suspicion of people who, after reading books like *Islam and the New Ethos* and *The Betrayal of Westernization*, had "immediately abandoned the tavern for the mosque, sat themselves on those ice-cold rugs doused with rosewater, and began preparing patiently for the next life which was not due for another fifty years" (ibid.). He chides people who believe in astrology, read books like *Love Sets You Free* and *Know Yourself*, and can still claim that these books could change their lives (ibid.). Osman's anxiety is not just restricted to the isolation he thinks he might face because of the book. He expresses his fear of misinterpreting the book. He feels the need to test the emotional overwhelming caused by the book against his ongoing rational, scientific training as a student of engineering. The romantic affect of reading, the visceral effect of the book continues throughout Pamuk's novel, sometimes in the book's presence and at other times in proxy.

In short, the book turns into the source of a daily plebiscite, a "constant affirmation of life," albeit in this context, to borrow from Bhabha again, a plebiscite about lives of the members of a nation of readers (*Location of Culture* 161). The desperate search for co-readers brings the acquaintanceship of Mehmet, another student at the university, and his friend Janan (*Canın* in Turkish, meaning soul-mate). Although Osman's adulation of the book, his raising the book to its mythical stature, continues throughout the novel, Pamuk works against his narrator to continuously demythify this experience for his readers. The opening sentences of the first three chapters, when read as a sequence, illustrate this ironic demythification: "I read a book one day" (Chapter 1); "the next day I fell in love" (Chapter 2); "I spent the next few days looking for Janan" (Chapter 3). In addition, Osman's first exchange with Mehmet subtly but remarkably conveys the melodrama that Osman has attached to his reading experience. During this exchange, Mehmet explains to Osman that he might be killed for having read the book. But Osman is convinced that there is a world beyond the book that he can find. Mehmet disagrees forecefully:

> "World shmorld!" Mehmet said "It doesn't exist. Think of it as tomfoolery perpetrated on children by an old sap. The old man thought he'd write a book to entertain adults just the same way he did children. It's doubtful he even knew what it meant. It's entertaining reading, but if you believe it, your life is lost."
> "There is a whole world in there," I said, as strong but stupid men do in the movies...
> "What makes you so sure of the existence of that life?"
> "Because I have the impression the book is telling the story of my life." He smiled amiably and walked away. (25)

Osman's daily plebiscite continues through Chapters 4 and 5, but the end of this affirmation is not far from sight. Osman continues to read the book; he copies it "sentence by sentence" (37) as he travels, initially on his own, through towns "which were carbon copies of each other" (46). After his miraculous union with Janan (59), their traveling continues, along the path on which "the history of all the peoples who had stirred up the dust on this terrain since the days of the Crusaders had settled layer after layer on [our] skins" (73). Immediately after this historical reference, in the same paragraph, Pamuk documents the architectural alphabet of these towns, "the statue of Atatürk, the Arçelik appliance dealership, the pharmacy and the mosque . . . the Koran school and the circumcision party that was approaching" (ibid.). After attesting to these "scraps, patches, and rags" that "add to the text of the nation without necessarily adding up"—reusing Bhabha's expression (*Location of Culture* 145)—the novel advances to a more complicated terrain where the alphabet of the nation will be threatened by foreign signs, and a new and expansive conflict will invite Osman's intervention. The sanctity of the book is henceforth openly questioned, and an unsettling clash of civilizations begins, led by the ultranationalist ideologue, Dr. Fine.

Chapter 6 is a turning point in Pamuk's novel. From here on, through the book and its enemies, Pamuk narrates a parodied struggle between East and West, as the narrator and his girlfriend travel under the false identities of Mr. and Mrs. Ali Kara. Rıfkı's book leaves the promise of the new life behind and surfaces as the object embroiled in a national and international conflict of political economy marked by cultural difference. At the end of the sixth chapter, the "girl in the blue jeans" who is about to die in a bus accident informs Osman and Janan (now Mr. and Mrs. Ali Kara) about dangers of the book. From her they learn for the first time about a certain Dr. Fine and "his struggle against the book, against foreign cultures that annihilate us, against the new fangled stuff that comes from the West, and his all-out battle against printed matter" (83).

A large part of the novel following this scene depicts Osman's accelerated absorption in this struggle. In order to convey the import of Dr. Fine and his struggle, I will interrupt my reading of the novel with a detour to another text with a title not dissimilar to that of Pamuk's novel and, as it will turn out at the end of the novel, that of Uncle Rıfkı's book itself. In order to arrive at the uncanny (*Unheimliche*) of the nation, I want to highlight a textual moment that influenced the design of the *Heim*, the modern Turkish nation-state. This text and its author could have secretly (*heimlich*) modeled Dr. Fine's character and his ideology. Although I will only be able to reveal uncanny coincidences, it might be productive to understand the present of the nation through a subjunctive. I now turn to a text that construes itself as instructive and places "the people" in precisely the originary, the homogenous empty time that Bhabha argues against in his essay.

About a decade before the collapse of the Ottoman Empire, the abolition of the caliphate, the change of Turkish script from Arabic to Latin, the banning of the fez, and all the other changes that stand today under the larger rubric of the Turkish Revolution and the foundation of the modern Turkish nation-state, an essay entitled "Yeni Hayat ve Yeni Kıymatlar" ("New Life and New Values") was published in *Genç Kalemler* (The Young Pens), an influential Turkish journal founded at the turn of the nineteenth century and, along with *Yeni Mecmua* (The New Magazine), a vehicle for the dissemination of nationalist ideals. The essay was published under the pen name Ziya Gökalp. In 1921, after the nationalist victory, it was found out that Gökalp was none other than Mehmed Ziya (1876–1924), the influential Turkish sociologist, writer, and poet, and at the time of his death in 1924, a member of the Turkish parliament.

Gökalp was one of the most influential Turkish thinkers of the early twentieth century; his writings inaugurated the design of the Turkish national identity in the new Republic born after the collapse of the Ottoman Empire. He wrote twenty books including poetry and fiction and about a hundred articles during the political turbulence in Turkey in the early twentieth century. His writings exhibit his profound awareness of the Turkish Islamic heritage combined with his engagement with Western thought, and thus are symptomatic of the culturally nebulous transitional period from the Empire to the Republic. Gökalp's writings emphasize the significance of *turkçuluk* (Turkishness), which he saw as a contrast to both an Ottoman[7] and a Western identity. Through his works, he initiated a discussion about the optimum appropriation of Western ideas of democracy, secularism, and political sovereignty in the new Republic to the advantage of the Turkish cultural identity. A clear delineation of Turks as an ethnic and a national group becomes the central concern of *Türkçülüğün Esasları* (Principles of Turkism, 1921) and *Türk Töresi* (Turkish Customs, 1922). Similarly, *Yeni Türkiye'nin Hedefleri* (Aims of New Turkey, 1923) brings to the fore the challenges faced by the new Republic. Gökalp was an intellectual who acknowledged Westernization as an essential parameter to measure development, yet unlike Atatürk he was not ready to turn his back completely on the Islamic heritage of Turkey. Gökalp's *Türkleşmek, Islamlaşmak, Muasırlamak* (Turkification, Islamization, Contemporization, 1912–1918) is an apt example of Gökalp's constant interrogation and problematization of a universal human identity and of his privileging of Turkish Islamic and nationalist difference.[8] In his invocation of Turkish civilization—as opposed to culture[9]—Gökalp always reverted to pre-Islamic Turkey and idealized this particular period as one when the drawbacks of the Ottoman Empire were absent. Nonetheless, he accepted Islam as an integral part of a communal (Turkish) cultural heritage. His writings frequently bear the anxiety of the loss of this heritage that might occur with a spate of Western-style education. In the history of Turkish thought, he surfaces as an intellectual who stands at the doorstep of Western industrial modernization while still negotiating feudalist and imperialist traditions of the Ottoman Empire with their roots in the fifteenth century. Although Gökalp's writings are expressions of cultural dilemmas that the Turkish-speaking people face at a historical moment of transition, they are by no means interrogative or suggestive. On the contrary, they tend to be rather authoritative, prescriptive, and directive to the extent of being almost pedantically propagandist. The essay "Yeni Hayat ve Yeni Kıymatlar" (New Life and New Values) is a prime example of Gökalp's confident and resolute approach to the instigation of nationalism in the people of Turkey.

"Yeni Hayat ve Yeni Kıymatlar" stipulates a new life and new values beyond the multicultural/multiethnic heritage of the Ottoman Empire ("Yeni Hayat" 55–60). The essay is replete with rigid instructions for the formation of the new Turkish identity in the twentieth century as envisioned by Gökalp. It is a call to the Turkish nation to leave behind the threatening heterogeneity of the Ottoman Empire and move toward an ethnically and racially homogenous national composition. Gökalp embarks upon his essay with a reference to the Young Turk Revolution of 1908 and the consequent administrative changes. He sees this event as a political revolution, and as a follow-up, he sets the demand for a sociocultural revolution in Turkey. By presenting the challenges of the social revolution as exponentially greater than those of the political revolution, Gökalp creates a hierarchical and logical progression of revolutions. Political revolution for Gökalp is based on ideas, which can be reasoned and, thus, are easier to adapt. A social revolution, which aims at overhauling the sentiments of the people, takes much longer, for, as Gökalp writes, the evolution of the sentiments is restricted by the fact that "they are the products of social habits developed in the course of several centuries" (56). He posits social habits as factors that distinguish Muslims from non-Muslims in the Ottoman Empire. At the end of his reflections on the revolution, he makes an abrupt turn to the non-Muslims: "There are non-Muslims among us. As they have remained outside active political life, they have been occupied primarily with economic activities. Since our Govt. had left all [religious] communities to organize themselves [under their religious leaders], their organizations became the basis of their social enterprises, and in this way our non-Muslim compatriots have been able to develop a special aptitude in economic enterprises" (56).

As can be noticed in this citation, professions and religious beliefs become part of the same equation for Gökalp. In a move that dangerously resembles Nazi perspectives on Jewish prosperity during the Third Reich, Gökalp presents a highly derogatory view of the millet system and its economic repercussions in the Ottoman Empire.[10] Not surprisingly, in the very next paragraph he spells out his own interpretation of the economic backwardness of Muslims by stating, "political preoccupations had forced the Muslims, however, to remain very weak in respect to economic and social activities" (ibid.).

After having created an ethnically and religiously segregated context to stress the urgent need for a social revolution, he assigns the Ottomans (Muslims in Turkey) their task: "the creation of New Life by discarding an older one" (ibid.). This involves, "obviously, a new form of economy, a new form of family life, new aesthetic standards, a new morality, a new conception of law, and a new political system" (ibid.). Gökalp sees the younger generation as the flag-bearers of this project. He reckons that once "the youth have taken the New Life as their goal, they will be in fact in search of these genuine values" (57). The genuine values that the youth should be in search of are not to be confused by the "vague goals" and "the utopia" of movements like feminism and socialism: "The followers of the New Life will not entertain such utopias, will not go forward towards preconceived goals with preconceived programmes as the utopians did in following their fictions. The New Life is a movement, but not a definite and straight-line movement. We cannot ascertain and predict the ends to which it will lead us and the consequences which it will bring forth" (ibid.).

For Gökalp, the new life is a scientific project with a definite methodology but no predetermined goals or final truths. The research, he suggests, would be based on recent practices and philosophical reviews and would avoid arbitrary speculation. However, this scientific project will not be for the betterment of all humanity. While referring to progress, Gökalp cites the aphorism, "tout par la science et pour l'humanité." For the followers of the new life, he rephrases it: "Every advance through science and for the fatherland. The first duty of the followers of the New Life is to work for the strengthening and elevation of the Ottomans by means of literature, science, and philosophy. *The New Life is not a cosmopolitan but a national life*" (58, my emphasis).

This characterization of the new life as one in service of the nation rather than all of humanity facilitates his return to the problem of non-Muslims; at this very instant he highlights cultural difference in order to outline European values that the non-Muslims in Turkey—like the Greeks, Armenians, and Bulgarians—have allegedly internalized: values that would be replaced by the new life. He describes non-Muslim residents of Turkey as "anxious imitators of European life. We, as I have explained, should create a new synthesis" (59). Muslims, according to Gökalp, by virtue of their *ümmet* (religious community), were not ready to imitate the European values: "since we belonged to a different *ümmet* we did not reproduce these models, believing that we should create a new mode of civilization from our own understanding. It is this belief which has given birth to our New Life" (ibid.). At the end of the essay, Gökalp raises a call for a new authentic Turkishness of the New Life, one that leaves any imitations behind: "The New Life will be created, not copied. Our new values will be economic, domestic, aesthetic, philosophic, moral, legal, and political values born out of the souls of the Ottomans. It will also show us that the foundations of the European civilization are worn, sick, and rotten, that they are destined to fall and disintegrate. We shall create a genuine civilization, a Turkish civilization, which will follow the growth of the New Life" (59).

A definition of the indigenous based on the majority religious community, a relegation of religious and ethnic minorities to the status of foreign, with an explicit disregard of the multinational composition of the Ottoman Empire frames Gökalp's blueprint for the fortress of Turkish nationalism in the twentieth century. Gökalp does not represent the productive ambivalence of a "cosmopolitan patriot" that Kwame Anthony Appiah describes in his recent essay "Cosmopolitan Patriots." The text of the nation is a monochrome, rigidly defined, and framed text, with little room for rags, shreds, and pieces from the outside. Gökalp's choice to relinquish multinational influences that altered the "souls of the Ottomans" over the centuries is a manifest omission of the geographical expanse and the related cultural diversity of the Ottoman Empire. For him, an *Urtext* of an idealized pre-Islamic Turkey serves as the basis for the shape of the New Republic, but with a generous incorporation of the scientific developments of the West.

Unsurprisingly, Gökalp's writings were encapsulated by his friend Atatürk in his famous slogan: *Ne mutlu Türküm diyene* (happiness is being a Turk)—an inscription that impregnated the project of the modern Turkish nation into the late twentieth century. While the nationalistic vocabulary was part of the Turkish political culture since the establishment of the Republic, the Motherland Party (ANAP), after claiming political power in 1983, reinforced an ideological superiority of the indigenous Islamic culture over the foreign. For twelve years, even under Tansu Çiller, Turkey's first woman prime minister, the state-sponsored response to the rise of the Kurdish nationalist movement—other than forceful suppression through the use of police power—was the revival of the slogan *Ne mutlu Türküm diyene*, propagating a systematic marginalization of everything perceived as foreign. With Çiller's (indirect) endorsement, the fundamentalist organization Gray Wolves demanded more than local control of the economy. Through their highly simplified populist accounts of Western values, which allegedly threaten local ancient cultural heritages, the Gray Wolves channeled public energy toward a programmatic subjugation of difference in the service of a homogenous cultural milieu.[11]

This telegraphically condensed reproduction of Turkish political developments conveys the nationwide cultural strife that Pamuk captures in his novel. By creating a figure like Dr. Fine, Pamuk identifies the inscriptions of a unifying, homogenizing, and absolutist text of a nation. He recalls an obsession with the past times, authentic values, and original identities in a paradoxical critique of globalization and multinational corporate expansion at the end of the twentieth century. This proposition serves as my entry into a discussion of Dr. Fine and Uncle Rıfkı. In the following discussion, I aim to render visible the legacy of Gökalp's prescriptive nationalism as a program where assertion of identity is concomitant with the suppression of difference.

Dr. Fine is first introduced in the novel by the girl in the blue jeans. He is the leader of an organization of merchants (translated as "dealers") united under the cause of "our goals." These merchants gather not in the metropolitan locations of Istanbul or Ankara, but in the provincial town of Güdül for a convention. It might be fruitful here to recount the atmosphere in Güdül, because the merchants' convention sets the tone for Dr. Fine's final rant against globalization. When Osman and Janan enter Güdül, the first signs they read are "a cloth banner summoning children to the summer Koran school" and an advertisement for "circumcision performed the good old way, not by laser" (*New Life* 86). Upon reaching the venue of the convention, the couple witnesses the merchants' commitment to reversing the flow of time. They behold "a device that cloaks time"; "the first Turkish-made gizmo that detects pork in any given product"; and most noticeably, "a windup clock that provides the answer to the problem of the call to prayer.... This clock automatically settled the Westernization-versus-Islamization question through a modern device: Instead of the usual cuckoo bird, two other figures had been employed, a tiny imam who appeared on the lower balcony at the proper time to announce three times that 'God is Great!' and a minute toy gentleman wearing a tie but no mustache who showed up in the upper balcony on the hour, asserting that 'Happiness is Being a Turk, a Turk, a Turk'" (88).

The purpose of the convention is in line with Gökalp's proposal of employing technological development for the advancement of Turkishness. Yet the merchants' lifestyles are not entirely in accord with the old cultural values they claim to protect, which accounts for the residents' abhorrence of them. They oppose Western values yet do not observe the Islamic prohibition of alcohol and tobacco. The state ideology bears similar paradoxes. In his speech against the merchants, the governor expresses the religious concerns of the community, but in the same stroke conflates his nationalistic message with the religious discourse: "Are they [the merchants] here to insult everything that is held sacred in our town? Our devotion to our religion, our prophet, our sheiks, and the statue of Atatürk has for centuries been demonstrated amply in our mosques and on our holy holidays.... Was it for this that Atatürk chased out the Greek Army?... We prefer death to life without honor" (102f.). Despite these delineated differences, the local governing body and the merchants come together on issues of national pride and hatred of the foreign as they assert that they "worship Allah, not the Cross, or America, or Satan," and (therefore) declare their unwillingness to "succumb to drinking Coca-Cola" (102).

Dr. Fine's ideas on the state of Turkish civilization reflect the glorified, pure, moralistic views characteristic of Gökalp. His disposition is "patient and . . . affectionate" but also "instructive" (*New Life* 122). Dr. Fine, expressing his dislike for the kids in the neighborhood, calls them petty thieves and announces his conviction that "the downfall of all great civilizations and the disintegration of their memories was first signaled by the moral degradation of the young. The young had the capacity to forget the old as quickly and painlessly as they could imagine the new" (124). Dr. Fine also seeks connection with the past through a restoration of the production and utilization of indigenous objects. For him, objects are the "unadulterated annals of time" (130). He earned the title of doctor during his military service because "he was cognizant of details that came in handy for small repairs, such as the eight-thread nut required for a certain bolt or the cranking speed of a field telephone" (123). He enjoys the nickname "because he loved equipment and enjoyed taking care of it, and because he had recognized that discovering the unique properties of each object constitutes the highest good" (ibid.). He exhibits a penchant for objects because he is convinced that like human beings, "objects had the capacity to remember" and "the faculty to record what happened to them and preserve their memories" (ibid.). The world for him is made up of the intercommunication of the inanimate: "substances inquire after each other, come to an agreement, whisper to one another, and strike up a harmony, constituting the music we call the world" (ibid.). His collection of objects of a bygone time includes "whetting stones that never wore down, hand-woven rugs, locks made out of hammered iron, sweet smelling wicks for kerosene stoves, simple versions of refrigeration" (124), which preserve a temporal but also a spatial memory from Istanbul to Anatolia. Furthering his obsession with objects, he fondly recalls the time he had "first become aware of the magical, necessary and poetic concept of time that was transmitted to us from objects when we came into contact using or touching some simple thing like a spoon or a pair of scissors" (125).

But for Dr. Fine, these intercommunicative vibes exist only in indigenous products, in tools made within the country. Their replacement causes a loss of the sense of time. He recounts to Osman the sad time when the local yogurt drink was replaced by "PERT (he said it as if he were saying Dirt)" and the traditional sorbets were replaced by "the imitation stuff called Mr. Turk Cola, which was soon replaced by the real Coca-Cola" (127). He opened a store to sell the German glue UHU rather than "our glues that are made of pine resin," and "Lux hand soap" rather than "our clay soap." These objects immediately became the cause of a temporal disjuncture. As soon as he put these in his store, he realized "that not only could he no longer tell the time, he did not know what time it was" (ibid.). This is in adherence with his convictions that objects have a national memory. It was for this reason that he had abandoned the idea of selling imported goods and had "continued stocking only those products that had traditionally been available to his forefathers" (128). These goods are for him "our greatest treasure," so he can establish "the sovereignty of our own unadulterated annals of time which were in danger of being annihilated" (130).

The only bridges between Western and Turkish cultures for Dr. Fine are watches, clocks, and timepieces. In order to trace the movements of his son (Osman's friend) Mehmet, he employs a number of spies with the code names Omega, Movado, Seiko, Sersikof, and Zenith. Nonetheless, his own interpretation of the purpose of keeping time distinguishes the West from the Islamic civilization:

> Our timetables and timepieces are our vehicles to reach God, not the means of rushing to keep up with the world as they are in the West. There never was a nation on earth as devoted to timepieces as we have been; we were the greatest patrons of European clockmakers. Timepieces are the only products of theirs that have been acceptable to our souls. That is why clocks are the only things other than guns that cannot be classified as foreign or domestic. For us there are two venues that lead to God. Armaments are the vehicles of Jihad; timepieces are the vehicles for prayer. They have managed to silence our guns. Now they have hatched these trains so that our time will also be silenced. Everyone knows that the greatest enemy of the timetable for prayers is the timetable for trains. My dead son was well aware of this fact, and that's why he spent months on buses to retrieve our lost time. . . . Remember this: when our people get some money together, the first thing they buy is a watch. (160)

Dr. Fine is thus the perfect caricature of the "steady onward clocking of calendrical time" with which the pedagogues of the nation give it its "sociological solidity" (Bhabha, *Location of Culture* 158). Any deviation from the onward march of this time would be a conspiracy against the nation, much like Dr. Fine's conviction that "There was a great conspiracy against him, his way of thinking, the products to which he had devoted his life, against everything that was vital for this country" (*New Life* 126). The spread of Coca-Cola symbolizes for Dr. Fine a significant challenge to the unadulterated annals on the verge of annihilation, a disruption in the schedule of the nation, and therefore a part of a "Great Conspiracy" of the West. In a bizarre consequent conflation of the ideational and the material, Dr. Fine identifies the original moment of the Great Conspiracy as Gutenberg's invention of the printing press. The merchants at the convention in Güldül foreshadow his sentiments about the printed word: "It was a state of true happiness, but Satan was displeased by our happiness; and he who is Satan conceived of the Great Conspiracy. One of the pawns of the Great Conspirator was a man named Gutenberg, known to be a printer and emulated by many, who reproduced words in a manner that outstripped the production of the industrious hand, the patient finger, the fastidious pen: and words, words, words broke loose like a strand of beads and scattered far and yonder. Like hungry and frenzied cockroaches, words invaded the wrapping on bars of soap, on cartons of eggs, on our doors, and out in the street" (107). The zeal to preserve the annals of time from adulteration makes Dr. Fine the leading enemy of Rıfkı's book. After his son (Mehmet) abandons him, he develops a particular animosity toward books: "What literature? . . . What book? . . . The culprit is not only that particular book, the book that snared my son, but all the books that have been printed by printing presses; they are all enemies of the annals of our time, our former existence" (131). The only kind of books that earn his respect are either those scripted by hand, because of the hand's relation to the pen, or those that "informed the farmers how to deal with the mice, steered on the right direction some absentminded person who had lost his way, reminded the misguided of their own traditions, or informed and educated the naive child about the nature of the world through illustrated adventures" (ibid.). He is resolutely against those "that promised us [the Turks] the serenity and enchantment of paradise within the limitations set by the world, those which the pawns of the Great Conspiracy mass-produced and disseminated . . . in their concerted effort to make us forget the poetry of our lives" (132). He holds them responsible for "the plague of forgetfulness that blows here on the winds from the West, erasing our collective memory" (ibid.).

Concluding his theories against the printed word, against foreign goods, Dr. Fine believes that on the great day when history gets rewritten "no quarter shall be given to public opinion, to newspapers, or to current ideas, none to petty morality and insignificant consumer products, like their bottled gas and Lux soap, their Coca-Cola and Marlboros with which the West has duped our pitiful compatriots." He ends his rant, "I am a genius" (138).

I cite Dr. Fine at length to lay bare certain remarkable similarities between his and Ziya Gökalp's notions of a nation's birth and lineage and the linked idea of indigenous superiority. In Pamuk's novel, Dr. Fine emerges as the exaggerated version of Gökalp, the nationalistic excess that valorizes the indigenous, resists multinational corporate power, and in a highly calculated move, ideologizes and assures an absolutist impermeability of culture. Gökalp's anticosmopolitan stand is located more than half a century before the accelerated economic globalization of the twentieth century. Dr. Fine, on the other hand, wages his ideological war on two different fronts. Through his network of merchants, who work together to ban the consumption of foreign-made goods, he participates in a direct resistance against economic globalization. In a parallel move, through his war against books and printed materials, which he views as an essentially Western pathological condition, he propagates his nativist, purist, anticosmopolitan agenda, fought mostly on the cultural front. The achievement of Pamuk's novel is not a crude depiction of "Turkey's crisis of identity between East and West," as the *New York Times* reviewer D. M. Thomas formulates. By giving Dr. Fine the best lines in his novel, Pamuk succeeds in construing a highly sophisticated and stringent but also engaging and entertaining critique of antiglobal economic nationalism. Furthermore, by presenting Uncle Rıfkı as a dead author whose specter haunts the narrator and the novel, Pamuk takes issue with cultural nativism, thus boosting the cosmopolitan ambition and confidence of *The New Life*. In the rest of my discussion of the novel I elaborate on the extratextual significance of certain traces in the novel as I engage with Rıfkı and his book, in order to explore the possibility of reading in Pamuk's novel a Turkish-German dialogue.

While laying down the basic tenets of the New Life, Gökalp presents the following plan for its dissemination: "They will be written in a book form by our young intellectuals, whom we shall ask to write on the subjects in which they have specialized. Everyone's contentions will be respected. The 'Outlines' on the values of the New Life will be published in cheap booklets; and although the values proposed in them will be nothing more than mere incomplete sketches of the genuine values, they will certainly gain acclaim and wide acceptance" ("Yeni Hayat" 58). The slim volume promising the new life in Pamuk's novel is a booklet, picked up by Osman at a secondhand bookstall. Instead of Gökalp's vision of restoring a nationalistic order through a reinforcement of familiar age-old traditions, Rıfkı's book instigates unfamiliarity with the terrain as well as with the culture. The professed confidence in a scientific methodology of Gökalp's new life project disintegrates in the hands of Osman, a rational student of engineering. But beyond these formal similarities, Rıfkı's book drastically departs from the programmatic booklets envisioned by Gökalp. It is in these dissimilarities, deviations, and departures from the pedagogy of nationalistic new life that Pamuk's novel's cosmopolitan moorings, his cosmopolitical claims, manifest themselves. But before that discussion, a last word on the readers themselves. Osman, as mentioned earlier, is not alone in his complete identification with Rıfkı's book. Reports of Dr. Fine's spies are full of accounts of individuals with an identical experience. The readers, mostly male, initially immerse themselves entirely in the book, only to face disillusionment later on, when they get involved in a violent condemnation of the book. The lover of the girl in the blue jeans conforms to this pattern. First obsessed and then disenchanted by the book, he starts blaming it for the many broken lives and decides to join the people working against it. The girl in the blue jeans tries to convince him that "the book was innocent," "that there was a great many books much like it. I told him what is important is your own perception, what you read into it, but I could not make him listen" (*New Life* 83). Among all the readers of the book, Mehmet stands out as the one with the most rewarding reading. His succinct comments on the nature of the book during his last conversation address the hollowness of an extreme belief in a text:

> "A good book is something that reminds us of the whole world," he said. "Perhaps that's how every book is, or what each and every book ought to be. . . . The book is part of something the presence and duration of which I sense through what the book says, without it actually existing in the book. . . . Perhaps it is something that has been distilled from the stillness or the noise of the world, but it's not the stillness or the noise itself. . . . A good book is a piece of writing that implies things that don't exist, a kind of absence, or death. . . . But it is futile to look outside the book for a realm that is located beyond the words." (222)

Thus, Mehmet is able to demonstrate that the urgent search for a holistic explanation of life in the book is responsible for the disillusionment of the majority of its readers. The readers of Rıfkı's book stand in an unexamined agreement with the enemies of the book because they themselves aspire to a singular mode of interpretation. The enemies' wrath is based on the supposition that the book entails an exhaustive and absolute program that might denigrate the existing modes of life. On the contrary, Rıfkı's book on the new life crumbles the unflinching faith in a programmatic reorganization of modes of culture through texts. In highlighting critique, the possibility of multiple interpretations, and the dangers of complete submission to a text through Mehmet, Pamuk questions Gökalp's assured enumeration of the characteristics of new life and their acquisition, as well as his reliance on the booklets that would propel the new life. A total intellectual abdication to a text—or a complete abomination of it—both are depicted as symptoms of traumatized critical faculties serving at best as accomplices of hegemonic intolerance.

As Pamuk enumerates the perils of a singular interpretation, he simultaneously indicates the questionable nature of authenticity of creation, yet another fulcrum of Gökalp's "New Life." A complete identification with the book, as I mentioned earlier, assists this aspect. Moreover, events in the lives of the two characters follow a pattern: the reading of the book is followed by the obsession of one of the male readers; his female lover tries to curtail this obsession but fails; he sets out on a journey, witnesses accidents, and is soon disillusioned; at the end he dies. Similarly, the two main characters, Mehmet and Osman, have grown up reading the same children's books. Toward the end of the novel, Mehmet lives under the pseudonym Osman. The killer and his target, the victim and the perpetrator, both have the same name. When Osman meets pseudo-Osman, the remarkable physical similarities between the two are experienced in a moment of heightened homoeroticism. And while the readers of Rıfkı's book seem to copy each other's lives, copying the book becomes an activity in and of itself. In the height of his obsession with the book, Osman (the protagonist) indicates to Mehmet, "you think you are reading the book, yet you are rewriting it" (68). The rewriting occurs figuratively as well as literally. After reading the book Osman starts deftly copying it, just like Mehmet. Months later, when Osman finally meets Mehmet (now Osman), he learns that Mehmet spends his days copying the (banned) book in school notebooks and then distributing them. He gives Osman a detailed account of the process of copying: "What I do might appear simple, but it requires great care. I keep rewriting the book without missing a single comma, a single letter, or a period. I want everything to be identical, right down to the last period and comma. And this can only be achieved through inspiration and desire that is analogous to the original author's. Someone else might call what I do copying, but my work goes beyond simple duplication. Whenever I am writing, I feel and I understand every letter, every word, every sentence as if each and every one were my own novel discovery" (212).

But the meaning of copying here cannot be restricted to lack of originality. Pamuk deliberately obfuscates the divisions between objects and their images, originals and their imitations, the authentic and the inauthentic, the indigenous and the foreign in his novel. This obfuscation is most conspicuous, for example, in Pamuk's clever employment of references to the Koran. At the very beginning of the novel, Pamuk's description of Osman's first encounter with the book is very similar to descriptions of the Prophet Mohammed's revelation on the mountain of Ararat. Toward the end when Osman meets his doppelgänger Osman, he compares him to a *Hafiz*, a copier of the Koran.[12] These allusions to the Koran can be interpreted in several ways. On one level, a glimpse into the time-honored tradition of copying the Koran—copying and memorizing being rites of passage to newer interpretations—invokes a particular pedagogical strategy of learning by rote. On another level, this copying, imitating, and duplicating highlights certain points of intercultural confluence. At the end of his journeys, Osman visits Rıfkı's wife, Aunt Ratibe, and borrows part of Rıfkı's library. He starts copying sections of these books, one of which is a collection of citations from the writings of Ib'n Arabi (1165–1240). Osman copies the following passage: "I came across a book . . . and I knew from the handwriting that the text had been written by the son of His Honor Abd-ur-Rahman, the Chief Magistrate of Aleppo. When I came back to my senses, I found myself writing the section you are presently reading. And suddenly I knew that the section written by His Honor's son, which I had read in a trance, was identical to the section I am writing in this book" (257f.).

In the specific context of literature, the idea of copying the Koran exposes both the limits and the freedoms within several (national) literary traditions often also studied under the rubric of Islamic literatures. Since the Koran is often considered the fountainhead of literatures in the Islamic world, unsurpassed in its purity and beauty to represent the highest ideal of style, the rest of literature seeks to approximate the Koran or is somehow influenced by the Koran.[13] Even Osman, during his research on the sources of Rıfkı's book, thinks that "Uncle Rıfkı, when he was in the process of giving his own book a final shape, could have been thinking of the divinely revealed Book in which 'everything is written'" (262). This strategy of presenting the authentic as the always already inauthentic and the recent as the always already obsolete upsets Gökalp's notion of discovering the new life through a new aesthetics of the Ottomans. Indeed it is none other than the *Hafiz* Mehmet/Osman who, moments before his murder at the hands of Osman, spells out Pamuk's idea of the impossibility of an original, authentic moment:

> "You are really after the Original Cause, aren't you?"
> "You are questing for things that are pure, uncorrupted and clear. But there is no prime mover. It's futile to search for the key, the word, the source, the original of which we are all mere copies." (227f.)

Rıfkı's *New Life*, reversing Gökalp's statement, is thus copied and not created.

However, it would be hasty to settle on the assumption that Rıfkı's book is a new version of the Koran. *The New Life* also contains several circumspect references to the Koran's "misinterpretation" in Rıfkı's book. As mentioned earlier, the reader of the novel never gets to know all of the contents of Rıfkı's book. He does learn that during his initial readings of the book Osman mentions his carrying it "surreptitiously as if it were a sin" (10). While combing through the spies' reports about the book and its readers in Dr. Fine's mansion, Osman reads about a young student from Erzurum who wallpapered his room with pages from the book and had an altercation with his roommates, for one of them claimed that "there was a slur against Prophet Mohammed in the pages" (153). Osman also learns that five of the readers have been killed by Dr. Fine's spies (watches), and a couple of political organizations had taken a special interest in two of them: "Since one of the murdered persons was a student of journalism who had done translations for the foreign news service of the *Sun* papers, the Journalists Association for Patriotic Action pretended to have taken an interest in the incident, announcing that the Turkish press would never bow down before senseless terrorism. The other killing involved a waiter . . . whose hands were full of empty bottles of a popular yogurt drink; Islamic Youth Raiders had disclosed that the dead waiter had been a member, declaring at their press conference that the homicide had been perpetrated by the agents of the CIA and Coca-Cola" (154f.). As Janan narrates her conversations about the book, she quotes Mehmet, saying, "Most people want neither a new life nor a new world. So they kill the book's author" (68).

These references are not just extensions of the discourse of intolerance toward *any* book. Viewed against the backdrop of a controversy known for its world-wide repercussions in the late twentieth century—

the Salman Rushdie affair—these references are Pamuk's direct allusions to a major cultural conflict. To quickly refresh our memory, the issues at stake in the Rushdie affair can be summarized as follows: an innovative interpretation of a religious text by an author; world-wide resistance to this creative expression by members of a religious community; immediate suppression of creative independence through a life-threat against the author by a religious leader; state-sponsored censorship due to fear of religious riots in countries in Asia and Africa; an unavoidable reinforcement of the image of Asians and Africans (especially immigrants) as illiberal and intolerant bigots. In the context of my reading, the issue that deserves special mention is the mutual denigration of imprecisely defined Western and Eastern cultures by self-appointed representatives from both sides.[14] While Scotland Yard was busy ensuring the protection of both Rushdie and No. 10 Downing Street (the symbolic protection of freedom of speech), champions of cultural authenticity like Syed Shahabuddin in India or the Ayatollah himself in Iran were blaming Rushdie's Western education and his literary production influenced by the West as the root cause of Rushdie's moral and ethical failure. Similar to Gökalp's contentions about the "worn, sick, and rotten" elements of European cultures, polemicists against Rushdie used a pathological vocabulary in their accounts of Western values. The Journalistic Association's resolution against senseless terrorism in Pamuk's novel contains traces of a real statement issued by the Press Association of Turkey following the murder of Ugur Mumçu, a young journalist who had published against the Fatwa, and the assassination attempt on Aziz Nesin, who translated and published sections of *The Satanic Verses*.[15] Through its allusions and oblique references to these political events, Rıfkı's book in Pamuk's novel becomes an intervention in a larger ethical and cultural war. In the Turkish context, Pamuk takes issue with the nationalistic fervor and an exaggerated cultural pride in the New Republic, which rests somewhere between Gökalp's defamation of Western cultural values and Atatürk's proactive Westernization. In addition he contests the complete negligence of religion and top-down secularization in the early years of the republic, which resulted in the return of the repressed as the right-wing Gray Wolves in the 1990s. Ib'n Arabi's presence in the novel draws particular attention to interpretative traditions within Islam, subject to selective amnesia by the right wing in both the East and the West. Ib'n Arabi, born in Murcia, Spain, is one of the greatest scholars of Theosophical Sufism, an Islamic interpretational discourse that adopted a number of traditions of Neoplatonism and Gnosticism from the West as well as those of Hinduism and Taoism from the East. One of its initial contributors, as-Suhrawardi, who was killed in Aleppo in 1191, combined elements of Persian (Zoroastrian) and Egyptian (Hermetic) traditions. Ib'n Arabi himself had a cosmopolitan education. He is believed to have been instructed in Sufism by two Spanish women saints in Seville. Later in his life, he had a dramatic encounter with Ib'n Rushd (Averroës 1126–1198) and immediately impressed the great Aristotelian philosopher. All these scholars are part of the genealogy of Turkish Sufism, with Mevlana Rumi as its most well-known representative. Rumi himself is claimed by both Iranians and Turks because of the geographical location of his city, Konya, where Janan and Osman embark upon their bus journeys to towns with "refugees from Afghanistan peddling Holy Korans no bigger than my thumb" (*New Life* 60). With these extranational, cosmopolitan references—especially when juxtaposed with Gökalp's rejection of cosmopolitanism—Pamuk disputes the originality and purity of an unadulterated new life of Turkishness based solely on an Islamic heritage. On the global level, by ending his book with a mention of the place and the time of its conception—"Istanbul. 1992–1994" (296)—Pamuk facilitates a reading in the context of an international controversy, thus wresting the new life from Gökalp's national parentheses. *The New Life* constantly strives to become cosmopolitan, not national.

Beyond the references to the Koran and its misinterpretations, *The New Life* entails Pamuk's engagement—at times cryptic, at times straightforward—with a repertoire of literary texts from the West that further extend the transnational, cosmopolitan dimension of his own novel. As Dr. Fine enchants Osman with his rant against books "which the pawns of the Great Conspiracy mass-produced and disseminated . . . in their concerted effort to make us forget the poetry of our lives," it is impossible for the reader to think of the "field mouse that zipped past [them]" (132) as anything but a reminder of Lewis Carroll's *Alice in Wonderland*. Furthermore, Uncle Rıfkı's illustrated comics for children, *Nebi in Nebraska* and *Peter and Pertev*, read by Osman and Mehmet during their childhoods, and carefully taken away from Mehmet's room by Dr. Fine, are Turkish versions of the American *Lone Ranger* and *Tom Mix* comics. The books that Osman borrows from Uncle Rıfkı's wife after his death, books he might have been reading during the writing of the book, include works of Sir Arthur Conan Doyle, Mark Twain, Jules Verne, and Dante, to mention a few. These inclusions constantly challenge the notion of an insulated cultural heritage and diffuse the rigid boundaries of a national literature. Since Novalis and Rainer Maria Rilke play a very special role in Pamuk's novel and Rıfkı's book, I now try to imagine their significance.

As *The New Life* lays bare the vacuous nature of the concept of the national within the Turkish context, its incorporation of German literati like Novalis and Rilke motivates a reading in a context beyond Turkey. The prologue to *The New Life* is a line from Novalis's romantic classic *Heinrich von Ofterdingen*: "The others experienced nothing like it even though they heard the same tales."[16] Like *Heinrich von Ofterdingen*, *The New Life* contains structural elements of an *Erziehungsroman* with a young man's self-exploration and intellectual development through a journey or several journeys at the center of the plot. At the very outset of both works, the narration of an unknown person stirs up a youth's otherwise tranquil life. For Osman, it is Rıfkı's book that seems to reflect the course of his own life, and for Heinrich it is a dream spoken by someone for whom the world perhaps appeared the way it did to Heinrich. As Osman sits in his room "shuddering and swinging ... legs with the excitement" (*New Life* 5) due to Rıfkı's book, Heinrich "lay restless on his bed and thought about the stranger and his stories" (*Henry* 5). Similar to Osman's astonishment at the influence that the book exercises on him, Heinrich wonders "why I was the only one to be so touched by his stories" (*Henry* 5). Defamiliarization of the existing world and a desire to familiarize oneself with the hitherto unknown further unite the experiences of Osman and Heinrich. Osman listens to "the everyday roar of the city, the tinkle of the yogurt vendor's bell in the street, car engines, all the sounds familiar to me [him], as if I [he] were hearing outlandish sounds" (*New Life* 5). Heinrich believes that he would be able to hear and understand the voices of animals, trees, and rocks (*Henry* 5). Osman imagines himself to be in "a country where I knew neither the lay of the land nor the language and the customs" in "least expected places" (*New Life* 4f.). Heinrich dreams of "immeasurable distances and wild, unfamiliar regions" (*Henry* 5f.). While Osman sees "bedraggled people, faint letters, lost towns, lost lives, phantoms" (*New Life* 5), Heinrich witnesses "many kinds of people, in war, in wild tumult, and in quiet huts" (*Henry* 6). The initial phase of epiphany in both the narratives involves a long night of chaotic experiences and events that end with the deaths of the protagonists followed by their return to the world of experiences at the break of dawn, equipped with a heightened sense of clarity and awareness. The following descriptions of this experience preempt the course of events in both novels and exhibit a remarkable interchangeability. Osman:

> It was as if a singular world, a complete creation with all its colors and objects, were contained in the words that existed in the book; thus I could read into it with joy and wonder all the possibilities in my own mind. . . . It was much later, after I had been totally overtaken by the world the book described, that I actually saw death appear in the half-light before dawn, radiant as an angel. My own death.
>
> I suddenly understood that my life had been enriched beyond my ken. (*New Life* 6f.)

And Heinrich:

> He went through an infinite variety of experiences, he died and came to life again, loved most passionately, and was then separated from his loved ones forever.
>
> Finally toward morning as daybreak appeared, his soul became calmer, and the images became clearer and more abiding. (*Henry* 6)

This intertextual correspondence is extended to reflections on the function of art and literature in both novels. The merchants in *The New Life* represent a utilitarian perspective on the arts. Dr. Fine, their self-proclaimed representative, is not too distant from the ideas of Ziya Gökalp, for whom literature must finally serve as a manual or a guidebook for uplifting the country. The merchants in *Heinrich von Ofterdingen* extend a similar privilege to practical skills. They first speak of the arts in the context of Swabia, the fatherland of Heinrich's mother. Commending her plans to expose her son to Swabia, they extol the way skills, crafts, and the arts work toward enriching each other: "The arts and crafts multiply and are ennobled" (*Henry* 27). But unlike skills and crafts that occupy the workday, arts for them are rejuvenating indulgences meant for "recreation and variety" in the evening. Before praising the "delightful singers," the "glorious painters," and the dance floors in Swabia with their "comely figures," the merchants express their love for the balanced work and entertainment culture of Swabia: "the more diligently the days are spent in the pursuit of gain, the more exclusively are the nights devoted to the stimulating enjoyment of the fine arts and social intercourse" (ibid.). Like Gökalp, or the merchants in Güdül, the merchants accompanying Heinrich to Swabia believe in specialization in earthly, that is, material, things through experience and practice. Heinrich's mention of his teacher, the *Hofkaplan* (court chaplain) is met with skepticism, for he (the

Hofkaplan) is for the merchants an abstract thinker so involved in the "knowledge of the supernatural world" that he has little "insight and authority" (*Henry* 29) in earthly affairs. These convictions inform their ideas on poetry, which unlike painting or music—art forms with a visual or an auditory appeal—is abstract and ungraspable. Painting and music become higher forms of art due to the "patience and diligence" with which a "practiced hand" together with the "proper eye" (*Henry* 31) can result in an enthralling listening or visual experience. Writing poetry, for them, remains a mysterious process, the secrets of which do not hold much fascination. Only when rendered as a song, a result of practice and patience, can a poem merit their attention. The merchants thus stand close to Dr. Fine, whose respect for handwritten books emanates from the relationship between the pen and the hand and from the practice demanded by calligraphy, and for his followers the replacement of the cuckoo-bird with the Muslim priest is the apt culmination of engineering and cultural ideas.

These are just a few observations on the correspondence between two *Erziehungsromane* from two very different times and very different cultures. Through a presentation of these few similarities, I neither intend to prove that *The New Life* is a twentieth-century "Osman von Istanbul," nor do I want to demonstrate that the inspirational source of Pamuk's novel is a work from German Romanticism. This would assure my regression into the traditional studies on intercultural sources and influences, which tend to suggest that a frame-by-frame comparability alone defines intercultural dialogues, thus establishing that the *The New Life* is a Turkish-German novel.[17] This approach would invoke the same poignant question from Mehmet, "You are really after the Original Cause, aren't you?" (*New Life* 227), and contradict my own preference for multiplicity of sources and interpretations that has been at the core of my reading. I shall, therefore, dispense now with the activity of listing similarities. Instead, I want to speculate on the significance of the figures of Novalis and, later, Rilke in Pamuk's project.[18] This will require another small, albeit a very significant detour into the works of Uncle Rıfkı, the author of the Book.

Apart from being a regular contributor to a magazine for railroad buffs, Uncle Rıfkı is the author and illustrator of widely read children's comics of a very special nature. Although the main purpose of these comics is to provide the children with local counterparts of American adventure comic-book heroes like Tom Mix and Billy the Kid, Uncle Rıfkı does not aim at a Gökalp-style replacement of these with Turkish figures. In his address to the children at the beginning of one of his books he states, "Dear children . . .wherever I see you after school . . . I always see you reading about Tom Mix or Billy the Kid's adventures in cowboy magazines. I too love those brave and honest cowboys and Texas rangers. So I thought that if I told you the story of a Turkish kid among American cowboys, you might like it. Besides, this way you will be exposed *not only to heroes who are Christians*, but through the adventures of your plucky Turkish compatriots you will *also* come to cherish the ethics and the national values that our forefathers have bequeathed to us" (118, my emphasis). Rıfkı's comic-book characters from Turkey do not prove the superiority of the Ottomans over the Turkish non-Muslims or that of the Turks over the rest of the world. Nebi, the Turkish kid in *Nebi in Nebraska*, meets his Native American friend Tom at the Chicago World's Fair and assists him in saving his tribe in Nebraska from the alcoholism encouraged by white settlers. Ali, the protagonist of *Mary and Ali*, meets Mary at the docks in Boston and tries to help her find her absent father in St. Louis and Iowa before returning to Istanbul. Peter, the Bostonian kid in *Peter and Pertev*, learns about secularization and enlightenment from his Turkish friend Pertev. In *Heroes of the Railroad*, Peter and Pertev fight against Wells Fargo and Mobil Oil as these companies resist the construction of a coast-to-coast railroad. Changes brought about by railroad construction in Turkey during the 1930s enable Pertev to speculate on its importance in the United States. In all of these stories, it is not one national, ethnic, or religious group that is privileged over the other. Uncle Rıfkı's comics do not stop at providing the young readers with immediately identifiable characters. The characters, through their various interactions with children from around the world, resist the division of the world between us and them and inculcate in the readers a transnational connectedness and the necessity of international cooperation for solving problems. Unlike Ziya Gökalp, and later Atatürk, unlike Dr. Fine and his followers, Uncle Rıfkı, the reader of both Dante and Ib'n Arabi, shifts the focus from the nationalistic motto "Happiness is being a Turk."

It should not be surprising now that in an invocation of German Romanticism, it is not the *Volkstümlichkeit* of Jacob and Wilhelm Grimm that merits Pamuk's attention. Unlike the *Märchen* of the Brothers Grimm, which nationalized the folklore by virtue of documenting it in a book form, Uncle Rıfkı's comics, part of the series Weekly Adventures for Children, internationalize the experiences of an Ali and a Mary, a Nebi and a Tom, a Pertev and a Peter. Pamuk's dialogue with German Romanticism is not carried out at the level of a programmatic cultural identity formation characteristic of authors like Achim von Arnim, Ludwig Tieck, and the Grimm brothers. Novalis, writing during the last years of the eighteenth century, was not explicitly interested in the Germanness or the Germanization of the arts. It is the faith in fantasy, a search for a world beyond the graspable, the fathomable, the concrete, and the reasonable, characteristic of Novalis, which transforms into the prologue to *The New Life*. Pamuk's turn to Novalis can be best explained in his (Pamuk's) incessant effort in this novel to emancipate literature from its material, moralistic, or regional (nationalistic) allegiance and in his desire to restore a fantasy-filled, albeit not depoliticized cosmopolitanism.

In this romanticized cosmopolitics, cities with a long history of religious and ethnic diversity become the site of fantasy and imagination. As Rıfkı's comics and *The New Life* reiterate the importance of tolerance, they join hands with Novalis when he presents a brief, yet by no means undue, discussion on the movement away from the monotony of the provincial toward the diversity of the cosmopolitan. Heinrich's ideas on the transcendental nature of the aesthetic endeavor cannot be assigned to Eisenach or Augsburg—provincial points of embarkation and disembarkation on his journey. It is the journey between these provincial locales, the trail that becomes the classroom. A significant incident on the way to Augsburg happens in Thuringia, where, in the Castle of the Knights, Heinrich hears the Crusaders' song. He is told that it is echoing through all of Europe (*Henry* 67). Heinrich is just about overwhelmed by the song when he hears another song in a woman's voice in broken German conveying the yearning for homeland, followed by the crying of a child and some soothing words in the voice of that woman. He decides to follow the sound and meets Zulima, the woman from Arabia. After a heavy dose of praise for Europe and the German fatherland from the Knights, Heinrich listens to Zulima's nostalgic account of her homeland. At the core of Zulima's monologue is not the superiority of Arabia and the Arabs but a message of tolerance and understanding beyond prejudice:

> By no means believe the stories they tell you about the cruelty of my countrymen. Nowhere were prisoners treated more magnanimously, and your pilgrims to Jerusalem were hospitably received; only they were seldom worthy of it. Most of them were good-for-nothing wicked men, who disgraced their pilgrimages with knavish deeds and hence, to be sure, often fell into the hands of righteous vengeance. How tranquilly the Christians could have visited the Holy Sepulcher without the need of starting a terrible, useless war which has embittered everything, spread endless wretchedness, and separated the East

from Europe for ever. What importance did the name of the possessor have? Our sovereigns reverently honored the Sepulcher of your Holy One, whom we also regard as a divine prophet; and how splendidly could his Holy Sepulcher have become the cradle of a happy mutual understanding and the occasion of everlastingly beneficent alliances! (*Henry* 61)

Zulima reminds Heinrich of the unnecessary violence and misunderstandings caused by the Crusaders in Thuringia, and Janan resists Osman's leap into the hellhole of fanaticism in the town of Güdül. In both the tales, cosmopolitan centers that facilitate tolerance of difference remind the reader of the unproductive exercise of privileging the provincial, authentic homogeneity. For Heinrich it is Jerusalem and for Osman it is Istanbul, where throughout the course of history, differences between East and West are simultaneously accentuated and blurred.

Furthermore, taking into account the multiethnic, multireligious elements of these two cities, the movement away from Eisenach acquires a special meaning. Eisenach, as is well known, is the city where Martin Luther translated the Bible. As the Novalis scholar Wm. Arctander O'Brian brings to our attention in his book *Novalis: Signs of Revolution*, at the center of Novalis's highly controversial vision of a spiritually unified Europe in *Die Christenheit oder Europa* is his discontent with the "holy orthodoxy" (*die heilige Allgemeingültigkeit*) and the "absolute popularity" (*die absolute Popularität*) of the Bible. O'Brian elaborates:

> Protestantism ... mistook the Book itself—rather than its sense—for the central mystery of faith. ... Hardenberg [Novalis] humorously affirms Protestantism's fetish of the Book. ... Hardenberg knows quite well in all his writings that letters and philology are necessary means for the production of sense. Protestantism, however, mistook them for ends. ... For Hardenberg, Protestantism neglected the invisible signified; its fetishism of the Book, its autotelism, proceeds ... without any self-ironizing detour toward the absolute. Its philology—its love for the word—abolishes, rather than erects, a sense of the invisible; that is, of any signified, including the one proper to religion, that of the unity beyond signification. (O'Brian 236f.)

It is safe now to infer that the pedagogical authority of the Word, the (literal and figurative) originary text of the nation, the authoritative essay for nationalism and against cosmopolitanism, the holy Koran, or Uncle Rıfkı's book, all of them are challenged by the performative deviations of the Pamuk-Novalis dialogue. During his inspection of Mehmet's room in Dr. Fine's mansion, as Osman reads through Uncle Rıfkı's comics, he comes across a line in *Peter and Pertev*: "the Things written in the book are now left behind me!" (*New Life* 120). This line surprises Osman, for the speaker is "a character who had dedicated himself to the war against illiteracy" (ibid.). Later, Mehmet, in his account of his meeting with Uncle Rıfkı accepts that Uncle Rıfkı had not taken his consistent request to reveal the secrets of the book seriously. Nahit (another pseudonym used by Mehmet) realizes only much later that "He was right, though. Now I know he had no secret to reveal" (*New Life* 224). I will take up the secret of the angel, but only after one last reference to a sign.

As I now bring my discussion on Novalis and Pamuk to an end, I want to point out a special moment in *Heinrich von Ofterdingen* when Novalis simultaneously disputes and reaffirms the authority of the letter. This is the moment when Zulima and Heinrich take leave of each other. She offers him a lute that belongs to her brother, who is now in Persia studying with a poet. Heinrich asks instead for her hair-band, which has an inscription in "unknown letters" (*Henry* 63). She gladly parts with it, telling him the inscription is her name written in Arabic. The movement away from Eisenach now comes to symbolize movement away from the fetishization of the letter—but a letter from the Latin alphabet. Eisenach was also the seat of Luther's writings against the Muslims, the generic word for whom was *Turk*. With Zulima's example of Jerusalem in the context of religious tolerance, Novalis highlights the intersections between Islam and Christianity. The hero of Novalis's *Ofterdingen*, at the end of his first lesson on the repercussions of Christian fanaticism and on the need for tolerance, is left with indecipherable letters of a foreign alphabet that nonetheless become reminders of a part of human history shared by the two religions.

The space shared between Islam and Christianity, which Novalis points out in *Heinrich von Ofterdingen*, is rediscovered by the twentieth-century author Rainer Maria Rilke, Pamuk's other (German) accomplice in purging the homogenous purity of nations, cultures, religions, and literatures. The figure of the Angel at the center of Uncle Rıfkı's book is ostensibly one of the angels in Rilke's *Duino Elegies*. During his reading and rereading of a Turkish translation of *Duino Elegies*, Osman finds out that the angels in the *Elegies*, as Rilke himself had written to his Polish translator, "had less to do with the angel of the Christian heaven than with the angelic figures in Islam, which was a fact Uncle Rıfkı had gleaned from the [Turkish] translator's short foreword" (*New Life* 261). In the obsessive research that follows, Osman tries to establish the differences between the angels of Islam and those of the Christian heaven, only to realize that "aside from trivial differences such as the Koran referring to angels as a separate class of beings, or that the fiendish crew in Hell was also considered to be of angelic descent, or that the Biblical angels provided a stronger connection between God and His creatures, there was little else to prove Rilke right about his distinction concerning the angels of Islam versus those in the Christian heaven" (*New Life* 261).

Indeed in his letter of November 13, 1925, Rilke wrote to his Polish translator, Witold Hulewicz, that "The 'Angel' of the Elegies has nothing to do with the Angel of the Christian heaven (but rather with the angelic figures of Islam)" (Rilke, *Briefe* 374). Nonetheless, the similarities that Rilke points out are not so much morphological. Rilke's reason for distancing himself from Christianity is its emphasis on otherworldiness and eternity (*Jenseits und Ewigkeit*), which stand in opposition to the finite, the here seen and touched (*das hier Geschaute und Berührte*), which according to him are at the center of his elegies. But before Rilke takes issue with the separation of the earthly and the otherworldly, he expresses his discomfiture with the possibility of a single authoritative interpretation, a move that situates him at the third apex of a triangle already inhabited by Pamuk and Novalis. At the very outset Rilke asks Hulewicz, "And am *I* the one, who will give the right explanation of the Elegies?" (*Briefe* 374, original emphasis). Rilke thus raises the same question that Pamuk pursues in *The New Life*, a pursuit that he shares with Novalis. Moreover, Pamuk's citation from the Ninth Elegy—in which the orthodoxy of the word in the Age of the Sayable (*die Sägliche Zeit*) is interrogated—further reinforces this question: "Are we on this earth to say: House, Bridge, Fountain, Jug, Gate, Fruittree, Window—at best: Column, Tower. . . ? but to *say* these words you understand with an intensity the things themselves never dreamed they'd express" (*New Life* 257).

All of these works, *The New Life, Heinrich von Ofterdingen*, and the *Duino Elegies*, reiterate intersecting historical foundations and condone interpretative multiplicity in their presentation of the individual's relationship to the work of art. Pamuk's Turkish novel resists the utility of art for the advantage of a national collective but also questions if art is a solution to personal pathos and misery. In a novel in which the protagonist, Osman, is an embodiment of Rilke's elegiac cry, Pamuk distances himself from his work through an ironic move and urges the reader to treat him and his work with disbelief. In a long passage on Chekhov, "that talented, consumptive, modest Russian," Pamuk addresses the readers directly and states his dislike for "readers who try giving an esthetic [sic] dimension to their broken and sorry lives with sentiment which they call Chekhovian, bragging about their misery in an effort to render it beautiful and sublime" (*New Life* 242). He expresses his contempt for "exploitative writers ... who pinch rough drafts of Chekhovian protagonists in order to present them in other lands and climes, exposing us to their wounds and pains" (*New Life* 242f.). What follows is a statement that serves a twofold purpose. On the one hand, it defies Gökalp's prescription for a nativist (Eastern or Ottoman) authenticity; on the other hand, it mocks the very foundation of a tradition of literary studies that insists on reinforcing a national/geographical pedigree of literary genres:

> So Reader, place your faith neither in a character like me, who is not all that sensitive, nor in my anguish and the violence of the story I have to tell. ... Besides, this new-fangled plaything called the novel, which is the greatest invention of Western culture, is none of our culture's business. That the reader hears the clumsiness of my voice within these pages is not because I am speaking raucously from a plane which has been polluted by books and vulgarized by gross thoughts; it results rather from the fact that I still have not quite figured out how to inhabit this foreign toy. (*New Life* 243)

Toward the end of the novel, just before his death in the bus accident, Osman finds out that the source of the angel for Uncle Rıfkı was the angel on the wrappers of The New Life Caramels. Osman decides to visit the town of Eskihehir to meet with Süreyya, the owner of the candy company and the author of doggerels on the candy wrappers. Süreyya tells him that his own source of inspiration was none other than Marlene Dietrich, *The Blue Angel* in the film version of Heinrich Mann's *Professor Unrat*. Desire—existential, sensual, intellectual—thus becomes the motivation of history, and *The New Life* completes the beginning of an extraordinary mode of thinking and feeling with and beyond Germany and Turkey.

"But I am going to urge us to see the novel as a testing ground for a distinction between cosmopolitanism, with its emphasis on dialogue among differences, and a different, more monological form of humanism," writes Kwame Anthony Appiah in his essay "Cosmopolitan Reading" (207). In his reading of Tsisti Dangarembga's *Nervous Conditions*, Appiah develops a distinction between a "homogenizing or monological universalism and the dialogical universalism of cosmopolitanism" (214). Appiah characterizes *Nervous Conditions* as a novel without the "telltale marks of the author addressing an Other from Elsewhere" (212). He takes issue with Richard Rorty's essentializing view of the West (217–24) to envision a "pragmatist" reading of a novel in which "strategies of narration [were] borrowed from a wider world than Africa" (204). "What is necessary to read novels across gaps of space, time, and experience," reflects Appiah, "is the capacity to follow a narrative and conjure a world" (224).

In *The New Life*, Orhan Pamuk explodes the myth of a writer from the East who has admittedly "not quite figured out how to inhabit this foreign toy." Turkish scholars like Mehmet Tekin, for whom the burden of reading is not always about identifying telltale marks of an author from elsewhere—an East-West identity crisis—can thus confidently comment on the unique place of the *Yeni Hayat*, unmatched for its interest and the weight of its argument (Tekin, "Yeni Hayat" 712). Tekin identifies the difference in Pamuk's writing, yet extols the novel for being well crafted and stylish and unique in the tradition of *our* novels. For a less alert reader like D. M. Thomas, a novel that heavily draws on Western texts will still appear as the work of a carpet weaver gone color-blind and, therefore, as inaccessible; the responsibility of reading conveniently shifted to the quality of translation. It is precisely the differing, sometimes mutually contesting import of this possessive pronoun *our* that I have tried to demonstrate in my reading of *The New Life*. The novel reconfirms that transcultural literary confluences are facilitated by, but not solely dependent on, transnational migration. The aesthetic modes of expression of a nation are in a constant dialogue with those of other nations. Historical experiences and a shared cultural memory undoubtedly precipitate in artistic production within the geographical boundaries of a nation, thus amplifying the idea of a national identity. Nonetheless, these very narrations of a nation work at odds with their (imposed) commitment to further nationhood. In other words, artistic production perpetually questions, challenges, indeed, resists nation-states' attempts to control and to delineate the indigenous and the foreign, thereby complicating the very idea of a national art or a national literature. National literatures might encapsulate and articulate the shared memories of nations in certain languages and certain literary idioms unique to those languages and nations. Yet these very idioms address not only the specific nation from where they emanate but incorporate artistic idioms from other nations, thereby revealing the networks of a cosmopolitan literariness, a kind of literary globality. *The New Life* does not ask to be inserted in the list of nations as metaphors that Bhabha creates in his essay. On the contrary, it disentitles the nation of its metaphor. The conflict between the pedagogical and the performative in Pamuk's novel suggests modes of thinking beyond what Bhabha postulates as metaphoricity. *The New Life* is a novel that pushes the limits of our reading. It demands to be read beyond the metonymy of what Bhabha identifies as a "homogenous empty time" (158) in Anderson's *Imagined Communities*. In Pamuk's *New Life*, the nation emerges as a belated "contemporaneity" (ibid.). This belated contemporaneity might be delivered by the angel of history—regardless of whether he is called Gabriel or Gibreel—but it will be the reader's responsibility to read this contemporaneity of the belated in the narration of a nation. This reading will be chaotic, upsetting, unsettling. As Osman himself registers, "The pleasure of reading, which natty old gentlemen complain is lacking in our culture, must be in the musical harmony I heard reading the documents and murder reports in Dr. Fine's mad and orderly archive" (*New Life* 85).

AFTERWORD
Minorities, Literatures, and Recursive Leaps of Faith

> *We remain strangers, many meetings hence*
> *We shall becomes lovers again, how many congregations hence?*
> FAIZ AHMED FAIZ, 1971

These lines were authored by Faiz Ahmed Faiz, whose poetry belongs on the same shelf as Bertolt Brecht, Pablo Neruda, and Nazim Hikmet. Faiz's biography is inscribed with political frontiers and boundaries, which he crossed and altered, transforming himself and his readers in the process. He was born in undivided India in 1910 and chose to stay in what became Pakistan after the partition of the country in 1947. He was a scholar of English, Urdu, Arabic, and Persian literatures, even though his poems were mostly composed in Urdu. In 1971, following the further division of the Indian subcontinent—this time into Bangladesh—Faiz wrote one of his most famous poems, "Dhaka se Vapsi Par" (On Returning from Dhaka), about the atrocities committed by the majority Sunni Muslims on Shia Muslims and Hindus in the early 1970s. The state apparatus of General Yahya Khan, the military leader of Pakistan, orchestrated the massacre and rape of religious minorities not just in the city of Dhaka but in all of East Pakistan, contemporary Bangladesh. Indira Gandhi, the former prime minister of India, privileged the politics of religious difference as she—assisted by the Indian Armed Forces—engineered the new national boundaries of Bangladesh. The drama of postcolonial brutality, appearing first as a tragedy during the Hindu-Muslim riots of 1947, reappeared as a farce, as religious differences were reaccentuated and reinforced and familiarity replaced by hatred and violence.

I read the above-cited opening couplet of the poem as a statement on the pathos of divided communities. On behalf of the victimized minorities, Faiz asks the majority—to which he himself belongs—for reasons for the perpetual neglect, suppression, exploitation, and estrangement of minorities. He calls for an end to exclusion, to estrangement, and seeks familiarity. Familiarity through congregation becomes the prerequisite for tolerance, recognition, even acceptance of difference.

Faiz's plea for familiarity and hospitality and his emphasis on the necessity of congregation resonate—albeit differently—in Derrida's work *On Cosmopolitanism and Forgiveness* (2001). Especially in the section "On Cosmopolitanism" (3–24), Derrida reflects on cosmopolitanism as a concept and strategy to reflect upon questions of home and belonging. Derrida emphasizes "l'être-soi chez soi" (being at home with oneself)—"l'ipsété meme" (the other within oneself, 17)—and elaborates upon the limitations imposed upon the "law of hospitality" that pervert and obstruct the very inclusion of Others into a host society (16f.). Building upon Hannah Arendt's accounts of "violations of hospitality" (16), Derrida argues for a reconsideration of Immanuel Kant's famous *Definitive Article in View of Perpetual Peace*: "the law of cosmopolitanism should be restricted to the conditions of universal hospitality" (19). Derrida reveals the limitation of Kant's proposition, which stops at the right to hospitality as a "right to visitation" (*Besuchsrecht*) and not a "right to residence" (*Gastrecht*, 21). In order for cosmopolitanism to transpire from a utopian principle to ethical practice, for Derrida, hospitality surfaces as the prime prerequisite to counter exclusion (22f.).

Questions pertaining to hospitality for immigrants in the host society have been at the center of a number of scholarly debates and discussions for over two decades now. These questions have long been cast in terms of the ethics and politics of multiculturalism, both inside and outside the academic community. Multiculturalism as an academic discipline offered modes to surmise a systematic understanding of a social reality made of numerous linguistic, ethnic, and national frontiers and boundary lines, sharing the lived space of a city or a nation. In the Anglo-American academy, developments in perspectives on sociopolitical recognition of minority ethnic cultures can be credited on the one hand to a number of scholars of Euro-American heritages, who have pursued their critical and interrogative intellectual training as citizens from the tumultuous events in Europe and North America in the 1960s and have persistently put forth daring and stimulating questions. Charles Taylor's definitive work *Multiculturalism and the Politics of Recognition* (1994) brought to the fore the necessity of a state-sponsored acknowledgement of cultural, linguistic, and religious differences in a society like Canada. Will Kymlicka's debatable, albeit provocative, engagement with *Multicultural Citizenship* (1995) shifted the focus from the politics of recognition to a politics of participation through distinct societal cultures of polyethnic rights, especially in the case of the first peoples of Canada. Brian Barry has taken issue with the vicious repercussions of the divisive politics of multiculturalism and argued for a reconsideration of social redistribution of resources in *Culture and Equality* (2002). In a more sophisticated treatment of the same problem, Seyla Benhabib, in her study *Claims of Culture* (2002), has painstakingly assessed questions of redressing injustice and inequality among groups in an age when multiculturalism might seem to foster nothing but a furthering of confined and restricted identity politics.

These scholars have been in dialogue and debate with those of Asian or African heritages. Scholars such as Gayatri Chakravorty Spivak, Paul Gilroy, Homi Bhabha, Rey Chow, Kwame Anthony Appiah, and Bhikhu Parekh, among others, have been at the forefront of multiple struggles for the shift from the Euro-American hegemony in critical considerations of the world. Bhikhu Parekh's focus on the ambivalence of culturally derived differences within philosophical accounts of mono- and multiculturalism from Greek monism to the Salman Rushdie affair supplies an exceptional breadth and depth to his book, *Rethinking Multiculturalism* (2000). Kwame Anthony Appiah's recent work, *The Ethics of Identity*, brilliantly investigates the associative duties of what may be perceived as an individualistic identity politics. Paul Gilroy's Wellek lectures, published as *Postcolonial Melancholia* (2005), have drawn a close and much needed attention to the apparent breakdown of the multicultural project; his emphasis on the necessity of conviviality reiterates the crucial significance of familiarity through congregation. Through these and other discussions and debates, scholars have tried to understand the rapidly accelerated pace with which mass migration has been changing traditionally homogenous societal structures in the West since the Second World War.

Apart from political and sociological scholarship, in the realm of literature, aesthetic expressions of direct and indirect experiences of the new situation caused by mass migration—usually in the majority language of the country of residence—gained a new qualifier: minority, or multicultural. Scholarship on this literature extended questions of political representation into the realm of artistic and aesthetic representation. Contested questions of home and belonging, assertions of cultural identities, and exclamations of racist reactions found expression in literature by and about the ethnic immigrant minorities.

Precisely these ambivalences of culturally derived differences, associative duties of identity politics, and the necessity of congregation and conviviality in order to cross borderlines have shaped and informed my own understanding of multiculturalism in more encompassing, more transgressive, and therefore, perhaps less divisive vocabularies of affiliation and disaffiliation. I have tried to understand them under the rubric of *Cosmopolitical Claims*. However, in translating these vocabularies from sociopolitical thought to literary criticism, I have remained attentive to the admonitions and modalities offered by three other scholars mentioned above. With Gayatri Chakravorty Spivak's continuing vigilance in postcolonial studies, I have tried to move away from the self-congratulatory mode of multicultural literary studies, which derives solace and comfort in criticizing (mis)representations and self-representations of minorities in literature (*Postcolonial Reason* 169). My specific inquiries into the nature, status, and role of the subaltern ethnic subject or the ethnic author as the native informant in Nadolny's *Selim* have helped in configuring exchange mechanisms between the marginal Other and the majority self. Extending these concerns to my reading of Özdamar's *Seltsame Sterne* has been an attempt to present the figuring of the native-informant ethnic woman—a figure of literary autobiography—as a participant observer and a documenter of certain subaltern pasts. Furthermore, an engagement with Homi Bhabha's elaborations on cultural hybridity alongside Rey Chow's conceptualization of ethnic abjection and Pheng Cheah's critique of migrant hybridity have assisted in grasping an irresolute and, therefore, problematic establishment and reception of a purportedly hybrid author (Zaimoğlu) and his marginalized subject (Ertan Ongun) as the authentic native informants. Finally, Bhabha's critical assessment of the pedagogical and the performative of the nation has assisted in comprehending the gravity of cosmopolitical claims of a dissident outsider within a nation. Therefore this book is more noticeably in dialogue with Gayatri Chakravorty Spivak, Rey Chow, Pheng Cheah, and Homi Bhabha.

However, the process of writing and thinking through these issues—of guests and hosts, immigrants and citizens, marginalized and mainstream—in the manner and mode outlined above has been stimulated by a number of other, equally important textual, critical, and worldly moments. These moments have invigorated and fortified my interest in writing this book beyond my assistant-professorial obligations toward tenure and publication. In the following three sections, I wish to reconstruct three moments that have given contour to divisive cultural lines in my own personal memory. More importantly, these moments have encouraged me to examine subalternity, diasporic memory, hybridity, and dissidence to doctrinaire national belonging as part of cosmopolitics. It is my hope that these moments will illustrate all the significant problems about the politics of "self-evident" difference and the pressure for homogenous assimilation and integration of the ethnics, which I have discussed throughout this book.

THE TEXTS

A New History of German Literature (2004) is based on Paul Celan's stimulating dictum, "[j]edes Gedicht is datierbar" (every poem is datable). In the succinct and highly insightful introduction to this volume, David E. Wellbery writes:

> The date each poem or work of literature bears is internal to the work itself, the temporal center around which it crystallizes. The meaning of literary texts—their capacity to testify to human experiences and to resonate in the lives of their readers—is inseparably tied to the singularity of their moment, to their primary historical character as contingent events. Paradoxically, in the inherited form of literary historical writing, it is just this character of literature that goes missing. Traditional literary histories treat individual texts and performances not just as singular occurrences, but as illustrative instances of some force, tendency, or norm such as the spirit of an age or a nation, a class bias, or an aesthetic ideal. To grasp the historical character of a literary text is, according to this way of thinking, to see the individual case as typical of something else, and therefore as replaceable. This operation effaces literature's "datable" singularity and contingency. A major aim of *A New History of German Literature* is to find a mode of presentation that restores access to this dimension of literature. (xvii)

Wellbery's contentions about traditional literary history and the superiority of the kind of dating and datablility that he proposes are, of course, open to debate and discussion but beyond the scope of this afterword. What is noteworthy, if contestable, about Wellbery's project is the gesture of the movement away from the inherited toward the search for the singularity and contingency of the enterprise of literature. Thus Wellbery brings together scholars and critics of German cultural production—literature, linguistics, philosophy, history, sociology, not all of them Germanists—who reflect on a specific date, a year, or a span of a couple of years and build around it an essay about a specific work of literature, a literary impulse, a genre, an institution, a strategy of reading, even an attack on literature and suppression of literary freedom. In a bid to transform the structure and content of literary-historical production, the words *history*, *German*, and *literature* acquire new meanings to capture the "revolutionary transformation of narratives" (xxi). To illustrate with two examples, Orrin Robinson's entry for the year 1523 is a comment on "Luther's Bible and the Emergence of Standard German" (231–35); Klaus Berghahn, in his essay on August 26, 1792 (455–59), engages with an aesthetic revolution that finds recognition beyond the German nation through the honorary French citizenship bestowed upon Friedrich Schiller. Written for a time when the reader's home is "almost anywhere" and the archives of literature seem to be a Google-search away, the volume aims at providing what Wellbery calls "a random access history, providing multiple points of entry and allowing for various reading agendas" (xxii). Random access memory, to refresh our understanding of the term, is the process of transferring information to or from memory in which every memory location can be accessed directly rather than being accessed in a fixed sequence.

The indebtedness of Wellbery's idea of random access literary history to the term "random access memory" is obvious. What is more significant for the discussion here are the following questions: first, in this *New History of German Literature*, does the reader have the same random and direct access to the literature of minorities as to the long tradition of mainstream institutions of German culture that the book presents and represents? Second, in setting up the archive of German cultural institutions, what kinds of beginnings are being carved out for the multicultural production? What are the documents, how are they being cataloged? Last, but not least, in a literary historical project that claims not to privilege a sequential access to a continuous collective German identity, are there any productive discontinuities and ambivalences that form and inform the hyphenated German subject, the immigrant, the marginal, the minority? Are these discontinuities rendered legible by the multicultural contributors to the volume?

The answers cannot be promptly affirmative, perhaps due to the nature of the volume itself (it is a reference book) or perhaps due to the very limited space provided to minority discourse within German literature. In other words, neither the editors nor the two contributors on multiculturalism—Leslie Adelson and Deniz Göktürk—can be held solely responsible for the reader's lack of access to the memory locations of the minority. My intention here is not to illustrate another victimized narrative of minority literatures by pointing out the benevolent neglect to which they are subjected. On the contrary, I wish to establish that even now, as the code and the program that determine our reading agenda for multicultural literature in Germany are written and rewritten, certain viruses that render the random access memory corrupt and inaccessible are often overlooked.

In this thousand-page literary history, minorities finally make an entrance on page 912 ("Migrants and Muses"), as Leslie Adelson—whose scholarship has constantly enriched our understanding of multiculturalism and literature in Germany—draws our attention to the 1979 publication of the German translation of the Turkish author Güney Dal's novel *Wenn Ali die Glocken läuten hört* (When Ali Hears the Bells Toll). In her reading of Kadir Derya, the hero of Dal's novel, Adelson presents the oppression of immigrant laborers, their social discrimination, and the suppression of their cultural and political identity, which Dal captures with a high degree of linguistic sophistication and creativity, both in the Turkish original and in the German translation. Adelson's situating of Dal and other contributors to *Gastarbeiterliteratur* within the larger framework of German literary history is extremely fruitful, even as I might disagree with Adelson about the choice of the date. Nineteen seventy-nine might have been the year of the German publication of the Turkish novel *Is Sürgünleri* (Exiles of Labor, 1976), but the novel's historical singularity and contingency lies in 1973, the year of the OPEC oil crisis and the *Anwerbestopp* (hiring freeze) of guest workers in Germany. Nonetheless, Adelson, whose most recent work, *The Turkish Turn in Contemporary German Literature* (2005), is a milestone in studies of literatures of ethnic minorities in Germany, seems forced to conflate the *Gastarbeiter*-focused writings of the 1960s, 1970s, and 1980s with those written after the reunification of Germany. Thus Yoko Tawada, a Japanese-German author who writes mostly about language and identity, somehow appears to belong to the same category as Emine Sevgi Özdamar. The reading agenda—for lack of allowed space or other factors—gets obfuscated by the plethora of works, authors who inhabit and crowd this historical location of undifferentiated and unorganized time; the essay almost becomes a refugee camp where the heroes of literary discrimination find shelter. Missing from this shelter for writers of color is, of course, Sten Nadolny, an ethnic German author who wrote a most challenging and self-critical account of the *Gastarbeiter*-experience in his novel *Selim oder Die Gabe der Rede* (1990), which has been rescued from ill-equipped readings by Adelson herself.

The second entry on multiculturalism, "Spectacles of Multiculturalism" by Deniz Göktürk, is a close reading of the *Karnival der Kulturen* organized by the city of Berlin every year. Göktürk's essay critically amplifies a statement by Johannes Rau, the former president of Germany, along with Brazilian music and sounds of minority writers in lectures presented in the series Deutschland neu Lesen (Rereading Germany) at the Haus der Kulturen der Welt in Berlin. Göktürk's aim is clearly to demonstrate the convoluted nature of the creation of ethnic identities through mass-cultural phenomenon such as a carnival, but the access to this phenomenon is not the same as access to the French Revolution (1789) or German Unification (1871). The limitation to two entries on contemporary minority cultures impedes the encounter that characterizes any exhilarating experiences of reading that Wellbery promises in his introduction. The impact of mass migration on German culture, or even the influential and innovative reading strategies of Adelson and Göktürk, remain inaccessible in the *New History*.

When Russell Berman and Azade Seyhan edited the *New German Critique*'s special issue on Minority Literature in 1989, they emphasized the pitfall of a stultified oppressor–oppressed equation. Sigrid Weigel and Leslie Adelson demonstrated the need for nuanced readings of feminist issues, which would resist, for example, the rescuing of a Turkish woman through an emancipatory agenda. Then how does one account for the limitations as demonstrated above? The reason lies partially in the limited execution of criticism within one's own field of study. The necessity for self-reflection that the Adelson-Gökberk debate in the early 1990s highlighted seems to have had little effect on the agenda for reading minority literatures. With the exception of Seyhan's *Writing Outside the Nation* (2001) and Adelson's most recent work, *The Turkish Turn* (2005), the majority of articles on minority literature in Germany—some of them mentioned in my own study—demonstrate an uninterrupted history of development of this literature. Identities are created and constructed, authentically and in an undisturbed, unchallenged fashion, both in literature and in its professional readings. Regimes of representationalist police declare whiteness and Christianity as the only pathological discrepancies, which they then cure through their establishment of a non-Christian, non-White self-representational accuracy. Everyone gets a room of one's own; every room is without a view. The Other becomes a career; the multiculturalist critic sits in the center of the room for the fear of being visited by the bailiff as in Chekhov's "Ward No. 6." For fear of being labeled conservative, critics of minority literature and scholars of multiculturalism stop short of criticizing their own field. Computer scientists read programs by reading the flow of execution, which can quickly become labyrinthine. A leap of faith is the alternative: when one comes to a functional call, instead of following the flow of execution, one assumes that the function works correctly and returns the appropriate value. Random access history becomes inaccessible due to an inopportune application of, to borrow for the last time from computer science, "a recursive leap of faith."

THE CRITICS

Aside from these limitations, I have intended to develop strategies of reading literature that would stress the overcoming of an exclusion to which a literary tradition had been subject by virtue of being labeled minority literature, indeed by merely accentuating its Otherness. If marginalization is only one of the manifestations of exclusion, the other one is exoticization. In privileging (artistic) self-representation of the Other over representation, critics either polemicize against artists who attempt to depict the Other for their lack of the "concrete experience of the oppression of the Other" or they preface their own critical enterprise with endless disclaimers enunciating their own status in the famous race-class-gender triangle. The activity of sharing knowledge is belabored by the great guilt of "cognizing" the other, or alternatively, someone else's intervention is easily subjugated for the apparent lack of multicultural guilt. Given that something called an innocent discourse bereft of desire and interest does not exist, and the narrative voice, in creating its objects of knowledge, does participate in a (hegemonic) practice of cognition, the question that needs to be asked is: is it essential for the so-called hegemonic-majority voice to undergo the concrete experience of oppression or become the Other by playing the native in order to be able to theorize about the Other? In other words, is an appropriate discourse on the Other possible only when the Other speaks for him/herself, or is there any redeemable factor left in speaking for/about/as the Other?

My cosmoplitical readings emerge as reactions to a specific context of the numerous scholarly works we have read after Edward Said's *Orientalism* (1978), in which criticizing the Western intellectual's capability to mediate an interaction with the Other becomes the central occupation of the scholarly enterprise. Unreflectively conflating Said's careful and nuanced study of the construction of the Orient with Samuel Huntington's *The Clash of Civilizations* (1996), cultural *interactions* are repeatedly studied as cultural *encounters*, thus rather crudely carrying over the adversarial relationship between the colonizer and the colonized, the master and the slave, the oppressor and the oppressed, the majority and the minority, the white and the rest, to interpretations of (self-critical)

ethnocentrism of the left

aesthetic interventions in the Other in the socioeconomic environment at the end of the twentieth century.[1] What is preferred and privileged are self-representations, the insider view of any social reality, perhaps for its "truth" content. The repercussions are serious. Publishers and booksellers, academics and minority students all participate in an artless valorization of self-representation of minorities. Under the aegis of the grand multicultural exploration of the "voices of their own," a rather disingenuous enterprise forges ahead as a symptom of what Herbert Lindenberger describes as "the ethnocentrism of the left" ("Reading Lists" 157). The academic community, in a very well intended project of listening to the voice of the Other, becomes so obsessed with authenticity that it turns a deaf ear to any vocalization of the Other by a "hegemonic" voice.[2]

As I taught and thought about multiculturalism and literature in Germany, a kind of orthodoxy seemed to emerge, one that goes beyond headscarves and halal meat. This orthodoxy, I believe, pays undue attention to the minorities' finding their own voice through literature; the critics who enthusiastically follow this voice will listen to any voice—shrill, dull, squeaky, flat—as long as they (the critics) can exhibit the construction of Otherness and identity through socially victimized narratives. A moral code is thus established whereby the writer's ethnicity/class/sexual orientation/gender becomes the gate pass to knowledge about the Other. The cultural interlocutor suffers under the same old debate that demarcates theory from praxis, lived experience from mediated experience, the self from the Other. This creates a necessarily exclusionist politics whereby any narrativization of the minority by the majority is rendered incomplete, insufficient, or irreverent for the lack of experience with oppression. Validation of textual documentation of the experience of or with the Other depends entirely on the ethnic/sexual/racial status of the individual subject. In a utopian project that perhaps aims for a day of representation without any prejudices, the literature for which one strives is a literature of the *same* people, by the *same* people (implying perhaps, for the *same* people?), all in the name of the productive politics of cultural difference! The result is a reconstruction of all the borders that one wanted to deconstruct.

As a concluding unscientific postscript, I shall only state that multiculturalism and minority studies, once meant to open up the institution of literature, might close themselves by losing the power of self-critique. If we wish to reestablish the exhilarating experience of reading, we will have to return from the leap of faith and question every recursion carefully to establish the rationale of literary studies. The word *minor* will otherwise come to signify nothing else but—to follow an impulse from mathematics this time—"the irrational difference between two irrational lengths as described in the 76th proposition of the tenth book of Euclid's *Elements*."[3]

THE WORLDS

Years before I started thinking about cosmopolitanism as a strategy in order to understand multiculturalism and literature, at age thirteen I was exposed to the history of the world through Jawaharlal Nehru's *Glimpses of World History*. This collection of letters by Nehru, written from the Naini prison to his teenage daughter Indira Gandhi, was my first detailed exposure to the political events of the world. After a decade of reading nursery rhymes with their fairy-tale illustrations and outdated English textbooks still in use today in private schools in India, I graduated to stories about the French Revolution, the German and Italian unifications, English imperialism, and the Indian Revolt of 1857. Through these, along with the BBC World Service, magazines and newspapers bought at the A. H. Wheelers' kiosk at my hometown's train-station, and books bought from Chinese and Soviet bookmobiles, I was assured that there was a world, no matter how far back or forward in time, to which I had access despite the absence of the information highway. Thus, the fascinating worlds of *Robinson Crusoe* and *Tom Jones*, Hindi translations of *Crime and Punishment* and the *Three-Penny Opera*, together with the woman author Ismat Chughtai's Urdu short story "*Lihaaf*" (The Quilt) about lesbian relationships in semifeudal India were all part of a newness that I saw entering my world along with *Glimpses of World History* at my bedside. These books made me feel the fragrance of the world and some glimpses of its reality.

This was my juvenile literary heritage, which re-presented itself in my rediscovery of a piece by Nehru much later. A few years after the end of the Second World War, Jawaharlal Nehru wrote the following lines to his Italian socialist friend Maria Lorenzini: "The world is a difficult place to live in wherever we might be, and life becomes more and more complicated with its unending problems. If we are fortunate, we can sometimes feel the fragrance of it and some glimpses of reality" (Nehru 273). The significance of these two sentences is not their sentimentality but the source of the sentiments. The letter was written almost two years after Indian independence and the massacre that followed the partition of India and Pakistan, a year and a half after Mahatma Gandhi had been targeted by Hindu right-wing supremacists for his alleged appeasement of minority politics in India. I recreated this time-line for myself in March 1999, fifty years after Nehru wrote those lines, as I read them at the Stabi (Staatsbibliothek zu Berlin). Europe was at war again. This time, however, the war was marketed as NATO's intervention in Kosovo. Bill Clinton and Tony Blair sharpened their rhetoric against Milošević's ethnic cleansing operations; Gerhard Schröder defended the German army's offensive role in restoring the multiethnic character of Europe.

As the Reverend Jesse Jackson boosted American soldiers' morale in Pristina, the view of the Olympia Stadium from my small room in Berlin served as a constant reminder of another Jesse, the Olympian Jesse Owens, and the need to contribute to the discussion on race relations in a unified Germany. I was a resident of the Internationales Studentenwohnheim-Berlin—formerly a hotel for British soldiers and donated in 1995 to Studentenwerk-Berlin. The soldiers had been replaced by aspiring young scholars in their mid-to-late twenties—mathematicians, architects, sociologists, musicians, literary critics—from the former allied countries. (That I, as a citizen of India, was one of the residents, was certainly not a long overdue acknowledgement of British India's participation in the Second World War. My affiliation with Stanford University had guaranteed me a place in the building.) As print and electronic media made a case for the purging of Sarajevo, as billboards and buses in Berlin thanked the Allied countries for the Berlin Airlift, I was engrossed in a modest project of reflecting on the literature of and about the Turkish immigrant community in Germany. As the project developed, it became clearer to me that very much like the German citizenship laws, which treated immigrants and their children as second-rate citizens, the taxonomy developed by literary scholars attributed marginal status to literature written by immigrants. The discovery of this uncanny coincidence became the cornerstone of my inquiry into the question, "What is Turkish-German?" which became my dissertation, submitted to Stanford University.

Following my move to the American Midwest in the fall of 2001, as I was just about to initiate a revisiting and rethinking of the dissertation, the World Trade Center and the Pentagon were attacked. Any semblance of tolerance and acceptance of cultural difference seemed to immediately disappear. As a resident of the United States, I shared the shock, grief, and melancholia caused by the terrorist attacks. But I was also alarmed by the momentum with which the journalists, in tandem with the state, converted a nation that prides itself on free speech into a wasteland of ideologically homogenous indoctrination. The connection between the falling of the Twin Towers to multiculturalism might seem exaggerated, but one only needs to think of global connectedness today to grasp the import of such provocation. The word *ethnic*, which has unreflectively become replaceable with *multicultural*, especially in recent history, gives us an easy entry into what might seem a remote discourse. In the aftermath of September 11, one witnessed an unreasoned scrutiny of the world's "ethnics" at immigration ports and embassies around the globe. Especially in the United States, the words *ethnic* and *ethnicity* reacquired a problematically threatening status. With a palpable and programmatic resurgence of the religious binary of the Jihad and the Crusades, the moralistic binary of good and evil, the "coalition of the willing" attempted to numb the critical sensitivities of a nation vulnerable to these misgivings. Phrases such as "Attack on America," "War on Terror," and "America Strikes Back" flashed on television screens, and American national collectivity was defined through adherence to these phrases. At the same time, "Golden Eagle," "Infinite Justice," and then "Enduring Freedom" turned into shibboleths. Anyone who, like Susan Sontag, cast doubts about the feasibility of these grand ideas fell vulnerable to the risk of being declared an outsider, an America-hater. I asked a political scientist at my home institution, "What does 'Enduring Freedom' mean? Is it an enduring freedom *from* terrorism, an enduring freedom *of* the people of Afghanistan, or an enduring freedom *for* the First World nations to create historical monsters in the Third World with no sense of accountability?" I was told that I was being too "lit crit"—literary critical—as I was worried about all these prepositions.

As peanut-butter and jelly sandwiches and the somewhat more ethnic Tex-Mex meals of rice and beans—packed in Lawrence, Texas, and reportedly kosher or halal in accordance with the culinary traditions of the Afghans—were dropped in Afghanistan, the ethnics were purportedly emancipated from shackles of fanaticism and self-imposed dictatorships. The "Protestant Ethnics"—whom Rey Chow in her influential work aptly defines as those protesting against the idiom of a forced emancipation without the agency of the self—continued to be termed regressive mercenaries, enemies of freedom. In short, by way of ethnicity (now a code word for Islam), multiculturalism regained its Thatcherite regressive implications in the early twenty-first century.

In the German sociopolitical context, the reinvention of the ethnics was admittedly not as extreme as in American society. Indeed, one could argue that not 9/11, but January 1, 2000, the day of implementation of the new citizenship law in Germany, is, and should be, the defining moment for minorities in Germany and their state-approved inclusion. In other words, one could claim that the process of political recognition of the humanity of the *Gastarbeiter*—as expressed by Max Frisch, "One has summoned forces of labor, and human beings are coming"[4] (100)—was finally completed on January 1, 2000. Thus, one could concede that with this final gesture, headscarves or no headscarves, the Protestant Ethnic had finally won the multicultural war. The recognition of the non-European Other—an immigrant in Europe or still a resident of a non-European country—as a political equal of any Western subject was either close to being achieved or had been achieved already.

However, the questionable efficacy of this easy and naïve conclusion was proven to me beyond a shadow of doubt a couple of weeks after September 11. A senior German diplomat, a representative of the German nation-state but also a self-proclaimed expert on German literature of the classical period, delivered a talk at my home institution. The talk was initially titled "At Crossed Signals? Transatlantic Transitions, Global Agendas, and Current Challenges for European-American Relations." It was, however, September 11 that became the point of departure for the diplomat, who announced that afternoon that he was going to speak "as a European citizen." Immediately, the two world wars emerged as his main points of reference. Explaining Jacques Chirac's reserve in endorsing "the War" (semantic problem), the diplomat stated that for Europeans "war" brings back memories of mass destruction and annihilation, an experience to which the citizens of the United States never had immediate access. But, he said, "This is not the time to criticize, it is the time to show solidarity." Thus the promise of a semblance of pacifism was quickly lost in the insistence that powerful European nations would—at least at the time of his talk—fully support the United States in any action against terrorism. To substantiate his argument, the diplomat reported on how Tony Blair, Gerhard Schröder, and Jacques Chirac had personally assured President Bush of their complete support. Europe and North America had shared the same "civilizational" values of justice, democracy, and freedom, so it was obvious for him that they would come together to fight the unnamed common enemy.

Suddenly, the twentieth century seemed like an exchange that had only happened between and on the Berlin-D.C./London-D.C./Paris-D.C. highways, and hence, in the first major event of the twenty-first century, globalization notwithstanding, the powerful fraternity was ready to decide the course of the world again. Thus "we" in the western World could deal with—to paraphrase and selectively quote the diplomat—the "trauma and the struggle" caused by a "typical oriental expression" of "collective neurosis" of some people living in a country of otherwise "very simple" people struck by "misery and poverty" if "we" "strengthen" a "bipolar unity" and "get the bad guys." A cultural bureaucrat from Europe, with his debatable use and abuse of history, told a primarily American audience of students and scholars, "This is not the time to criticize; it is the time to show solidarity." The necessity for the dominance of the West over the subservience of the East was reestablished. The Owl of Minerva had a new job: to carry the wreckage of history, neatly gift-wrapped, from 10 Downing Street to 1600 Pennsylvania Avenue.

Today, a specter seems to go through the world—the specter of multiculturalism. Owners of political power in the centers of immigrant populations in the geographical West have united themselves in a holy witch-hunt against this ghost: the Pope and the Imam, Bush and Blair, German journalists and the French police. Where is the party in power or in opposition today that has not been decried for its appeasement of minorities, for its programs to advance any semblance of multicultural rights? Where is the opposition that has not hurled back the branding reproach of multiculturalism?

The presence of Marx in the last sentences is easily recognizable—although this is no attempt to write a multicultural manifesto. In his book *Cosmopolitanism*, Kwame Anthony Appiah calls multiculturalism "another shape-shifter, which so often designates the disease it purports to cure" (*Cosmopolitanism* xiii). I will go one step further and state that multiculturalism—the colored brainchild of postindustrial north-Atlantic ultraspace—finally died on September 11, 2001. I state this neither with a sense of unnecessary provocation nor with a feeling of remorse because, with this imagined death of an imagined idea, a fallacy seems to have thankfully come to an end. Since the late 1960s, with much progress made—both within and outside the academy—in accepting and acknowledging the presence and participation of ethnic and religious immigrant minorities within the largely white and Judeo-Christian societies of the West, a particular fallacy surreptitiously gained currency, the fallacy of inherent positive recognition, acceptance, and tolerance of minorities. The source of this fallacy lay not only in "culture sensitivity" trainings in the workplace, discussions on "diversity" in the executive boardrooms of universities and corporations, but also in an unfounded belief in a harmonious coexistence of humans of different races, ethnicities, and colors. The secret weapon for this fallacy was, of course, the hope for integration in the public sphere. Multicultural ethnics were part of the society as long as they were themselves in their little ghettos and behaved like the majority in the public sphere.

In the absence of total integration of the minorities, unfamiliarity continued to propagate itself. This unfamiliarity between communities already divided by race and class, ethnicity and religions, the estrangement of neighbors, the glaring absence of understanding and tolerance between citizens—resident-members of same cities—is now visible from New York to London to New Orleans to New Delhi to Berlin to, most recently, Paris. Following the terrorist attacks in New York and Washington, D.C., in 2001 and immediately after the London bombing in June 2005, the electronic and print media in Europe and North America seemed to be asking a rather naïve question: "how could our good neighbors, who seemed fairly assimilated in our societies, turn out to be terrorists?" In asking this question, they overlooked a more important question: "What are the consequences of incessant neglect, ignorance of social isolation, and discrimination against minorities?" Following hurricane Katrina in late summer 2005, levees of race and class broke in New Orleans, and out of the floodwaters emerged the Third World within the First World. The American media reacted with classic sentimental ignorance: "How and why this pain and suffering, why among of us—the richest and the most powerful nation in the whole world?"

Through all of these historical markers of the early twenty-first century, the idea of congregation seems to be threatened and eclipsed by years of segregation, of repeated reinforcements of frontiers and borderlines of class, religion, race, ethnicity, and gender. In the West, especially, the "ethnics"—members of that "perilous" collective who, according to the conservative imagination, weaken the social fiber of a civilized society—seem to be resurfacing.

As I was bringing this manuscript to an end, Faiz's couplet could be read on the flames burning Parisian suburbs.[5] As a curfew—temporally restricted movement—on the citizens of Paris was presented by Jacques Chirac as the only alternative to accelerate movement toward peace,[6] the unfamiliarity with the coinhabitants, the estrangement of and from immigrants, and a rampant neglect of minority citizens came to the fore again. Derrida's tension between "visitation" and "residence" found its most extreme and violent manifestations in and around Paris. As of the second week of November 2005, the reaction to years of discrimination, suppression, and negligence had spread out of Paris to other cities in France. Similar reactions were reported in German cities such as Berlin and Cologne. Contrary to the statement of the spokesperson for the German government—"we do not have Parisian conditions here"—the isolated but powerful incidents in these cities duplicated the violence of

Paris.[7] Meanwhile Orhan Pamuk, who in his acceptance speech for the German Peace Prize had declared the impossibility of a Europe without Turkey, was indicted in his own country for treason. His dissidence against the Turkish nation, registered recently in his insistence that the Turkish nation acknowledge the Armenian genocide in Turkey, was threatened with a reward of up to three years in jail. The case was dropped, but it was a significant reminder that the dissident Others of the nation would be threatened with exclusion and prevented from receiving any hospitable treatment from the project of the nation.

In these times of exclusion and lack of congregation, contrary to the pronouncements of the German diplomat, this book is about sustaining critique—of the state, the nation, the language, the community, and the ethnicity—while showing solidarity. It arises out of the necessity to chart the claims of the so-called Others with "self-evident differences" who have crossed ethnic and linguistic boundaries and are shaping and informing the cultures and civilizational values of Europe through the power of critique. Writing this book has been an exercise in explaining the difficulty and complications of a cosmopolitan conversation at the turn of our century, in which embassies and immigration counters at airports controlled the hopes and aspirations of millions of people around the world. We live in a world where, as Faiz writes, "we ask every stranger the whereabouts of our last home." In trying to imagine this world and my world through various literary addresses, I have learned one thing. From the media to scholarly discourse, there seems to be an emphasis to move beyond "self-evident differences." In searching for a cosmopolitan conversation, I am all for moving beyond the exploitation of self-evident differences. However, cosmopolitical claims cannot be registered without accounting for selves that evidence differences, evidences that differentiate selves, and differences that evidence selves.

NOTES

INTRODUCTION

1. I write "returned" because the optimism of negotiating imagined frontiers forms an integral part of Rushdie's *Imaginary Homelands: Essays and Criticism, 1981–1991*. I detect a very different tone in *Step across This Line* (2003), also a collection of Rushdie's nonfiction writings. The pervasiveness of ideological and cultural divisions in international politics gives Rushdie's later writings a distinctly somber, if not entirely pessimistic, view of boundaries and frontiers.

2. Unless specified, all references to Germany before the reunification in 1990 refer to the former Federal Republic of Germany (West Germany).

3. See Saskia Sassen, "Immigration Policy in a Global Economy," *SAIS Review* (Summer/Fall 1997): 1–19; Yasemin Soysal, *Limits of Citizenship* (Chicago: U of Chicago P, 1994); David Harrocks and Eva Kolinsky, *Turkish Culture in German Society Today* (Providence: Berghahn, 1996).

4. For recent discussions see Harald Weinrich, "Chamisso, Chamisso Authors, and Globalization," *PMLA* 119 (2004): 1339–46, and Irmgard Ackermann, "Der Chamisso-Preis und der Literaturkanon," in *Die andere deutsche Literatur. Istanbuler Vorträge*, ed. Manfred Durzak and Nilüfer Kuruyazıcı, 47–51 (Würzburg: Königshausen and Neumann, 2004).

5. Sten Nadolny, *Selim oder Die Gabe der Rede* (München: Piper, 1990). For a discussion of this novel, see Chapter 1. For a discussion of Özdamar, see Chapter 2; Zaimoğlu, Chapter 3.

6. For a discussion of Pamuk, see Chapter 4.

7. For discussions of Turkish entry into the European Union see Erik Jan Zürcher, *The European Union, Turkey and Islam*.

8. All translations from German into English are mine, unless otherwise specified.

9. Benhabib credits Derrida for the word *iteration*: "no originary source or meaning, or an original to which all subsequent forms must conform" (*Rights* 179).

10. In Chapter 4, I perform the same task in reference to Turkey with a discussion of an essay, "New Life and New Values" (1913), by the Turkish sociologist, writer, and poet Ziya Gökalp (1876–1924).

11. In the German academy, recognition of literature by non-German authors is at first formulated in terms of the oppositional, rebellious potential of *Gastarbeiterliteratur*. German scholars' early engagement emphasizes the role of this literature as a platform against discrimination and marginalization, as a forum to give voice to the otherwise silenced guest workers. Helmut Koch, for example, writes, "Die '*Gastarbeiterliteratur*' ist per definitionem eine rebellische" (Potratz

4). Irmgard Ackermann and Harald Weinrich (1986) and Hans-Dieter Grünefeld emphasize the aspiration of authors to register and resist the social marginalization of the *Gastarbeiter*. However, scholarship on *Gastarbeiterliteratur* soon acknowledges that this literature, with its beginnings on the margins, was slowly changing into a direct address to the nation's mainstream and that it had moved beyond only depicting discrimination, isolation, and strife within and outside of the workspace. See Irmgard Ackermann and Harald Weinrich, eds., *Eine nicht nur deutsche Literatur*; Horst Hamm, *Fremdgegangen Freigeschrieben*; Wolfgang Riemann, *Das Deutschlandbild in der modernen türkischen Literatur*; Monika Frederking, *Schreiben gegen Vorurteile*; *Zeitschrift für Literaturwissenschaft und Linguistik* 14. Jahrgang (1984), Heft 56; Hans Grünefeld, "Literatur und Arbeitsmigration. Probleme Literaturwissenschaftlicher Gegenstands- und Begriffsbestimmung in Ausländer oder Gastarbeiterliteratur? Geschichte und Aktuelle Situation einer neuen Literatur in Deutschland"; Marianne Krüger Potratz, ed., *Schreibend einen Ort suchen—: Gastarbeiterliteratur, Lesungen, Information: Wintersemester 1985–86*.

12. In light of the fact that most non-German ethnic authors publishing in German were not themselves *Gastarbeiter*, the term *Ausländerliteratur* (literature of foreigners) gains currency. In a stark refutation of this term, Heidrun Suhr captures the contradictions of these two literary categories in her essay "Ausländerliteratur: Minority Literature in the Federal Republic of Germany." While commenting on the publications of Südwind, she confirms that even though it was expected that workers would contribute to the anthologies, "following the assumption that the social group that experiences societal conflicts is also best able to comment on them and to suggest solutions, most foreign authors were not guest-workers" (Suhr 81). Suhr identifies the condescending neutrality conveyed by the term *Ausländerliteratur*, which reduces the literary works of these authors to little emblems of cultural pluralism. Her analysis has recently been extended in Rita Chin's illuminating study of the reciprocity between the processes of policy making and literary critical scholarship. Chin affirms: "*Gastarbeiterliteratur* emerged at the same time as the category of *guest worker* underwent fundamental redefinition" (45, original emphasis). Independent of the later debates on the term *Gastarbeiterliteratur* in Germany and the United States, the initial Turkish reception of literature by Turkish emigrants emulates German terms: *Dış göçün türk yazın* (emigrant writings in Turkish) and *gürbet yazın* (foreign writings), written by *Alman Türkler* (German Turks) about *yaban işçileri* (foreign guest workers). See Gitmez, "Türk Yazınında Dış Göç."

13. One of the first usages of this term can be traced to the conference at the Evangelische Akademie Iserlohn in 1985; it gained currency by being included in a reader for *Interkulturelle Erziehung und Kommunikation/Ausländerpädagogik* at

the Westfälischen Wilhelms-Universität in Münster compiled in 1985. Despite the admonition against strict categorization, both from authors and from scholars like Grünefeld, the conference papers reveal an extended exercise in dogmatizing literary categories. Instead of a rigorous engagement with the narratives, the conference proceedings demonstrate discussions on themes and motives, as well as style and plot, with some of the studies explicitly expressing their affiliation to applied linguistics and sociolinguistics. The effort to bridge the aesthetic with the political appears at best as sidelined. A methodologically confused scholarship shuttles between literary history and literary sociology (*Literatursoziologie*), thus becoming entrapped in its own dialectic of exclusion due to a benevolent neglect of the text. On the one hand, Turkish-German writings become sites of cultural identity construction, communicating the propensity of mainstream German culture to move toward a multiculture, but on the other hand, they parallel the development of the subdiscipline of German as a foreign language (*DaF*) in the 1980s. The promotion of a new, in-between culture through contact and transfer of two different cultures takes precedence in a number of scholarly works. The project found its intellectual basis in literary hermeneutics as proposed by Hans Georg Gadamer. Proceedings of the major conferences of the Gesellschaft der Interkulturellen Germanistik can be found in *Perspektiven und Verfahren interkultureller Germanistik*, ed. Alois Wierlacher, and *Blickwinkel*, ed. Alois Wierlacher. See also Bernd Thum and Genthies-Louise Fink, *Praxis interkultureller Germanistik*. Peter Zimmerman and his colleagues critique the essentialization of the project of *interkulturelle Germanistik* in *Interkulturelle Germanistik. Dialog der Kulturen auf Deutsch?* ed. Peter Zimmerman. Leslie Adelson, in her article on Sten Nadolny's *Selim oder Die Gabe der Rede* ("Opposing Oppositions"), points out the flaws in the strategies developed by *interkulturelle Germanistik*. She privileges, instead, a deconstructive model of cultural studies that acknowledges cultures as projects that are always in the state of being. Adelson was confronted by Ülker Gökberk in her rebuttal, "Culture Studies und die Türken." I will be commenting on this debate in Chapter 1. Karl Esselborn has commented on the dominance of the "intercultural" mode of thinking in his article "Deutschsprachige Minderheitenliteraturen."

14. See Kuruyazıcı, "Warum Grenzüberschreitungen?" (*Die Andere Deutsche Literatur* 7–9). See also McGowan, "Brücken und Brücken-Köpfe" (ibid. 31–40).

15. One of the highlights of the *NGC* special issue lies in the critical reexamination of literary terminology. See Suhr, "Ausländerliteratur" 71–103, and Teraoka, "Talking 'Turk'" 104–28. Suhr discusses the fact that writers of Gastarbeiterliteratur were not guest workers. Teraoka focuses on the act of naming the Other in order to then theorize about the Other. It is in this spirit that Teraoka emphasizes the modes through which the minority Other transports his or her own idiom to the language of the majority (self)—one that encourages the self to "suspend its

own sure beliefs that it can even begin to listen carefully to what the Other is saying" (128).

16. For another discussion of Deleuze and Guattari see Seyhan (*Writing Outside* 23–30).

17. Benhabib decries debates in cognitive and moral relativism that have accentuated the "we" and "they," the "West and its others," which have "turned on a holistic view of cultures and societies as internally coherent, seamless wholes" (Benhabib 25), but she does not decry intercultural dialogue itself as a propagator of cultures as seamless wholes. In fact, Benhabib's pointed criticism of Gadamer's *Horizontverschmelzung* is part of her critique of cultural relativism (Benhabib 34–35).

18. By emphasizing the changeability of culture, I do not immediately imply that culture is an entrapment and, therefore, necessitates emancipation. I discuss this point in greater detail in Chapters 3 and 4 with reference to Pheng Cheah's essay "Given Culture."

19. Huyssen makes these observations prior to his discussion of memory of the Holocaust in the Turkish-German writer Zafer Şenocak's novel *Gefährliche Verwandschaften* (Perilous Kinship). Huyssen specifically criticizes Yasemin N. Soysal's imagination of the diaspora as "an extension of the nation-state model" ("Diaspora" 150). Soysal's conceptualization of "postnational citizenship" has also been criticized by Leslie Adelson (*Turkish Turn* 8–9). See Soysal, "Citizenship and Identity: Living in Diaspora in Postwar Europe" in Hedetoft and Hjort, eds., *The Postnational Self* (137–151).

20. In their discussion of Kant, Robert Fine and Robin Cohen observe, "The cosmopolitan idea was no more than a recognition of the fact that 'the peoples of the earth have entered in varying degrees into a universal community and it has developed to the point where a violation of rights in one part of the world is felt elsewhere.'" See Fine and Cohen, "Four Cosmopolitan Moments," in Steven Vertovec and Robin Cohen, *Conceiving Cosmopolitanism*.

21. For a discussion of Universalism and Ethnocentrism see Benhabib, *Claims* (24–48). For a specific discussion on Kant's Cosmopolitan Right see Benhabib, *Rights* (25–48).

22. Spivak defines the native informant "as a name for that mark of Expulsion from the name of Man—a mark crossing out the impossibility of ethical relation" in texts by Kant, Hegel, and Marx (*Critique* 6). I discuss the figure of the native informant again in Chapter 1.

23. I stand in complete agreement here with Adelson's admonishment against loose borrowing of terms from postcolonial theory to describe the position of Turks in Germany. This kind of loose borrowing establishes an oppressor–oppressed binary between the Turks and Germans that is *unreflectively* imagined in terms of

the European self as a colonizing power and the non-European as the colonized or postcolonial Other. This arises both from the jump from the minor to the minority, and from what Lawrence Grossberg aptly diagnoses as "the dominant deployment of Said . . . to establish a simple chain from colonialism to the construction of cultural identities to the production of subjects, and sometimes, the 'discovery of resistance'" (Grossberg 96). Indeed this kind of authentication of the Other has led to the establishment of the immigrant author as the "local informant," as Aijaz Ahmad observes in "Languages of Class" (in *In Theory*). In the case of authors from ex-colonies residing in metropolitan locations of the West, the author either becomes or aspires to become the sole informant of the country of birth—in some cases the ex-colony—or in curious ways is established as the only reliable critical authority on the cultures of the homeland. In the specific case of immigrants in Germany, the immigrant becomes the sole informant of the country of birth, or at most, the spokesperson for the immigrant collectivity. This unsophisticated embracing of postcolonial theory is best illustrated in Lubrich and Clark's article "German Studies Go Postcolonial" (625–34). The authors identify postcolonial studies as a field that attempts to "re-value texts, artistic representations, and all other kinds of voices from the former colonies, from international migrants and from cultural minorities" ("German Studies" 629). In relating this predicament to German studies, they quickly note, "the most prominent literary figures in contemporary Germany [are] of Turkish background (Feridun Zaimoğlu, Emine Sevgi Özdamar)" ("German Studies" 630).

24. It is a fact that despite the absence of colonies, and long before it became a unified nation, Germany had a continuing intellectual engagement with the non-West. This fact necessitates keeping in mind that Germany's lack of self-realization as a colonial power and its late self-assertion as a national collective distinguishes the discourse of cultural Other in Germany from that in Great Britain and France. Germany did not have the extended opportunity to define itself with and against its colonies, as was the case for Great Britain and France. The change in the political organization of the world after the Second World War created a peculiar situation for Germany. The immigrants arrived when the German national collective self was already ideologically bifurcated. Moreover, while the first wave of immigrants to Britain and France came from their former colonies, Germany's new immigrants came from Italy, Spain, the former Yugoslavia, Greece, and Turkey. Cf. Spivak, *Critique* 6–7; see also Mani, "The Self of the Other."

1. THUS SPAKE THE *GASTARBEITER*

1. Cf. Picardi-Montesardo 3–10.
2. Reconstructed from Jung et. al 50–73.

3. "One has summoned forces of labor, human beings are coming." English translation by Leslie Adelson (*Turkish Turn* 124). Frisch's statement is cited frequently, even now, in numerous scholarly works on immigrants in Germany. Adelson rightly criticizes the sentimental invocation of this statement, which is not my intention. I consider Frisch's text an extremely timely observation on the questions of national identity, on the role of Switzerland, on the position of foreign workers in Switzerland, and on the issues of a larger European political and social community.

4. At the end of the 1960s, poetry and prose writing competitions were organized by a Christian missionary for members of the Italian community. In 1974, A. Pesciaioli, an Italian electrician, founded ALFA (Associazione Letteria Facolta Artistiche). In 1975, the bilingual magazine *Incontri* was founded, and in 1976 FISC (Federazione Italiana Sport e Cultura). Finally, in 1983, the missionary newspaper *Corriera d'Italia* was founded. A detailed account of the Italian writers can be found in Ackermann and Weinrich, *Eine nicht nur deutsche Literatur*. See also Frederking, *Schreiben gegen Vorurteile*.

5. Translation into English by Leslie Adelson (*Turkish Turn* 27).

6. To summarize the novel very briefly: during the years of Adenauer's economic miracle, a German student, Alexander, on his way to the military service, meets a few Turkish guest workers on a train, including Selim. A few years later, in the politically turbulent Berlin of the 1960s, Alexander, now disenchanted by the students' movement, develops a close friendship with Selim. Alexander is struggling to become a good orator; Selim has the gift of gab. Alexander is planning to start a school of communication; Selim would be satisfied if he could own a small pub. Years later, Selim kills a pimp while trying to rescue a friend's daughter from a brothel in Hamburg. He is arrested and sentenced to jail, and Alexander decides to write a novel about him. Throughout the novel, Alexander wonders in numerous vignettes if he will succeed in doing justice to Selim's character, if he is creating his own Selim as he writes; most importantly, will Selim read his novel? Meanwhile Selim is deported to Turkey and gradually the two friends lose contact. Once, Dirk, one of Selim's children in Germany, visits Alexander, who is now a financially successful speech writer and communication expert. They both try to get Selim's address from his friends in Berlin but do not succeed. Alexander decides to go Turkey in order to find Selim. His search is unsuccessful, and in the end he creates a phantasmagoric tale about meeting with Selim and about his final journey to Germany.

7. See Traub, "Ein türkischer Winnetou." See also Weinbörner, "Vom Türken und Deutschen"; Rüb, "Verliere den Faden"; Führer, "Den Geist des Romans aufs."

8. With Edward Said's *Orientalism* providing the theoretical underpinnings

for her reading, Sabine von Dirke asks, "does the novel aim at containment of Otherness, or does it promote difference and the idea of multiculturalism?" (von Dirke 62). She inquires whether Nadolny is still trapped in oppressive practices toward the foreigner as a minority that exclude this foreign Other from the discourse and allow the Other to return only as "image, spectacle, false representation?" (ibid.). She scrutinizes Nadolny's novel for a *true* representation of the foreigner, one that is presumably emancipated from oppressive narrative strategies like condescending exoticism, on the one hand, and xenophobia on the other. To do so she collects textual evidence to prove that Nadolny's ideas about Selim are "fraught with clichés based on underlying cultural stereotypes of Orient and Occident" (ibid.).

Leslie Adelson, in her extremely insightful reading of *Selim*, suggests that Nadolny is indeed able to deconstruct the difference between the Occident and the Orient, the self and the Other. She indicates the complex processes that underlie the construction of cultural identities, whether they are Turkish or German. She tries to overcome the polarization between the (cultural-insider) author's and the (cultural-outsider) reader's "supposed exchange of meaning" ("Opposing Oppositions" 306) propagated by a hermeneutics-inspired *interkulturelle Germanistik*. Adelson is invested in Bhabha's notion of fluidity of the self and the Other in any cultural location, which manifests itself through a textual and/or societal performance. Unlike von Dirke, for whom Turkish and German identities somehow exist in a permanent binary, Adelson uses Bhabha's concept of hybridity to refute singularizing notions of ethnic identities. Her case in point is the creation of Turkish national identity under Atatürk, which she eloquently phrases as "a performative orientation towards Europe" (ibid. 309), evidence of a sociotextual performance ushered in by a change in the state structure. Adelson argues, and I agree, that a productive reading of texts by Turkish-German authors or texts by German authors about the Turks in Germany can result from juxtaposing the complexity of twentieth-century historical narratives of the two nations. This would provide a methodological alternative to critical positions that essentialize Turkish and German identities on the basis of ethnic difference. Nadolny's novel, which attempts to escape this essentialization, is thus for Adelson a path-breaking intervention.

Three years after the publication of Adelson's article, Ülker Gökberk published a response. Gökberk presents the interest in multicultural texts within German studies in the United States as a symptom of ideological as well as paradigmatic concerns, the latter arising from a crisis in German studies and out of the individual professional concerns of U.S. Germanists (Gökberk 98). She believes that such concerns—and the publish-or-perish paradigm of American universities—have led to the lack of a self-reflective dimension on the part of the scholar. I partially agree with Gökberk's observation. Because the immediate purpose of this chapter is not a critique of the profession of German studies, I will concentrate on another crucial point Gökberk makes: she is right in pointing out that in the criticism or valorization of the voice of the Other through a hegemonic intervention, critique is conflated with historical reconstruction, thus aiming again at some search for truth. She makes a stronger case for discussions of majority issues in collaboration with the minority issues, and not in isolation. Nonetheless, in an attempt to valorize Nadolny's allegedly hegemonic participation, she inadvertently establishes another truth-claim: that of the secularized political history of Turkey under Atatürk.

9. For a discussion of Whiskey Sisodia in Rushdie's *Satanic Verses* see Walkowitz, *Cosmopolitan Style* 131–32.

10. Therefore, instead of choosing "Third Worldist" texts to assess the voice of the native informant, she attempts to discover the figure of the native informant in the interstices of the muddy mainstream of Western philosophy: Kant, Hegel, and Marx. Spivak lays bare Kant's proposition of the Aborigine's inaccessibility to culture and accounts for the absence of the Aborigine/the Primitive from the concept of the Sublime (7–37). She reconstructs Hegel's account of the unconscious Other of the *Bhagwad Gita* and exposes the timelessness of that Other for a contemporary reader (37–67). With her critique of Marx's "Asiatic Mode of Production," she uncovers the surplus, the excess, the Ex(Orbitant) positioning of the native informant (67–111). Spivak's text thus demonstrates the complicity of a textual tradition that "non-obviously" forecloses the aboriginal, the primitive, the colonial, and then the native informant.

11. Within the standard narration there are instances when one or the other character challenges Alexander's investment in writing. Niyazi, for example, dislikes writing, for he thinks that "am Geschriebenen siehst du ja nicht einmal, wer spricht, Mann oder Frau!" (*Selim* 63). Alexander agrees with him.

12. For a discussion on the relationship between stereotypes, prejudice, and national characters in the European context see Walas, *Stereotypes and Nations*.

13. "We are so busy battling stereotypes in the description of Others that we end up refusing these Others any specificity at all. It is true that 'the Orient' is far too broad a category, including as it does both Syria and Japan; it is also true that the very existence of such a category teaches us a great deal about the obsessions of scholars and world travelers. But this does not mean that there is no such thing as a Japanese culture or Near-Eastern traditions—or that this culture and these traditions are impossible to describe. Do past attempts at describing them tell us about *nothing* except the observer's prejudices, or do they transmit, despite these prejudices, something of the societies observed?" (Todorov, "Race and Culture" 373f.)

14. Against von Dirke's reading, I would argue that Nadolny does not present Selim as the authorized spokesperson for "Turkish rhetoric," of a "representative" Eastern style of speech; even if one accepts the crass distinction of an emotional/anecdotal Eastern speech and a rational/factual Western speech, both Turkish and German characters defy this. Selim's uninhibited oral articulation, bereft of facts and figures, is not something that one finds in Mevlut, another guest worker, who is always ready to impress people with a generous inclusion of facts in his speech (*Selim* 21). Also different from Selim is Mesut, a very practical man with an apparently bright future. He hates Selim for his naïve, baby-like way of looking at things. Neither Mevlut nor Mesut exhibits effective speech. It is Selim whose oratory revolutionizes Alexander's established conception of good speech, which is why Alexander considers him a "natural teacher of rhetoric." Secondly, all the Turkish guest workers in the novel are very aware of the prejudices of the Germans and vocalize them at various instances.

15. On the cultural heritages of cities in the Ottoman Empire and after the Revolution, see Ergin, *Türkiye'de Şehirciliğin Tarihi Inkısafı*, and Ergin, *Türk Belediyeçilik ve Şehiçilik Tarihi Üzerine Seçmeler*.

16. There are other instances in the novel that I would like to address before I turn to the discourse of artistic representation. To continue on the cryptic Turkish-Greek heritage, Leslie Adelson remarks that Nadolny, in his declaration of the Greco-Roman wrestler, privileges the westernized Turk over Mevlut, a practicing, religious Muslim. Gökberk debates this point by emphasizing that the Westernization and secularization of Turkey was the only solution to the undemocratic coalition between religion and politics during the Ottoman Empire. The two scholars also disagree on the correct rendition of Turkish history. Adelson privileges the historian Sarif Mardin, for he pays due attention to the complexities involved in the top-down secularization, a performative orientation toward the West. Gökberk suggests the historical-sociological perspective of Niyazi Berkes to be a more reliable account. The matter has been exhausted in the debate already, but I do think that both of these scholars, in the context of Nadolny's *Selim*, stop short of mentioning or discussing the millet system of governing a multiethnic/multination empire. Ottoman minorities formed millets, or little self-governing units of their own, and had to pay certain taxes but had fairly well-protected rights that provided them the power to protect their heritage. Millets, which come from the Arabic word *milla*, meaning religion, were introduced to protect the rights of religious minorities. The word *Turk*, which became the name for all the peasants living in eastern Turkey, was deliberately embraced by Atatürk to designate post-1923 Turkish nationality. It brought along a homogenization of members of various little nation-states who were living in mainland Turkey. In a move from Pericles to Selim via Hitler and Churchill, these historical factors cannot be

dismissed. They do get neglected in the process of clearly demarcating the Other, presenting it as the product of a singular cultural heritage. For a discussion of the millet system and multiculturalism see Rodrigue, interview with Nancy Reynolds.

17. See Anatassiadou, "Sports d'élite au tournant du siècle." For the history of wrestling in Turkey, see Tekin, "Hatay'da Aba Güreşi Üzerine" and Sertoğlu, *Rümeli Türk Pehilvanları*.

18. See Appadurai, *Modernity at Large*.

19. Picardi-Montesardo, *Gastarbeiter in Literatur*.

20. The five lectures in the series Das Erzählen und die guten Absichten were delivered in 1990, the year of *Selim*'s publication. The published collection includes a total of eleven lectures by Nadolny. *Selim* is mentioned just twice, once to refer to a Turkish friend who served as a model for the novel (*Erzählen* 65) and once to refer to the inclusion of the film *Shoah* in the novel (*Erzählen* 66), which, Nadolny admits, he later regretted. The speeches provide an insight into Nadolny's activity as a novel writer, but more importantly, they are rich theoretical reflections on narration, language, and literature.

21. For a discussion on "post-positivist Realism," see Moya and Hames-Garcia 1–28 and 29–66.

2. SLOUCHING HISTORIES, LURKING MEMORIES

1. At the core of this essay is an exploration of "identity as wound" through deliberations on the works of Assia Djebbar and Jacques Derrida. However, the complex itinerary of Spivak's argument, as usual, complicates a comfortable juxtaposition of the two authors. I do not wish to expand on this itinerary in this chapter. It is helpful to point out that this complicated itinerary is marked at the outset by the question of language: French in Algeria, English in India. Furthermore, by way of preparing her readers for the drama of identitarian assertion in front of the audience in West Bengal (origin), and her non-Bengali, non-Indian readers elsewhere, Spivak strategically pauses on two languages that signify originary high cultures: Latin and Sanskrit. Spivak refutes the idea of etymology as an instrument of comparability and compatibility of cultures—their "identity in difference," so to speak—as she demonstrates the dissimilarities between the Latin word *idem* and the Sanskrit *idam* as signifiers of identity. In addition, while setting the stage for her self-identification, her "Acting Bits" of "Identity-Talk" in Calcutta, Spivak points out how she is hailed as "the daughter of Bengal" by a newspaper published in Calcutta, her non-Indian surname, Spivak, conveniently dropped.

2. As Spivak reports, Hassan inscribes lines from the novel onto photographs of children who "lost their country in 1948." For reproductions of Hassan's work see Spivak, "Acting Bits" 160–64.

3. Huyssen translates the title as "Dangerous Kinship" or "Dangerous Affini-

ties," noting that the novel invokes "literary memories of titles such as Choderlos de Laclos's *Les liaisons dangereuses* or Goethe's *Wahlverwandschaften*" ("Diaspora" 157). The title is translated in Leslie Adelson's *Turkish Turn* as "Perilous Kinship." Adelson discusses Huyssen's article at various points in *Turkish Turn*: in the introduction (11, 27), and later, prior to her discussion of Şenocak's novel (79–83) in the chapter "Genocide and Taboo" (79–122).

4. See the introduction to this book for a discussion of Seyla Benhabib's distinction between *demos* and *ethnos*.

5. Born in Malatya, Turkey, Özdamar worked in a factory in Berlin (1965–67), received formal training as an actress in Istanbul (1967–70), worked as an intern at the Volksbühne in Berlin with noted directors Benno Besson and Matthias Langhoff (1976), and then as an actress in Paris with Benno Besson (1978–79). She has acted in films: Hark Bohm's *Yasemin* (1988) and Dorris Dörrie's *Happy Birthday Türke!* (1992). She has also written plays, *Karagöz in Alamania* (1982) and *Kelgolan in Alamania* (1991).

6. The complete title of the novel is *Das Leben ist eine Karawansarei: hat zwei Türen aus einer kam ich rein aus der anderen ging ich raus*. Cf. Luise von Flotow's translation *Life is a Caravanserai: Has Two Doors I came in one I Went Out the Other*. Von Flotow's translation was published a year before Azade Seyhan's *Writing Outside the Nation*. Seyhan translates the title as "Life is a Caravansary" (*Writing Outside* 141).

7. For a discussion of this controversy see Jankowsky, "'German' Literature Contested."

8. See Jameson, "Third World Literature." For a critique of this position see Aijaz Ahmad's chapter "Jameson's Rhetoric of Otherness" (*In Theory* 95–122). Rey Chow engages with both Jameson and Ahmad in her chapter "Keeping Them in Their Place" (*Protestant Ethnic* 95–127).

9. See Westwood and Bhachu, *Enterprising Women*. See also the *Southall Black Sisters Annual Report, 1986*. For works on Turkish-German women, see note 16 of this chapter.

10. Viewing the author as a native informant was a trend prevalent in the late 1980s and early 1990s, although such scholarship filters into the first decade of the twenty-first century. On the unreflected celebration of the authentic voice in the past five or six years, see Sandten, "In Her Own Voice"; Stephens, "Immigrant Women Writers"; and Mason, "The Other Voice."

11. Two examples of mediocre collections of short stories by Indian immigrants in the United States come to mind. See Chitra Banerjee Divakaruni's two volumes, *Arranged Marriage* and *The Mistress of Spices*.

12. See for example Mira Nair's highly orientalist and obscurantist ode to Indian sexuality in her film *Kama Sutra: A Tale of Love*.

13. Two fictional works written in the United States illustrating this point are Chang-rae Lee's *Native Speaker* and Kiran Desai's *Hullabaloo in the Guava Orchard*.

14. Although Adelson refers to the literary critical scholarship on Turkish women's writings, I would like to add that a number of nonfictional studies of Turkish immigrant women also engage in this kind of "double othering." Anthropological works on Turkish women in Germany inevitably deal with the "Probleme" or the "Problematik" of these women in a culturally different milieu. See, for example, Wengemeyer and Sengör, "Problematik der Frau," and Grottian, "Probleme von Frauen aus der Türkei." A number of book-length works on Turkish-German women repeat this inadvertent condescension. See, for example, Stienen, *Leben zwischen zwei Welten*; Franger, *Wir haben es uns anders vorgestellt*; Karasan-Dirks, *Die Geschichte der Fatma Hanim*. Again, my intention is not to undermine the importance of the problems faced by immigrant women. Nonetheless, one needs to pause and question what motivation a scholar has to approach her subjects with the presumption that their world is replete with problems. On the social level, this condescending attitude manifests itself in political rhetoric, as well as in common parlance, in the form of statements like "I understand the problems of community X growing up in country Y" or in questions like "How was it growing up as a member of ethnicity X in country Y?"

15. For examples of such analyses see Zielke-Nadkarni, *Frauenfiguren*; Fischer, "Intercultural Alterity or Borderland Experience"; Wierschke, *Schreiben als Selbstbehauptung*; Veteto-Conrad, *Finding a Voice*; Fischer and McGown, *Denn du tanzt auf einem Seil*.

16. Even since the time of Atatürk's Revolution, Turkish women authors have challenged the complete rejection of the Turkish cultural heritage in favor of Westernization. Halide Edip Adivar, Atatürk's friend and confidante, had a falling out with him on this very issue. In Adivar's most famous novel, *Sinnekli Bakkal*, the female protagonist assists her father in a grocery store and with Karagöz puppet shows but is brought up in the Islamic tradition as a *Hafiz* who earns her living by reading the Qur'an and chanting religious poems. For a discussion of East-West issues in Adivar's works, see Enginün, *Halide Edip Adivar'ın Erserlerinde Doğu ve Batı Meselesi*. Since the beginnings of an organized feminist movement in Turkey in the 1960s, the women's magazine *Kadınca* has published a number of articles dealing with this debate. Women authors such as Sevgi Soysal, Pinar Kür, Adalet Agaoğlu, and Duygu Asena have represented this tension in their works. Adalet Agaoğlu's *Ölmeye Yatmak* deserves special mention, for it discusses the double repression of women both by Islamist and Kemalist regimes. The protagonist, Ayşel, waiting to die, embodies the gap between the ideal of the total sexual freedom promised by Atatürk and the reality of social rules that separate the two sexes.

17. See also two articles by Ayşe Durakbaşa: "Cumhuriyet Döneminde Kemalist Kadın Kimliğinin Olusmu" and "Kemalism as Identity Politics in Turkey."

18. See Afet Inan, *Atatürk ve Türk Kadın Haklarinin Kazanlıması*, and Kandiyoti, "Emancipated but Unliberated?"

19. Seyhan discusses code-mixing of Turkish and German. Retention of German bureaucratic vocabulary in Turkish syntax by guest workers illustrates her point (*Writing Outside* 109).

20. However, the focus of this discussion is not on reading the work as a source of objective truths about Özdamar's life. Since the work identifies itself neither as an autobiography nor a memoir—nor unlike the first two works, as a novel—it leaves the question of genre open.

21. I am borrowing from Francesca Stafford's insightful article "Else's Elsewhere." Stafford discusses aspects of Lasker-Schüler's writing to propose a "utopian chronotype" (116)—one that transforms us from one space and time to another. While Stafford's reading successfully illustrates the efficacy of her model in her reading of Lasker-Schüler, I do not intend to read *Seltsame Sterne* only through the referential framework of Lasker-Schüler.

22. See Mühl's *Weg aus dem Sumpf* and Hubert Klocker's *Wiener Aktionismus*.

23. For related discussions see Karpat, *The Basic Causes of the Failure of Democracy in Turkey*, and Akin, Barchard, et al., *The Turkish Republic at Seventy-Five Years*.

24. Elsewhere I have pursued a parallel reading of Özdamar's *Die Brücke vom Goldenen Horn* with Brecht's *Der gute Mensch von Sezuan*. See Mani, "The Good Woman of Istanbul."

25. For commentaries on these specific directors and productions see Rischbieter, *Durch den Eisernen Vorhan*. For a discussion on Benno Besson see Neubert-Herwig, *Benno Besson*.

26. Huyssen references Daniel Levy and Natan Snaider's *Erinnerung im globalen Zeitalter*.

3. AUTHENTIC HYBRID?

1. Translation of the title by Petra Fachinger, *Rewriting Germany* 109.

2. For an exhaustive list see www.complit.fu-berlin.de/gastvortraege/gastvortraege.html#SamuelFischer-Gastprofessur.

3. Tom Cheeseman, in his insightful article "Akçam-Zaimoğlu-*Kanak Attak*," writes: "In a seminar held in Mainz in December 1999 as part of the proceedings on migrant writing in German, Zaimoğlu sat at a table with Franco Biondi, Gino (Carmine) Chiellino, Alev Tekinay and other representatives of the 'old school' of 'Gastarbeiterliteratur,' and loudly condemned the entirety of their work in similar terms: 'weinerlich,' 'wehleidig,' 'anbiedernd'" (190).

4. See Ahmad, "Politics" 1–20.

5. Chow cites from Cheah's essay "Given Culture."

6. Kristeva, *Powers of Horror* 2, 4.

7. This phrase appears in the blurb accompanying the article.

8. Susanne Gaschke's enthusiasm of discovery is evident in every line. The reader gets the feeling that Gaschke herself is, for the first time, realizing how successful the Turks in Germany are. Noticeable is the fact that nowhere in the article does she use the phrase *Türkisch-Deutschen* or *Deutsche-Türken*. Turks remain just Turks living in Germany, even as she registers racist incidents against them. Remarkable about these success stories is also the sheer lack of class-consciousness of the author as well as the interviewees. These individuals are presented as successful, without any reference to the fact that they all come from educated families and a middle-class, not lower-class, social milieu with more than some access to opportunities.

9. Detlef Grumbach, "Die Liga der Verdammten" *Süddeutsche Zeitung*, 19 June 1999: 7.

10. Sylt is an island with a summer program in literature offered for the privileged—a more expensive version of the Elder Hostel program in the United States. See Ahne, "Ein Türke auf Sylt."

11. See Theil, "Russendisko."

12. See Gerk, "Abenteuer Deutschland."

13. See Zaimoğlu, "Verzweiflung ist Dynamik."

14. See Rappe, "Zwischen Goethe und Kanake." LAKS stands for Landesarbeitsgemeinschaft der Kulturinitiativen und soziokulturellen Zentren in Hessen.

15. For the German press's enthusiam for Zaimoğlu's publications see also Lottman, "Ein Wochenende in Kiel mit Feridun Zaimoğlu." See also Terkessidis, "Das Fremde, Eigene"; Assheuer, "Was heißt hier deutsch?"; and Sommer, "Der Kopf zählt." Zaimoğlu has also written columns for *Die Zeit*. See Zaimoğlu, "Über das Verhältnis zwischen Kanksta und Dschörmans" and "Knabenwindelprosa." Kanak Attack, a group of young Turkish-Germans in Germany with centers in Berlin, Hamburg, and Munich, has a manifesto that can be read on the Web site www.passagiere.de/ka/manifest/manif_dt.htm.

16. Translation by Tom Cheeseman, as cited in Adelson, *Turkish Turn* 104–22.

17. Fachinger's brief remarks on the "Burial Story" that I discussed at the beginning of this chapter include a citation from Wallraff: "Buried among the living . . . Ali is taking refuge among the dead" (*Rewriting Germany* 109).

18. Adelson's discussion of Zaimoğlu (95–104) is followed by her discussion of Zafer Şenocak's *Perilous Kinship* (104–22). Adelson's reading mobilizes references to the Holocaust in *Kanak Sprak*, thus demonstrating the "touching tales" of Turks and Germans.

19. I have decidedly not offered an English translation here to give the reader a

glimpse of the Turkish-German code-switching that happens throughout the stories. This code-switching is more frequent when Ongun converses with other Turks, but it is not limited to such situations. Ongun's self-reflective moments are also full of Turkish words and phrases, which are often preceded or followed by exact or approximate German translations. The most common Turkish phrase, "amina koyum" (fuck the cunt), is never translated.

4. TURKISH-GERMAN REATTACHMENTS

1. The charge against Pamuk accuses him of using the word *genocide*. Pamuk claims he did not use that word but just broke the official taboo on state-orchestrated violence in Turkey. Pamuk has reiterated this clarification, even though he stands by his words. See Browning and Brand, "Orhan Pamuk, Turkey's controversial Faulkner."

2. See also Sakcur, "Hardtalk in Tukey: Orhan Pamuk."

3. The speech was delivered in Turkish. For a text of the entire speech in German translation see Pamuk, "*Friedenspreis* Acceptance Speech."

4. With seven novels published since 1983, Orhan Pamuk is regarded as Turkey's most prolific novelist. Pamuk has been received in Turkey as the most celebrated, most read, and—politically—most vocal author. He has received many international literary awards, although he has refused to accept the state award offered to him in 2001. Within four months of its publication in Turkish, 136,000 copies of the novel *Yeni Hayat* had been sold, a phenomenon for the Turkish market. Yet, as a novel, it was not as enthusiastically received by critics and scholars in Turkey as his earlier novels *Beyaz Kale* (White Castle) and *Kara Kitap* (Black Book) or his later works *Benim Adım Kırmızı* (My Name Is Red) and *Kar* (Snow). For scholarly discussions of selected novels see Esen, "Orhan Pamuk'un"; Akkoyun, "Değişik Metinler Kavşağında Bir Roman"; Sahin, "Türk Edebiyatında Modernizm-Postmodernizm Tartışmasının İlk Örneği"; Güneli Gün, "The Turks Are Coming." Pamuk was first profiled in *World Literature Today* in 2005; the November–December 2006 special issue will be on Orhan Pamuk.

5. See Thomas, "Crash."

6. The publishing house is called Babiali Publishers, a clear reference to the hero of "Ali Baba and the Forty Thieves" in the Arabic classic *Alif Laila va Laila* (Thousand and One Nights).

7. The word *Ottoman* in this particular sentence refers to the imperial culture of the Sultans. During the Ottoman Empire, the term *Turk* was used by the landed bourgeoisie and the nobility as a term for a peasant from Anatolia. One of the major goals of the Revolution was to redeem the word and give it a sense of pride. Mustafa Kemal Pasha thus came to be known as Atatürk: father of the Turks. Gökalp, in his essay, uses the term *Ottoman* as a synonym for the Muslims in the Ottoman Empire.

8. I will not be providing an elaborate discussion on the plethora of texts on Turkish nationalism written in the last eighty years or so. I will, therefore, focus on only one short essay by Ziya Gökalp, "Yeni Hayat ve Yeni Kıymatlar" (New Life and New Values), also published in Latin script as *Yeni Hayat; Doğru Yol*. For English translations of Gökalp's works see the bibliography to this volume. Gökalp's writings have been the subject of many critical works both in Turkish and English. For a comprehensive bibliography in Turkish see Binrak and Sefercioğlu, *Ziya Gökalp Bibliographyası*. Representative bibliographies include Gökseri, *Ziya Gökalp*, and Hakki Baltacıoğlu, *Ziya Gökalp*. Istanbul University's *Journal of Sociology* has two special issues on Gökalp. See *İstanbul Üniversitesi İktisat Fakültesi. Sosyologi Konferansları* 5 (1965) and 14 (1976). For works in English see Parla, *The Social and Political Thought of Ziya Gökalp*. I have recently learned about an MA thesis that discusses Gökalp and Pamuk, but I had not been able to access it at the time of publication of the manuscript. See Erginel, "Reconsidering Turkish Nationalism."

9. See, for example, Gökalp's essay "Culture and Civilization."

10. For a discussion on the millet system and its effects on the multiethnic/multinational composition of the Ottoman Empire, see Rodrigue, "Difference and Tolerance." For a discussion on secularism in modern Turkey see Sözer, "Laiklik ve Sekülarizm Hakkında Bazı Görüşler ve Düşünceler."

11. See Erinç, "Kültür de Kültür."

12. The Arabic word *hafiz* means scribe, but also protector. In the absence of printing technology, the copiers were thus the protectors of manuscripts.

13. See Arkoun, *Rethinking Islam*.

14. For an insightful discussion see Asad, *Genealogies of Religion*.

15. See www.alevism.net/repressions.html.

16. I was unable to trace the translation from which Pamuk cites Novalis in his novel. It could well be that Pamuk's citation from the Turkish translation of *Ofterdingen* was translated back into English. All English citations from Novalis are from *Henry von Ofterdingen*, translated by Palmer Hilty.

17. Meral Ozan has discussed introspection and romanticism in an intercultural context in his article "Der Weg nach Innen."

18. *Partial* support for this speculation comes from David Damrosch's discussion of world literatures as "elliptical refraction of national literatures" (*What Is World Literature* 281–86). Refuting René Wellek's formulation "the foreign trade of literature," Damrosch explains "elliptical refraction" as one that "doesn't lead to a transcendent universalism in which cultural difference is a mere 'heresy'" (284). While this particular formulation is useful to understand my discussion of Novalis in Pamuk, I am ambivalent about another explanation of "refraction" that Damrosch provides in a passage prior to the one I have cited. Explaining the "double" nature of refraction, Damrosch writes, "works become world literature by

being received into the space of foreign culture, a space defined in many ways by the host nation's national tradition and the present need of its own writers" (283). Since the entire discussion in this chapter accords centrality to the dubiousness of a national tradition, "elliptical refraction" reaches its limits once any national tradition is perceived as undifferentiated and in singularity. I cannot speculate on the source of the chasm between Damrosch's positive evaluation of difference and what he later phrases as the singularity of "a national tradition" and the "needs of its own writers."

AFTERWORD

1. Translation mine. For another translation, "On My Return from Dhaka," see Agha Shahid Ali, *The Rebel's Silhouette: Faiz Ahmed Faiz*, 86–87 (Salt Lake City: Peregrine Smith Books, 1991). Ali has translated this couplet as follows: "After those many encounters, that easy intimacy, we are strangers now—/After how many meetings will we be that close again." I do not see the need to elaborate on the Urdu word *Madaratein* with encounters and easy intimacy. In addition, I have tried to retain the structure of the Sher—the couplet—as well as the end of the couplet, the importance of which Ali explains in the preface to the collection.

2. An MLA bibliographical search with key words *identity, representation,* and *critique* gives access to at least 200 works, a number of which have the words *crisis* or *stereotype* somewhere in their subtitles. Similarly, the words *Orientalism* or *Orientalist* give about 400 results, a number of which try to demonstrate Orientalism in this or that author. In Henry Louis Gates Jr.'s *"Race," Writing, and Difference*, a number of participants investigate the Orientalist/racist perspectives on writings on the non-West. For a detailed critique see Arnold Krupat, *Ethnocriticism* (Berkeley: U of California P, 1992).

3. The other disadvantage is the containment of the "ethnic canon" on the margins. See for example David Palambo-Liu, ed., *The Ethnic Canon: Histories Institutions and Interventions* 1–30 (Minneapolis: U of Minnesota P, 1995).

4. See www.dictionary.oed.com.

5. Translation by Leslie Adeslon (*Turkish Turn* 124).

6. For a detailed account of developing violence and related stories, see www.lemonde.fr/web/module_chrono/0,11-0@2-3226,32-705641@51-704172,0.html.

7. See www.lemonde.fr/web/article/0,1-0@2-706693,36-709030@51-704172,0.html.

8. See www.spiegel.de/politik/deutschland/0,1518,383949,00.html.

BIBLIOGRAPHY

Ackermann, Irmgard. "Der Chamisso-Preis und der Literaturkanon." In *Die andere deutsche Literatur. Istanbuler Vorträge*, edited by Manfred Durzak and Nilüfer Kuruyazici, 47–51. Würzburg: Königshausen and Neumann, 2004.

Ackermann, Irmgard, and Harald Weinrich. *Eine nicht nur deutsche Literatur*. Munich: Piper, 1986.

Adelson, Leslie A. "Migrants' Literature or German Literature? TORKAN's Tufan. Brief an einen islamischen Brüder." *German Quarterly* 63 (1990): 382–89.

———. "Migrants and Muses." In *A New History of German Literature*, edited by David E. Wellbery and Judith Ryan, 912–17. Cambridge, MA: Harvard UP, 2004.

——— "Opposing Oppositions: Turkish German Questions in Contemporary German Studies." *German Studies Review* 17 (1994): 305–30.

———. "The Price of Feminism: Of Women and Turks." In *Gender and Germanness: Cultural Productions of Nation*, edited by Patricia Herminghouse and Magda Mueller, 305–19. New York: Berghahn Books, 1997.

———. "Response to Ülker Gökberk." *The German Quarterly* 70 (1997): 277–82.

———. *The Turkish Turn in Contemporary German Literature: Toward a New Critical Grammar of Migration*. New York: Palgrave Macmillan, 2005.

Adivar, Halide Edip. *Sinekli Bakkal*. 43rd edition. Istanbul: Atlas Kitabevi, 1989.

Adorno, Theodor W. "On the Question: What is German?" Translated by Thomas Y. Levin. *Theory, Culture, and Society* 2 (1985): 121–31.

Afet Inan, Ayşe. *Atatürk ve Türk Kadin Haklarının Kazanılması*. Istanbul: Milli Egitim Basimevi, 1966.

Agaoğlu, Adalet. *Ölmeye Yatmak*. Istanbul: Remzi Kitabevi, 1973.

———. *Die zarte Rose meiner Sehnsucht*. Stuttgart: Ararat, 1979.

Ahmad, Aijaz. *In Theory: Classes, Nations, Literatures*. London: Verso, 1994.

———. "The Politics of Literary Postcoloniality." *Race and Class* 36(1995): 1–20.

Ahne, Petra. "Ein Türke auf Sylt." *Berliner Tageszeitung* (4 November 2003): 3.

Akbulut, Nazire. *Das Türkenbild in der neueren Deutschen Literatur, 1970–1990*. Berlin: Köster, 1993.

Akçam, Dursun. *Alman ocağı: Türkler almanları anlatıyor = Deutsches Heim— Glück allein: Wie Türken Deutsche sehen*. Bornheim-Merten: Lamuv, 1982.

Akin, Sina, et al., eds. *The Turkish Republic at Seventy-Five Years*. Huntingdon, UK: The Eothen Press, 1999.

Akkoyun, Tülay "Değişik Metinler Kavsağında Bir Roman: Orhan Pamuk'un Kara Kitap'I." *Frankofoni* 14 (2002): 145–50.

Anatassiadou, Meropi. "Sports d'élite et élites sportives a salonique au tournant du siècle." In *Vivre dans l'empire Ottoman: sociabilités et relations intercommunautaires (XVIIe–XXe siècles)*, edited by François Georgeon and Paul Dumont, 143–60. Paris: Editions L' Harmattan, 1997.

And, Metin. *Cumhuriyet Dönemi Türk Tiyatrosu (1923–1983)*. Ankara: Türkiye Is Bankasi Kültür Yayinlari, 1983.

———. *A History of Theatre and Popular Entertainment in Turkey*. Ankara: Forum Yayinlari, 1963.

Anderson, Amanda. *The Powers of Distance: Cosmopolitanism and the Cultivation of Detachment*. Princeton: Princeton UP, 2001.

Anderson, Benedict. *Imagined Communities: Reflections on the Origin and Spread of Nationalism*. London: Verso, 1991.

Andrews, Walter G. "The Black Book and Black Boxes: Orhan Pamuk's *Kara Kitap*." *Edebiyât: The Journal of Middle Eastern Literatures* 11 (2000): 105–29.

———. "Contested Mysteries and Mingled Dreams Speaking for Ottoman Culture Today: From Gencebay to Pamuk." In *Cultural Horizons/Kültür Ufukları*, edited by Jayne L. Warner, 518–37. Syracuse, NY: Syracuse UP, 2001.

Anzaldúa, Gloria. *Borderlands/La Frontera*. San Francisco: Aunt Lute Books, 1999.

Appadurai, Arjun. *Modernity at Large: Cultural Dimensions of Globalizations*. Minneapolis: U of Minnesota P, 1996.

Appiah, Kwame Anthony. "Cosmopolitan Patriots." In *Cosmopolitics: Thinking and Feeling Beyond the Nation*, edited by Bruce Robbins and Pheng Cheah, 91–114. Minneapolis: U of Minnesota P, 1998.

———. "Cosmopolitan Reading." In *Cosmopolitan Geographies: New Locations in Literature and Culture*, edited by Vinay Dharwadker, 197–225. New York: Routledge, 2001.

———. *Cosmopolitanism: Ethics in a World of Strangers*. New York: W. W. Norton, 2006.

———. *The Ethics of Identity*. Princeton: Princeton UP, 2005.

———, and Henry Louis Gates Jr., eds. *Identities*. Chicago: U of Chicago P, 1995.

Arkoun, Mohammad. *Rethinking Islam: Common Questions, Uncommon Answers*. Translated by Robert D. Lee. Boulder, CO: Westview Press, 1994.

Asad, Talal. *Genealogies of Religion: Discipline and Reasons of Power in Christianity and Islam*. Baltimore: Johns Hopkins UP, 1993.

Assheuer, Thomas. "Was heißt hier deutsch? Der Nationalkonservatismus definiert seine Leitkultur." *Die Zeit* 30 (1998).

Atebyoğlu, Cem. "Tanzimat'an Cumhuriyet'e Spor." *Tanzimat'an Cumhuriyet'e Türkiye Ansiklopedisi (1473–1518)*. Istanbul: Iletisim Yayınları, 1985.

Baltacıoğlu, Ismail Hakki. *Ziya Gökalp*. Istanbul: Yeni Maatbaa, 1966.

Barry, Brian. *Culture and Equality: An Egalitarian Critique of Multiculturalism.* Cambridge, MA: Harvard UP, 2002.

Benhabib, Seyla. *The Claims of Culture: Equality and Diversity in the Global Era.* Princeton: Princeton UP, 2002.

———. *The Rights of Others: Aliens, Residents, and Citizens.* Cambridge: Cambridge UP, 2004.

Berger, John. *A Seventh Man: Migrant Workers in Europe.* New York: Viking, 1975.

Berghahn, Klaus. "An Aesthetic Revolution." In *A New History of German Literature*, edited by David E. Wellbery and Judith Ryan, 455–59. Cambridge, MA: Harvard UP, 2004.

Bhabha, Homi. *The Location of Culture.* London: Routledge, 1994.

Binrak, Ismet, and Nejat Sefercioğlu. *Dogumunun 95: Yildönümü Münasebetiyle Ziya Gökalp Bibliographyası.* Ankara: Türk Kültürünü Arastırma, 1971.

Biondi, Franco, and Rafik Schami. "Literatur der Betroffenheit. Bemerkungen zur Gastarbeiterliteratur." In *Schreibend einen Ort Suchen . . . Gastarbeiterliteratur, Lesungen, Informationen: Wintersemester, 1985–86*, edited by Marianne Krüger Potratz, 11–15. Münster: Westfälischen Wilhelms-Universität Münster, 1985.

Bittner, Jochen. "Ghetto im Kopf." *Die Zeit* 36 (28 August 2003). www.zeit.de/2003/36/Integration.

Bizim Almanca/Unser Deutsch (December 1984).

Blioumi, Aglaia. *Interkulturalität als Dynamik. Ein Beitrag zur deutsch-griechischen Migrationsliteratur seit den siebziger Jahren.* Tübingen: Stauffenburg, 2001.

———. "Interkulturalität und Literatur. Interkulturelle Elemente in Sten Nadolnys Roman *Selim oder die Gabe der Rede*." In *Migration und Interkulturalität in neueren literarischen Texte*, edited by Aglaia Blioumi, 28–40. Munich: Iudicium, 2002.

Boegehold, Alan L., and Adele C. Scafuro, eds. *Athenian Identity and Civic Ideology.* Baltimore: Johns Hopkins UP, 1994.

Böll, Heinrich. *Gruppenbild mit Dame.* Munich: dtv, 1974.

Boudjedra, Rachid. *La Repudiation.* Paris: Les Lettres Nouvelles, Denoël, 1969.

Brecht, Bertolt. *Der gute Mensch von Sezuan. Gesammelte Werke in acht Bänden. Band II: 1486–1607.* Frankfurt am Main: Suhrkamp, 1967.

———. *Three-Penny Opera.* Translated by Desmond Vesey and Eric Bentley. New York: Grove Weidenfeld, 1964.

Breckenridge, Carol A., Sheldon Pollock, Homi K. Bhabha, and Dipesh Chakrabarty, eds. *Cosmopolitanism.* Durham, NC: Duke UP, 2002.

Breger, Claudia. "'Meine Herren, spielt in meinem Gesicht ein Affe?' Strategien der Mimikry in Texten von Emine S. Özdamar und Yoko Tawada." In *Aufbrüche: Kulturelle Produktionen von Migrantinnen, Schwarzen und jüdischen Frauen in Deutschland*, edited by Cathy Gelbin, Kader Konuk, and Peggy Piesche, 30–59. Königstein/Taunus: Ulrike Helmer, 1999.

Brennan, Timothy. *At Home in the World: Cosmopolitanism Now*. Cambridge, MA: Harvard UP, 1997.

Brinker-Gabler, Gisela, and Sidonie Smith, eds. *Writing New Identities: Gender, Nation, and Immigration in Contemporary Europe*. Minneapolis: U of Minnesota P, 1997.

Browning, Frank, and Madeleine Brand. "Orhan Pamuk, Turkey's Controversial Faulkner." NPR transcript, 11 October 2005.

Brussig, Thomas. *Am kürzeren Ende der Sonnenallee*. Frankfurt am Main: Fischer, 2001.

Butler, Judith. "Collected and Fractured." In *Identities*, edited by Kwame Anthony Appiah and Henry Louis Gates Jr., 439–47. Chicago: U of Chicago P, 1995.

Çengiz, Metin. "Yine Orhan Pamuk Üzerine." *Edebiyat ve Elestiri* 9.54 (2001): 84–90.

Chakrabarty, Dipesh. *Habitations of Modernity: Essays in the Wake of Subaltern Studies*. Chicago: U of Chicago P, 2002.

———. *Provincializing Europe: Postcolonial Thought and Historical Difference*. Princeton: Princeton UP, 2000.

Chamisso, Adalbert von. *Peter Schlemihls wundersame Geschichte*. Stuttgart: Reclam, 1993.

Cheah, Pheng. "Given Culture: Rethinking Cosmopolitical Freedom in Transnationalism." In *Cosmopolitics: Thinking and Feeling beyond the Nation*, edited by Pheng Cheah and Bruce Robbins, 290–328. Minneapolis: U of Minnesota P, 1998.

———, and Bruce Robbins, eds. *Cosmopolitics: Thinking and Feeling beyond the Nation*. Minneapolis: U of Minnesota P, 1998.

Cheeseman, Tom. "Akçam- Zaimoğlu- *Kanak Attak*: Turkish Lives and Letters in German." *German Life and Letters* 55 (2002): 180–95.

Chin, Rita Chook-Kuan. *Rewriting the "Guest Worker": Turkish-German Artists and the Emergence of Multiculturalism in the Federal Republic of Germany, 1961–1989*. Ann Arbor: U of Michigan P, 2002.

Chow, Rey. *The Protestant Ethnic and the Spirit of Capitalism*. New York: Columbia UP, 2002.

———. *Woman and Chinese Modernity: The Politics of Reading between West and East*. Minneapolis: U of Minnesota P, 1991.

Damrosch, David. *What Is World Literature?* Princeton: Princeton UP, 2003.
Deleuze, Gilles, and Felix Guattari. *Kafka: Toward a Minor Literature*. Translated by Dana Polan. Minneapolis: U of Minnesota P, 1986.
Derrida, Jacques. *On Cosmopolitanism and Forgiveness*. Translated by Mark Dooley and Michael Hughes. London: Routledge, 2001.
———. *Of Grammatology*. Translated by Gayatri Chakravorty Spivak. Baltimore: The Johns Hopkins UP, 1976.
———. *Of Hospitality: Anne Dufourmantelle Invites Jacques Derrida to Respond*. Translated by Rachel Bowlby. Stanford, CA: Stanford UP, 2000.
———. *Politics of Friendship*. Translated by George Collins. London: Verso, 1997.
Desai, Kiran. *Hullabaloo in the Guava Orchard*. New York: Atlantic Monthly Press, 1998.
Dharwadker, Vinay. "Cosmopolitanism in Its Time and Place." In *Cosmopolitan Geographies: New Locations in Literature and Culture*, edited by Vinay Dharwadker, 1–13. New York: Routledge, 2001.
Diamond, Catherine. "Darkening Clouds over Istanbul: Turkish Theater in a Changing Climate." *New Theatre Quarterly* 14.4 (1998): 46–59.
Divakaruni, Chitra Banerjee. *Arranged Marriage: Stories*. New York: Anchor Books, 1995.
———. *The Mistress of Spices*. New York: Anchor Books, 1997.
Durakbaşa, Ayşe. "Cumhuriyet Döneminde Kemalist Kadın Kimliğinin Olusmu." *Tarih ve Toplum* 51 (1988): 39–43.
———. "Kemalism as Identity Politics in Turkey." In *Deconstructing Images of the Turkish Woman*, edited by Zehra F. Arat, 139–56. New York: St. Martin's Press, 1998.
Durzak, Manfred. "Schnittpunkte interkultureller Erfahrung: Am Beispiel deutsch-türkischer Begegnung in Sten Nadonlys Roman *Selim oder die Gabe der Rede*." In *Praxis interkultureller Germanistik: Forschung—Bildung—Politik. Beiträge zum II. Internationalen Kongreß der Gesellschaft für Interkulturelle Germanistik, Straßburg, 1991*, edited by Bernd Thum and Gonthier-Louis Fink, 291–304. Munich: Iudicium, 1993.
———, and Nilüfer Kuruyazıcı, eds. *Die andere deutsche Literatur. Istanbuler Vorträge*. Würzburg: Königshausen and Neumann, 2004.
Emre, Gültekin. *300 Jahre Türken an der Spree. Ein vergessenes Kapitel Berliner Kulturgeschichte*. Berlin: Ararat, 1983.
Enginün, Ihsen. *Halide Edip Adivar'in Eserlerinde Doğu ve Batı Meselesi*. Istanbul: Istanbul Üniversitesi Edebiyat Fakültesi Yayınları, 1978.
Ergin, Osman Nuri. *Türk Belediyeçilik ve Şehirçilik Tarihi Üzerine Seçmeler*. Istanbul: Istanbul Büyük Sehir Belediyesi, 1987.

———. *Türkiye'de Şehirçiliğin Tarihi Inkısafı*. Istanbul: Cumhuriyet Matbaası, 1936.

Erginel, Erdem. "Reconsidering Turkish Nationalism: A Critical Reading of Ziya Gökalp and Orhan Pamuk." Unpublished MA thesis, Eastern Mediterranean University Doægu Akdeniz Universitesi in Famagusta, Turkish Republic of Northern Cyprus, 2000.

Erinç, Sikti M. "Kültür de Kültür, Kültürde Kültür." *Cogito* (Fall 1994): 107–11.

Esen, Nüket. "Orhan Pamuk'un Romanlarinda Anlatim Çesitliliği." *Varlik* 4 (April 2001): 11–14.

Esselborn, Karl. "Deutschsprachige Minderheitenliteraturen als Gegenstand einer kulturwissenschaftlich orientiereten interkulturellen Literaturwissenschaft." In *Die andere Deutsche Literatur. Istanbuler Vorträge*, edited by Manfred Durzak and Nilüfer Kuruyazıcı, 11–22. Würzburg: Königshausen and Neumann, 2004.

Fachinger, Petra. *Rewriting Germany from the Margins: "Other" German Literature of the 1980s and 1990s*. Montreal: McGill-Queen's UP, 2001.

Faiz, Faiz Ahmad. "On My Return from Dhaka." In *The Rebel's Silhouette: Faiz Ahmed Faiz*, edited and translated by Agha Shahid Ali, 86–87. Salt Lake City: Peregrine Smith Books, 1991.

———. *The Rebel's Silhouette: Faiz Ahmed Faiz*. Edited and translated by Agha Shahid Ali. Salt Lake City: Peregrine Smith Books, 1991.

Felski, Rita. *The Gender of Modernity*. Cambridge: Harvard UP, 1995.

Finney, Gail. *Women in Modern Drama: Freud, Feminism, and European Theater at the Turn of the Century*. Ithaca: Cornell UP, 1989.

Fischer, Monika. "Intercultural Alterity or Borderland Experience: Minor Literatures of Germany and the United States." PhD diss., University of Oregon, 1997.

Fischer, Sabine, and Moray McGown, eds. *Denn du tanzt auf einem Seil. Positionen Deutschsprachiger MigrantInnenliteratur*. Tübingen: Stauffenberg, 1997.

Franger, Gaby. *Wir haben es uns anders vorgestellt. Türkische Frauen in der Bundesrepublik*. Frankfurt am Main: Fischer, 1984.

Frederking, Monika. *Schreiben gegen Vorurteile. Literatur türkischer Migranten in der Bundesrepublik Deutschland*. Berlin: ExPress Edition, 1985.

Friedman, Jonathan. "Global Crisis, the Struggle for Cultural Identity and Intellectual Porkbarreling: Cosmopolitans versus Locals, Ethnics, and Nationals in an Era of De-Hegemonisation." In *Debating Cultural Hybridity: Multi-Cultural Identities and the Politics of Anti-Racism*, edited by Pnina Werbner and Tariq Madood, 70–89. London: Zed Books, 1997.

Friedman, Thomas L. *The World Is Flat: A Brief History of the Twenty-First Century*. New York: Farrar, Straus and Giroux, 2005.

Friedrich, Heinz, ed. *Chamissos Enkel. Literatur von Ausländern in Deutschland*. Munich: dtv, 1986.

Frisch, Max. "Überfremdung." In *Öffentlichkeit als Partner*, 100–13. Frankfurt am Main: Suhrkamp, 1967.

Führer, Ruth. "Den Geist des Romans aufs schönste überlistet." *Frankfurter Rundschau*, 20 January 1990.

Gadamer, Hans Georg. *Wahrheit und Methode. Grundzüge einer philosophischen Hermeneutik*. Tübingen: Mohr, 1990.

Gaschke, Susanne. "Nie mehr Migrations-Ali." *Die Zeit* 35 (21 August 2003).

Gates, Henry Louis Jr., ed. *"Race," Writing, and Difference*. Chicago: U of Chicago P, 1986.

Gerk, Andrea. "Abenteuer Deutschland. Feridun Zaimoğlu schreibt sprachstark über Stofftiersammler und noch Härteres." *Frankfurter Rundschau* (10 October 2001): 15.

Gilroy, Paul. *Postcolonial Melancholia*. New York: Columbia UP, 2005.

Gitmez, Ali. "Türk Yazınında Dış Göç." *Türk Dili. Dil ve Edebiyati Dergisi/Aylik Dil ve Yazin Dergisi Özel Bölüm* (September 1981): 145–67.

Göçke, Orhan. "Das Bild der Türken in der deutschen Presse." PhD diss., Universität Gießen, 1987.

Godzich, Wlad. *The Culture of Literacy*. Cambridge, MA: Harvard UP, 1994.

Gökalp, Ziya. "Culture and Civilization." In *Turkish Nationalism and Western Civilization*, translated by Niyazi Berkes, 104–09. New York: Columbia UP, 1959.

———. *The Principles of Turkism*. Translated by Robert Devereux. Leiden: E. J. Brill, 1968.

———. *Turkish Nationalism and Western Civilization*. Translated by Niyazi Berkes. New York: Columbia UP, 1959.

———. *Yeni Hayat; Doğru Yol*. Ankara: Devlet Kitaplari, 1976.

———. "Yeni Hayat ve Yeni Kıymatlar." In *Turkish Nationalism and Western Civilization*, translated by Niyazi Berkes, 55–60. New York: Columbia UP, 1959.

Gökberk, Ülker. "Culture Studies und die Türken: Sten Nadolnys *Selim oder die Gabe der Rede* im Lichte einer Methodendiskussion." *The German Quarterly* 70 (Spring 1997): 97–122.

Gökseri, Ali Nüzhet. *Ziya Gökalp: Haytı, Sanati, Eseri*. Istanbul: Varlik Yayinevi, 1959.

Göktürk, Deniz. "Kennzeichen: weiblich/türkisch/deutsch; Beruf: Sozialarbeiterin/Schriftstellerin/Schauspielerin—Türkische Autorinnen in

Deutschland." In *Frauen Literatur Geschichte. Schreibende Frauen vom Mittelalter bis zur Gegenwart*, edited by Hiltrud Gnüg and Renate Möhrmann, 516–32. Stuttgart: Metzler, 1999.

———. "Spectacles of Multiculturalism." In *A New History of German Literature*, edited by David E. Wellbery and Judith Ryan, 965–69. Cambridge, MA: Harvard UP, 2004.

———. "Turkish Delight-German Fright: Migrant Identities in Transnational Cinema." *Transnational Communities—Working Paper Series* [An Economic & Social Research Council Research Programme at the University of Oxford], (January 1999): 1–14.

Göle, Nilüfer. *The Forbidden Modern: Civilizations and Veiling*. Ann Arbor: U of Michigan P, 1996.

Goodbye, Lenin! DVD. Directed by Wolfgang Becker. Culver City, CA: Sony Pictures Classics, 2004.

Greber, Erika. "Öst-Westliche Spiegelungen: Der Doppelgänger als kulturkritische Metapher." *Deutsche Vierteljahrsschrift für Literaturwissenschaft und Geistesgeschichte* 66 (1992): 539–94.

Grossberg, Lawrence. "Identity and Cultural Studies—Is That All There Is?" In *Questions of Cultural Identity*, edited by Stuart Hall and Paul du Guy, 87–107. London: Sage, 1996.

Grottian, Giselind. "Probleme von Frauen aus der Türkei beim Umgang mit medizinischen Diensten." *Curare—Braunschweig* 9 (1986): 143–48.

Grumbach, Detlef. "Die Liga der Verdammten." *Süddeutsche Zeitung* (19 June 1999): 7.

Grünefeld, Hans-Dieter. "Literatur und Arbeitsmigration. Probleme Literaturwissenschaftlicher Gegenstands- und Begriffsbestimmung." In *Ausländer oder Gastarbeiterliteratur? Geschichte und Aktuelle Situation einer neuen Literatur in Deutschland*, edited by F. A. Keinenburg and Rüdiger Sareika, 4–31. Iserlohn: Evangelische Akademie Iserlohn, 1985.

Gün, Güneli. "The Turks Are Coming: Deciphering Orhan Pamuk's Black Book." *World Literature Today* 66 (1992): 59–63.

Guth, Stephan. "Zwei Regionen—eine Literaturgeschichte? Zwei zeitgenössische Romane aus Ägypten und der Türkei und die Möglichkeit einer übergreifenden Periodisierung nahöstlicher Literaturen." *Welt des Islams: International Journal for the Study of Modern Islam* 34 (1994): 218–45.

Hakkı Baltacıoğlu, Ismail. *Ziya Gökalp*. Istanbul: Yeni Maatbaa, 1966.

Hall, Stuart, and Paul du Gay, eds. *Questions of Cultural Identity*. London: Sage, 1996.

Hamm, Horst. *Fremdgegangen Freigeschrieben*. Würzburg: Königshausen and Neumann, 1988.

Hannerz, Ulf. "Cosmopolitans and Locals in World Culture." In *Global Culture: Nationalism, Globalization, and Modernity*, edited by Mike Featherstone, 237–51. London: Sage, 1990.

Harrocks, David, and Eva Kolinsky. *Turkish Culture in German Society Today*. Providence: Berghahn, 1996.

Hensel, Jana. *Zonenkinder*. Reinbek: Rowohlt, 2003.

Hestermann, Sandra. "The German-Turkish Diaspora and Multicultural German Identity: Hyphenated and Alternative Discourses of Identity in the Works of Zafer Şenocak and Feridun Zaimoğlu." In *Diaspora and Multiculturalism: Common Traditions and New Developments*, edited by Monika Fludernik, 329–73. Amsterdam: Rodopi, 2003.

Hoffman, Dieter. *Postmoderne Erzählstrukturen und Interkulturalität in Sten Nadolnys Roman* Selim oder die Gabe der Rede*: Interpretation, Kommentar, Materialien*. Frankfurt am Main: Peter Lang, 2001.

Hollinger, David A. "Not Universalists, Not Pluralists: The New Cosmopolitans Find Their Own Way." In *Conceiving Cosmopolitanism: Theory, Context, and Practice*, edited by Steven Vertovec and Robin Cohen, 227–39. Oxford: Oxford UP, 2002.

———. *Postethnic America: Beyond Multiculturalism*. New York: BasicBooks, 1995.

Huntington, Samuel P. *The Clash of Civilizations and the Remaking of World Order*. New York: Simon and Schuster, 1996.

Huyssen, Andreas. "Diaspora and Nation: Migration into Other Pasts." *New German Critique* 88 (2003): 147–64.

İstanbul Üniversitesi İktisat Fakültesi. *Sosyologi Konferansları* 5 (1965). Istanbul: Istanbul Yayini.

İstanbul Üniversitesi İktisat Fakültesi. *Sosyologi Konferansları* 16 (1976). Istanbul: Istanbul Yayini.

Jäger, Lorenz. "Die Türkei und die europäische Identität." *Frankfurter Allgemeine Zeitung* 14 August 2002. www.bpb.de/themen/HQSACT,,0,Die_T%FCrkei_und_die_europ%E4ische_Identit%E4t.html.

Jakobson, Roman. *Language in Literature*. Edited by Krystyna Pomorska and Stephen Rudy. Cambridge, MA: Belknap Press, 1987.

———. "Two Aspects of Language and Two Types of Aphasic Disturbances." In *Language in Literature*, by Roman Jakobson, 95–120. Cambridge, MA: Belknap Press, 1987.

Jameson, Fredric. "Third World Literature in the Era of Multinational Capitalism." *Social Text* (Fall 1986): 65–88.

Jankowsky, Karen. "'German' Literature Contested: The 1991 Ingeborg-Bachman-Prize Debate, 'Cultural Diversity,' and Emine Sevgi Özdamar." *German Quarterly* 70 (1997): 261–76.

Jung, Matthias, Thomas Niehr, and Karin Böcke. *Ausländer und Immigranten im Spiegel der Presse. Ein diskurshistorisches Wörterbuch zur Einwanderung seit 1945.* Wiesbaden: Westdeutscher Verlag, 2000.

Kahf, Mohja. *Western Representations of the Muslim Woman: From Termagant to Odalisque.* Austin: U of Texas P, 1999.

Kama Sutra: A Tale of Love. DVD. Directed by Mira Nair. Vancouver: Trimark Pictures, 1997.

Kanak Attack. www.passagiere.de/ka/manifest/manif_dt.htm.

Kandiyoti, Deniz. "Emancipated but Unliberated? Reflections on the Turkish Case." *Feminist Studies* 13 (1997): 317–38.

Kant, Immanuel. "Perpetual Peace: A Philosophical Sketch." In *Kant: Political Writings.* 2nd edition. Edited by Hans Reiss, translated by N. B. Nisbet. Cambridge: Cambridge UP, 1991.

Kappert, Petra. "Almanya, Almanya—zum Deutschlandbild in der zeitgenössischen türkischen Literatur." *Zeitschrift für Türkeistudien* 1 (1988): 148–61.

Karasan-Dirks, Sabine. *Die Geschichte der Fatma Hanim in Köln.* Göttingen: Herodot, 1983.

Karpat, Kemal. *The Basic Causes of the Failure of Democracy in Turkey: An Interpretation.* Berlin: Berliner Institut für Vergleichende Sozialforschung, 1981.

Katzelmacher. VHS. Directed by Werner Fassbinder. New York: Wellspring, 1972.

Klingst, Martin. "Wer ist uns Willkommen?" *Die Zeit* 45 (30 October 2003). zeus.zeit.de/text/2003/45/Zuwanderung.

Klocker, Hubert, ed. *Wiener Aktionismus. Wien 1960–1971.* Klagenfurt: Ritter, 1989.

Konuk, Kader. *Identitäten im Prozess: Literatur von Autorinnen aus und in der Türkei in deutscher, englischer und türkischer Sprache.* Essen: Die Blaue Eule, 2001.

———. "'Identitätssuche ist ein [sic] private archäologische Graberei': Emine Sevgi Özdamars inszeniertes Sprechen." In *Aufbrüche: Kulturelle Produktionen von Migrantinnen, Schwarzen und jüdischen Frauen in Deutschland,* edited by Cathy Gelbin, Kader Konuk, and Peggy Piesche, 60–75. Königstein/Taunus: Ulrike Helmer, 1999.

Kristeva, Julia. *Powers of Horror: An Essay on Abjection.* Translated by Leon S. Roudiez. New York: Columbia UP, 1982.

Krupat, Arnold. *Ethnocriticism: Ethnography, History, Literature.* Berkeley: U of California P, 1992.

Kurdakul, Sükran. *Şairler ve Yazarlar Sözlüğü.* Istanbul: Inkilap Kitabevi, 1989.

Kuruyazıcı, Nilüfer. "*Selim oder die Gabe der Rede.* Verschiedene Lesemöglichkeiten des Romans von Sten Nadolny." *Alman Dili ve Edebiyati Dergisi* 9 (1995): 21–31.

———. "Warum 'Grenzüberschreitungen'?" In *Die Andere Deutsche Literatur: Istanbuler Vorträge,* edited by Manfred Durzak and Nilüfer Kuruyazıcı, 7–9. Würzburg: Königshausen and Neumann, 2004.

Kymlicka, Will. *Multicultural Citizenship: A Liberal Theory of Minority Rights.* Oxford: Clarendon P, 1995.

Lebe, Mehmet Emin. "Almanya Sanicisi." *Türk Dili. Dil ve Edebiyati Dergisi/Aylik Dil ve Yazin Dergisi* 336 (September 1979): 180–84.

Lee, Chang-rae. *Native Speaker.* New York: Riverhead Books, 1995.

Lenz, Siegfried. *Deutschstunde.* Hamburg: Hoffmann und Campe, 1968.

Levy, Daniel, and Natan Sznaider. *Erinnerung im globalen Zeitalter. Der Holocaust.* Frankfurt am Main: Suhrkamp, 2001.

Lewis, Bernard. *Emergence of Modern Turkey.* New York: Oxford UP, 2002.

Lindenberger, Herbert. "On the Sacrality of Reading Lists: The Western Cultural Debate at Stanford University." In *The History in Literature: On Value, Genre, Institutions,* 148–62. New York: Columbia UP, 1990.

Lottman, Joachim. "Ein Wochenende in Kiel mit Feridun Zaimoğlu, dem Malcom X der deutschen Türken." *Die Zeit* 47 (1997). www.zeit.de/archiv/1997/47/zaimogl.txt.19971114.xml.

Lubich, Oliver, and Rex Clark. "German Studies Go Postcolonial." *Eighteenth Century Studies* 35 (2000): 625–34.

Lützeler, Paul Michael, ed. *Spätmoderne und Postmoderne.* Frankfurt am Main: Fischer, 1991.

Mani, B. Venkat. "The Good Woman of Istanbul." *Gegenwartsliteratur. Ein germanistisches Jahrbuch* 2 (2003): 29–49.

———. "Phantom of the 'Gastarbeiterliteratur': Aras Ören's *Berlin Savignyplatz.*" In *Migration und Interkulturalität in neueren literarischen Texte,* edited by Aglaia Blioumi, 28–40. Munich: Iudicium, 2002.

———. "The Self of the Other: Contemporary German Scholarship on Trans-, Inter-, and Multiculturalism." *Monatshefte* 97 (2005): 679–96.

Marmon, Shaun. *Eunuchs of the Holy Cities.* Oxford: Oxford UP, 1993.

Mason, Mary G. "The Other Voice: Autobiographies of Women Writers." In *Women, Autobiography, Theory: A Reader,* edited by Sidonie Smith and Julia Watson, 321–24. Madison: U of Wisconsin P, 1998.

Matrinovitch, Nicholas N. *The Turkish Theater.* New York: Theater Arts Inc., 1933.

McGowan, Moray. "Brücken und Brücken-Köpfe: Wandlungen einer Metapher in der türkisch-deutschen Literatur." In *Die Andere Deutsche Literatur: Istanbuler Vorträge,* edited by Manfred Durzak and Nilüfer Kuruyazıcı, 31–40. Würzburg: Königshausen and Neumann, 2004.

Mignolo, Walter. "The Many Faces of Cosmopolis: Border Thinking and Critical Cosmopolitanism." In *Cosmopolitanism,* edited by Carol A. Breckenridge, Sheldon Pollock, Homi K. Bhabha, and Dipesh Chakrabarty, 157–88. Durham: Duke UP, 2002.

Mohanty, Satya P. "The Epistemic Status of Cultural Identity: On *Beloved* and the Postcolonial Condition." In *Reclaiming Identity: Realist Theory and the Predicament of Postmodernism,* edited by Paula M. L. Moya and Michael R. Hames-Garcia, 29–66. Berkeley: U of California P, 2000.

Moya, Paula M. L., and Michael R. Hames-Garcia, eds. *Reclaiming Identity: Realist Theory and the Predicament of Postmodernism.* Berkeley: U of California P, 2000.

Mühl, Otto. *Weg aus dem Sumpf.* Nürnberg: AA-Verlag, 1977.

Nadolny, Sten. *Die Entdeckung der Langsamkeit.* Munich: Piper, 1983.

———. *Das Erzählen und die guten Ideen. Die Göttinger und Münchener Poetik-Vorlesungen.* Munich: Piper, 2001.

———. *Netzkarte.* Munich: List, 1981.

———. *Selim oder die Gabe der Rede.* Munich: Piper, 1990.

Necatigil, Behçet. *Edebiyatimizda Eserler Sözlüğü.* Istanbul: Varlik Yayınları, 1989.

Nehru, Jawaharlal. Letter to Maria Lorenzini 2 July 1949. *Jawaharlal Nehru: Thoughts,* 273. New Delhi: Jawaharlal Nehru Memorial Fund, 1985.

Nekimken, Albert Lee. "The Importance of Bertolt Brecht on Society and the Development of Political Theater in Turkey." PhD diss., University of California at Riverside, 1978.

Neubert-Herwig, Christa, ed. *Benno Besson. Theater Spielen in Acht Ländern. Texte—Dokumente—Gespräche.* Berlin: Alexander Verlag, 1998.

"Special Issue on Minorities in German Culture." *New German Critique* 46 (Winter 1989).

Nietzsche, Friedrich. *Also sprach Zarathustra.* Frankfurt am Main: Reclam, 1989.

Novalis. *Die Christenheit oder Europa.* Stuttgart: Reclam, 1984.

———. *Henry von Ofterdingen.* Translated by Palmer Hilty. New York: Frederick Ungar Publishing, 1964.

Nussbaum, Martha C. "For Love of Country: Debating the Limits of Patriotism." In *For Love of Country?* edited by Joshua Cohen, 3–17. Boston: Beacon Press, 1996.

Nüzhet Gökseri, Ali. *Ziya Gökalp: Hayti, Sanati. Eseri.* Istanbul: Varlik Yayinevi, 1959.

O'Brian, William Arctander. *Novalis: Signs of Revolution.* Durham, NC: Duke UP, 1995.

Ören, Aras. "Dankrede zur Preisverleihung." In *Chamissos Enkel. Literatur von Ausländern in Deutschland,* edited by Heinz Friedrich, 25–29. Munich: dtv, 1986.

Özakin, Ayşel. *Die Leidenschaft der Anderen.* Hamburg: Luchterhand, 1984.

———. *Soll ich hier alt werden?* Munich: Goldmann, 1987.

Özan, Meral. "Der Weg nach Innen bei Novalis und Pamuk." *Edebiyat Fakültesi Dergisi/Journal of the Faculty of Letters* 17 (2000): 137–50.

Özdamar, Emine Sevgi. *Die Brücke vom goldenen Horn.* Cologne: Kiepenheuer and Witsch, 1998.

———. *Das Leben ist eine Karawanserei.* Cologne: Kiepenheuer and Witsch, 1992.

———. *Life Is a Caravanserai.* Translated by Luise von Flotow. London: Middlesex UP, 2000.

———. *Mother Tongue.* Translated by Craig Thomas. Toronto: Coach House, 1994.

———. *Mutterzunge.* Cologne: Kiepenheuer and Witsch, 1990.

———. *Seltsame Sterne Starren zur Erde.* Cologne: Kiepenheuer and Witsch, 2003.

Özel, Banu. "Reclaiming History in Orhan Pamuk and Toni Morrison." PhD diss., San Francisco State University, 2004.

Packer, George. "Name Calling." *New Yorker* (8 and 15 August 2005): 33–34.

Palambo-Liu, David, ed. *The Ethnic Canon: Histories, Institutions, and Interventions.* Minneapolis: U of Minnesota P, 1995.

Pamuk, Orhan. *Friedenspreis* Acceptance Speech. www.friedenspreis-des-deutschen-buchhandels.de/de/96387.

———. "I Stand by My Words. And Even More, I Stand by My Right to Say Them . . ." Interview with Maureen Freely. *The Observer* (23 October 2005). observer.guardian.co.uk/international/story/0,6903,1598633,00.html.

———. *The New Life.* Translated by Güneli Gün. New York: Vintage International, 1998.

Parekh, Bhikhu. *Rethinking Multiculturalism: Cultural Diversity and Political Theory.* Cambridge, MA: Harvard UP, 2000.

Parla, Taha. *The Social and Political Thought of Ziya Gökalp, 1876–1924.* Leiden: E. J. Brill, 1985.

Pazarkaya, Yüksel. "Stimmen des Zorns und der Einsamkeit in Bitterland." *Zeitschrift für Kulturaustausch* 35 (1985): 16–27.

———. "Was ist das Gastarbeiterliteratur." *Forum* 1 (1986): 130–32.

Peck, Jeffrey M. "Methodological Postscript: What's the Difference? Minority Discourse in German Studies." *New German Critique* 46 (Winter 1989): 203–08.

Picardi-Montesardo, Anna. *Die Gastarbeiter in der Literatur der Bundesrepublik Deutschland.* Berlin: ExPress Edition, 1985.

Pierce, Leslie. *The Imperial Harem: Women and Sovereignty in the Ottoman Empire.* New York: Oxford UP, 1993.

Plutarch. *The Rise and Fall of Athens: Nine Greek Lives.* Translated by Ian Scott-Kilvert. London: Penguin, 1960.

Podlecki, Anthony J. *Pericles and His Circle.* London: Routledge, 1998.

Pollock, Sheldon, et al. "Cosmopolitanisms." In *Cosmopolitanism*, ed. Carol A. Breckenridge, et al., 1–14. Durham, NC: Duke UP, 2002.

Potratz, Marianne Krüger, ed. *Schreibend einen Ort suchen—: Gastarbeiterliteratur, Lesungen, Informationen. Wintersemester 1985–86.* Münster: Westfälischen Wilhelms-Universität Münster, 1985.

Pratt, Mary Louise. *Imperial Eyes: Travel Writing and Transculturation.* New York: Routledge, 1992.

Rappe, Michael. "Zwischen Goethe und Kanake." (2002). www.laks.de/public/aktiv/interv-zai.htm.

Reich-Reinicki, Marcel. "Discussion of Emine Sevgi Özdamar." *Das literarische Quartett.* ZDF-Show (5 June 1998).

Riemann, Wolfgang. *Das Deutschlandbild in der modernen türkischen Literatur.* Wiesbaden: Harrassowitz, 1983.

Riesenberg, Peter. *Citizenship in the Western Tradition: Plato to Rousseau.* Chapel Hill: U of North Carolina P, 1992.

Rilke, Rainer Maria. *Briefe in Zwei Bänden.* Edited by Horst Nawelski. Frankfurt am Main: Insel, 1991.

———. *Duino Elegies: A Bilingual Edition.* Translated by Stephen Cohn. Evanston, IL: Northwestern UP, 1989.

Rischbieter, Henning, ed. *Durch den Eisernen Vorhang. Theater in geteilten Deutschland 1945 bis 1990.* Berlin: Propyläen, 1999.

Robinson, Orin W. "Luther's Bible and the Emergence of Standard German." In *A New History of German Literature*, edited by David E. Wellbery and Judith Ryan, 235–39. Cambridge, MA: Harvard UP, 2004.

Rodrigue, Aron. "Difference and Tolerance in the Ottoman Empire." Interview with Nancy Reynolds. www.stanford.edu/group/SHR/5-1/text/rodrigue.html.

Rüb, Matthias. "Verliere den Faden und gewinne die Welt." *Frankfurter Allgemeine Zeitung* (24 March 1990): B5.

Rushdie, Salman. *Imaginary Homelands: Essays and Criticism, 1981–1991*. London: Granata Books, 1991.

———. *Midnight's Children*. New York: Penguin, 1991.

———. *The Satanic Verses*. New York: Viking, 1988.

———. *Step across This Line: Collected Nonfiction, 1992–2002*. London: Vintage, 2003.

Sabuncu, Sevgi. *Tante Rosa: Hikâyeler*. Ankara: Dost Yayınları, 1968.

Sahin, Seval. "Türk Edebiyatında Modernizm-Postmodernizm Tartışmasının İlk Örneği: *Kara Kitap*." *Hece: Aylik Edebiyat Dergisi* 7.77–79 (May–July 2003): 266–82.

Said, Edward. *Orientalism*. New York: Vintage Books, 1994.

Salih, Sabah A. "East, West: Orhan Pamuk's *The White Castle*." *Notes on Contemporary Literature* 31 (November 2001): 6–7.

Sandten, Cecile. "In Her Own Voice: Sujata Bhatt and the Aesthetic Articulation of the Diasporic Condition." *Journal of Commonwealth Literature* 35 (2000): 99–119.

Sari, Zafer. *Hatay'da Aba Güresi*. Antakya: Hatay Folklor Aristirmalari Dernegi, 1992.

Sassen, Saskia. "Immigration Policy in a Global Economy." *SAIS Review* (Summer/Fall 1997): 1–19.

Schechner, Richard. *Performance Theory*. New York: Routledge, 2003.

Scheinhardt, Saliha. *Drei Zypressen*. Berlin: ExPress Edition, 1983.

———. *Frauen, die sterben, ohne dass sie gelebt hätten. Erzählungen*. Frankfurt am Main: Dageli, 1991.

———. Interview with Andrea Zielke-Nadkarni. In *Frauenfiguren in den Erzählungen Türkischer Autorinnen Identität und Handlungsspielräume*, edited by Andrea Zielke-Nadkarni, 7. Pfaffenweiler: Centaurus, 1996.

Schmidt, Helmut. "Der Teppich braucht keine neuen Flicken." *Die Zeit* (27 January 1989).

Seeba, Hinrich. "Germany—A Literary Concept: The Myth of National Literature." *German Studies Review* 17 (1994): 353–69.

Sertoğlu, Murat. *Rümeli Türk Pehlivanları: Kurtdereli Mehmet ve Adali Halil*. Ankara: Kültür ve Turizm Bakanlığı Yayınları, 1987.

Sevilen, Muhittin. *Karagöz*. Ankara: Kültür ve Turizm Bakanligi, 1986.

Sevin, Nureddin. "Türk Golge Oynun Kaynagi Üzerine." In *I. Uluslarrarasi Türk Folklor Semineri Bildirilesi 8–14 Ekim, 1973*, 56–63. Ankara: Basbakanlik Basimevi, 1974.

Seyhan, Azade. "Introduction." *New German Critique* 46 (Winter 1989): 3–9.

———. "Lost in Translation: Re-Membering the Mother Tongue in Emine Sevgi Özdamar's *Das Leben ist eine Karawanserei*." *German Quarterly* 69 (1996): 414–26.

———. *Writing outside the Nation*. Princeton: Princeton UP, 2001.

Shankland, David, ed. *The Turkish Republic at Seventy-Five Years*. Huntingdon: Eothen Press, 1999.

Sieg, Katrin. *Ethnic Drag: Performing Race, Nation, Sexuality in West Germany*. Ann Arbor: U of Michigan P, 2002.

Sölçün, Sargut. *Sein und Nichtsein. Zur Literatur in der multikulturellen Gesellschaft*. Bielefeld: Aisthesis, 1992.

Sommer, Theo. "Der Kopf Zählt, nicht das Tuch." *Die Zeit* 30 (1998). www.zeit.de/archiv/1998/30/199830.auslaender_.xml.

Southall Black Sisters Annual Report, 1986. London: Southall Black Sisters, 1986.

Soysal, Levant. "Labor to Culture: Writing Turkish Migration to Europe." In *Relocating the Fault Lines: Turkey beyond the East-West Divide*, edited by Güven Güzeldere and Sibel Irzik, 491–508. Durham, NC: Duke UP, 2003.

Soysal, Yasemin. "Citizenship and Identity: Living in Diaspora in Postwar Europe." In *The Postnational Self: Belonging and Identity*, edited by Ulf Hedetoft and Mette Hjort, 137–51. Minneapolis: U of Minnesota P, 2002.

———. *Limits of Citizenship*. Chicago: U of Chicago P, 1994.

Sözer, Bülent. "Laiklik ve Sekülarizm Hakkında Bazı Görüşler ve Düşünceler." *Cogito* (Fall 1994): 163–73.

Spivak, Gayatri Chakravorty. "Acting Bits/Identity Talk." In *Identities*, edited by Kwame Anthony Appiah and Henry Louis Gates, Jr., 147–80. Chicago: U of Chicago P, 1995.

———. "Can the Subaltern Speak?" In *Marxism and the Interpretation of Culture*, edited by Cary Nelson and Lawrence Grossberg, 271–313. Urbana: U of Illinois P, 1988.

———. *A Critique of Postcolonial Reason: Toward a History of the Vanishing Present*. Cambridge, MA: Harvard UP, 1999.

———. *In Other Worlds: Essays in Cultural Politics*. New York: Methuen, 1987.

———. "Intellectuals and Power: A Conversation between Michel Foucault and Gilles Deleuze." In *Language, Counter-Memory, Practice: Selected Essays and Interviews*, by Michel Foucault, 207–15. Ithaca: Cornell UP, 1977.

———. Interview by Sarah Harasym. In *The Postcolonial Critic: Interviews, Strategies, Dialogues*, edited by Sarah Harasym. New York: Routledge, 1990.

Stafford, Francesca. "Else's Elsewhere: Reading Marginalities in the Work of Else Lasker-Schüler." In *Aufbrüche: Kulturelle Produktionen von Migrantinnen, Schwarzen und jüdischen Frauen in Deutschland*, edited by Cathy Gelbin, Kader Konuk, and Peggy Piesche, 113–36. Königstein/Taunus: Ulrike Helmer, 1999.

Steinbach, Udo. "Eingeholt von der Wirklichkeit." *Kulturaustauch* 47, vols. 1 and 2 (1997).

Stephens, Rebecca-Lynn. "Immigrant Women Writers and the Specter of Multiplicity: Articulations of Subjectivity and Nationalism in the Texts of Julia Alvarez, Christina Garcia, Le Ly Hayslip, Jamaica and Bharati Mukherjee." PhD diss., Washington State University, 1997.

Stienen, Inga. *Leben zwischen zwei Welten. Türkische Frauen in Deutschland.* Weinheim: Quadriga, 1994.

Stokes, Martin. "'Beloved Istanbul': Realism and the Transnational Imaginary in Turkish Popular Culture." In *Mass Mediations: New Approaches to Popular Culture in the Middle East and Beyond*, edited by Walter Armbrust, 224–42. Berkeley: U of California P, 2000.

Strauß, Botho. *Rumor*. Munich: dtv, 1980.

Suhr, Heidrun. "Ausländerliteratur: Minority Literature in the Federal Republic of Germany." *New German Critique* 46 (1989): 71–103.

Suleri, Sara. "Woman Skin Deep: Feminism and the Post-Colonial Condition." In *Identities*, edited by Kwame Anthony Appiah and Henry Louis Gates, Jr., 133–46. Chicago: U of Chicago P, 1995.

Tatar, Maria, ed. *The Annotated Brothers Grimm.* New York: Norton, 2004.

Taylor, Charles. *Multiculturalism and the Politics of Recognition.* Princeton: Princeton UP, 1994.

Tekin, Mehmet. "Hatay'da Aba Güresi Üzerine." In *Hatay'da Aba Güresi. Z. Sari.* Antakya: Hatay Folklor Aristirmaları Dernegi, 1992.

———. "Yeni Hayat" *Hece* 6 (2002): 712–22.

Teraoka, Arlene Akiko. "Talking 'Turk': On Narrative Strategies and Cultural Stereotypes." *New German Critique* 46 (1989): 104–28.

Terkessidis, Mark. "Das Fremde, Eigene." *Die Zeit* 11 (2000). www.zeit.de/archiv/2000/11/200011.s-migration_.xml.

Theil, Stephan. "Russendisko. Wie Einwanderer das verschnarchte europäische Kulturestablishment aufmischen und auffrischen." *Die Welt* (5 April 2004): 4.

Thomas, D. M. "Crash: This Surreal Turkish Novel Involves a Magical Book, a Horrific Accident and a Disappearing Double." *New York Times* (22 May 1999): A1.

Thum, Bernd, and Genthies-Louise Fink. *Praxis interkultureller Germanistik.* Munich: Iudicium, 1993.

Todorov, Tzvetan. "'Race,' Writing and Culture." In *"Race," Writing and Difference*, edited by Henry Louis Gates Jr., 371–80. Chicago: University of Chicago Press, 1989.

Tomlinson, John. *Globalization and Culture*. Chicago: U of Chicago P, 1999.

Toulmin, Stephen Edelston. *Cosmopolis: The Hidden Agenda of Modernity*. New York: Free Press, 1990.

Traub, Rainer. "Ein türkischer Winnetou." *Der Spiegel* 2 (1990): 153–55.

Treichler, Paula A., Cheris Kramarae, and Beth Stafford, eds. *For Alma Mater: Theory and Practice in Feminist Scholarship*. Urbana: U of Illinois P, 1985.

Türk Dili ve Edebiyati Ansiklopedisi. Istanbul: Dergah Yayınları, 1987.

Überhoff, Thomas. "Sten Nadolny." In *Kritisches Lexikon zur deutschsprachigen Gegenwartsliteratur*, edited by Heinz Ludwig Arnold. Munich: text+kritik, 2002.

Vertovec, Steven, and Robin Cohen, eds. *Conceiving Cosmopolitanism: Theory, Context, and Practice*. Oxford: Oxford UP, 2002.

Veteto-Conrad, Marilya. *Finding a Voice: Identity and the Works of German-Language Turkish Writers in the Federal Republic of Germany to 1990*. New York: Peter Lang, 1996.

von Dirke, Sabine. "West Meets East: Narrative Construction of the Foreigner and Postmodern Orientalism in Sten Nadolny's *Selim oder die Gabe der Rede*." *Germanic Review* 69 (1994): 61–69.

Wagner, Richard. "What Is German?" *Richard Wagner Stories and Essays*, edited by Charles Osborne, 40–55. London: Owen, 1973.

Walas, Teresa, ed. *Stereotypes and Nations*. Cracow: International Cultural Center, 1995.

Walkowitz, Rebecca. *Cosmopolitan Style: Modernism beyond the Nation*. New York: Columbia UP, 2006.

Wallerstein, Immanuel. *The Modern World System*. New York: Academic P, 1974.

Wallraff, Günter. *Ganz unten*. Cologne: Kiepenheuer and Witsch, 1985.

Weigel, Sigrid. "Literatur der Fremde—Literatur in der Fremde." In *Hansers Sozialgeschichte der deutschen Literatur*. Band 12, *Gegenwartsliteratur seit 1968*, edited by Sigrid Wiegel and Klaus Briegleb, 182–229. Munich: Hanser, 1992.

Weinbörner, Udo. "Vom Türken und Deutschen, vom Reden und Schweigen." *Rheinischer Merkur* 7 (February 1990): 22.

Weinrich, Harald. "Chamisso, Chamisso Authors, and Globalization." *PMLA* 119 (2004): 1339–46.

Wellbery, David E., and Judith Ryan, eds. *A New History of German Literature*. Cambridge, MA: Harvard UP, 2004.

Wengemeyer, Sule, and Hale Sengör. "Problematik der Frau zwischen Traditiongebundenheit und Emanzipation." *Curare—Braunschweig* 9 (1986): 83–88.

Werbner, Pnina. "The Dialectics of Cultural Hybridity." In *Debating Cultural Hybridity: Multi-Cultural Identities and the Politics of Anti-Racism*, edited by Pnina Werbner and Tariq Madood, 1–28. London: Zed Books, 1997.

Westwood, Sallie, and Parminder Bhachu, eds. *Enterprising Women: Ethnicity, Economy, and Gender Relations*. London: Routledge, 1988.

Widman, Arno. "Why Don't the Germans Love to Read Their Own New Writers?" *The European* (28 January–3 February 1994): 12–13.

Wierlacher, Alois, ed. *Perspektiven und Verfarhren interkultureller Germanistik*. Munich: Iudicium, 1987.

———, and Georg Stötzel. *Blickwinkel: Kulturelle Optik und interkulturelle Gegenstandskonstition: Akten des III. Internationalen Kongresses der Gesellschaft für Interkulturelle Germanistik, Düsseldorf 1994*. Munich: Iudicium, 1996.

Wierschke, Annette. *Schreiben als Selbstbehauptung. Kulturkonflikt und Identität in den Werken von Aysel Ösakin, Alev Tekinay und Emine Sevgi Özdamar. Mit Interviews*. Frankfurt am Main: Iko, 1996.

World Culture Report, 2000: Cultural Diversity, Conflict and Pluralism. Paris: UNESCO, 2000.

Yesilada, Karin E. "Topographien im 'tropischen Deutschland': Türkisch-deutsche Literatur nach der Wiedervereinigung." In *Literatur und Identität. Deutsche-deutsche Befindlichkeiten und die multikulturelle Gesellschaft*, edited by Ursula E. Beitter, 303–39. New York: Peter Lang, 2000.

Yurtacan, Ibrahim Halil. "Türkler almanya'da neler yayınlıyolar." *Türk Kültürü* 28 (1990): 114–19.

Zaimoğlu, Feridun. *Abschaum. Die wahre Geschichte von Ertan Ongun*. Hamburg: Rotbuch, 1997.

———. "Feridun Zaimoğlu Über das Verhältnis zwischen Kanksta und Dschörmans." *Die Zeit* 51 (1997). www.zeit.de/archiv/1997/51/kanaksta.txt.19971212.xml.

———. Interview with Edith Kresta. *Die Tageszeitung* (18 February 1997).

———. *Kanak Sprak. 24 Mißtöne vom Rande der Gesellschaft*. Hamburg: Rotbuch, 1995.

———. "Knabenwindelprosa." *Die Zeit* 47 (1999). www.zeit.de/archiv/1999/47/199947.poplit_.xml.

———. "Verzweiflung ist Dynamik. Interview mit dem Kieler Autor Feridun Zaimoğlu." www.nadir.org/nadir/periodika/linx/linx-699/fer1.html.

Zeitschrift für Literaturwissenschaft und Linguistik 14. Jahrgang (1984), Heft 56.

Zielke-Nadkarni, Andrea. *Frauenfiguren in den Erzählungen Türkischer Autorinnen. Identität und Handlungsspielräume.* Pfaffenweiler: Centaurus, 1996.

Zimmerman, Peter, ed. *Interkulturelle Germanistik. Dialog der Kulturen auf Deutsch?* Frankfurt am Main: Peter Lang, 1989.

Zürcher, Erik Jan. *The European Union, Turkey, and Islam.* Amsterdam: Amsterdam UP, 2004.

INDEX

Abschaum. Die wahre Geschichte von Ertan Ongun, 38, 118–21, 137–45, 186, 215–16n19; and anti-heroism, 137; and authorial interlocution, 119–20, 136–45; and cosmopolitical claims, 144–45; and cryptic claims of hybridity, 39, 137–39, 143–45; and *demos* and *ethnos*, 145; and ethnicity and class, 120–21, 137–45; and human rights, 142; and hybrid vernacular, 118–20, 136–45; and hypermasculinity, 118, 119, 138–40; and *Kanak Sprak* and *Bitte nix Polizei*, 143–45; and *Migrantenkinder*, 142–43; and narrative authenticity, 121, 130–45; and religious difference, 137; and scatological language, 118; and sexual details, 139; and skinheads, 138; and Turkish solidarity, 138; and Turkish ethnicity and cultural difference, 137–38; vs. *Gastarbeiterliteratur*, 137

Adelson, Leslie, 15–17; and Appadurai, Arjun, 102; and Benhabib, Seyla, 22, 204n17; and Bhabha, Homi, 55, 56; and Gökberk, Ülker, 52, 53, 209n16; "Migrants and Muses," 188–89; "Opposing Oppositions," 203n13, 207–8n8; and Özdamar, Emine Sevgi, 102; "Price of Feminism," 99, 212n14; and Selim in "Opposing Oppositions," 52; and Selim in *Turkish Turn*, 53; and Seyhan, Azade, 17–19, 22–23, 102; *Turkish Turn*, 15, 16–18, 21–22, 23, 190, 214n16, 204n19, 204n23, 206n3, 211n3, 217n5; and Zaimoğlu, Feridun, 136, 214n18

Adenauer, Konrad, 46, 51

Adorno, Theodor Wiesengrund, 12–14; "Auf die Frage, 'Was ist Deutsch?,'" 12–13; and German national collectivities, 12–13; and National Socialism, 12; and Wagner, Richard, 14

aesthetics, 41
Ahne, Petra, 131, 214n10
Akbulut, Nazire, 52
Akçam, Dursun, 135
Anderson, Amanda: and cosmopolitanism, 40; and *Cosmopolitical Claims*, 41
Anderson, Benedict: and nation, 149; and seriality, 46
Andrews, Walter G., 148
Appadurai, Arjun: *Modernity at Large*, 23–25, 210n17; and culture, 23–25; and difference, 23–25; and new cosmopolitanism, 25; and Turkish guest workers, 55
Appiah, Kwame Anthony: "Cosmopolitan Reading," 32–33, 180; "Cosmopolitan Patriot," 160; *Ethics of Identity*, 185;
Arendt, Hannah, 184
Armenian genocide, 19, 146–47, 199, 215n1
assimilation, 7, 21–22, 48–49, 97, 118, 127–34
Atatürk, 39, 155, 160–61, 212n16, 215n7
Ausländerliteratur, as a categorical term, 14, 202n12, 203n15
autobiography, 38, 97; and Özdamar, 94–96; and self-referentiality, 125–26; and Spivak, Gayatri Chakravorty, 97

Bakhtin, Mikhail, 148–49
Barry, Brian, 185
Beck, Ulrich, 84, 87
Becker, Wolfgang, 107
Benhabib, Seyla, 9, 23, 53, 185; and Appadurai, Arjun, 24–25; and cosmopolitan federalism, 25; and interculturalism, 21–22, 204n17
Berghahn, Klaus, 188
Berman, Russell, 19, 190

Bhabha, Homi, 31, 34, 38, 39, 121–26, 133, 144, 154, 155, 164, 186, 207n8; and borderlines of history and language, 150–51; and criticism, 149–50; and cultural hybridity, 121–22; and "DissemiNation," 148–51; and figure of the Turk, 39, 54–58; and hybridity, 31, 52; and nation as *heimlich* and *unheimlich*, 149–51; and nation as metaphor, 149; and nation as pedagogical and performative, 148–49; and stereotypes and ambivalence, 63; and subaltern signification, 56–58; and temporality of the nation, 55, 148–49, 181–82; and Turkish guest workers, 136; and victimized foreigners, 55–57; and *vox populi*, 54–58
Bhaduri, Bhuvneswari, 80–81
Biondi, Franco, 1, 3, 4, 213n3
Bittner, Jochen, 129
Blioumi, Aglaia, 52
Böll, Heinrich, 51
border epistemology, 34–35
Brecht, Bertolt, 80, 104, 113, 115, 183
Breckenridge, Carol, 34
Breger, Claudia, 15; and Özdamar, Emine Sevgi, 100–01
Brennan, Timothy, 33–34
Brussig, Thomas, 107

Celan, Paul, 187
Chakrabarty, Dipesh, 34, 39, 90–92; and minority history, 89–93; and subaltern pasts, 89–93; and subaltern signification, 57–58
Chamisso, Adalbert von, 3–4, 120, 201n4; and *Peter Schlemihl*, 4
Cheah, Pheng: and cosmopolitics, 30–31; and Bhabha, Homi, 149–51; and critique of cultural hybridity, 186; and "Given Culture," 38–39, 124–25, 149–50, 204n18, 214n5; and migrants, 30–31
Cheeseman, Tom, 15, 135–36, 213n3, 214n16

Chekhov, Anton, 179–180, 190
Chow, Rey, 126; and coercive mimeticism, 125–26; and compulsory self-referentiality, 125; and cross ethnic representation, 61–63; and ethnic abjection, 186; and Other, 60–62; and *Protestant Ethnic*, 30, 39, 125–26, 195, 211n8, 214n5; and self-representation, 30; and stereotypes, 61–63
Chughtai, Ismet, 193
Çiller, Tansu, 160
citizenship, 7; and political membership, 9; and rights, 10
Clifford, James, 124–25
Clinton, Bill, 194
colonialism, 36–37, 191, 205n23
constitutional state, 10
co-optation, 7
cosmopolitanism, 4–6, 36; and ancient Greece, 26; and Anderson, Amanda, 40; and Appiah, Kwame Anthony, 180–81, 193, 197–99; and artistic representation, 29–30, 33–41; and Beck, Ulrich, 84, 87; and Calhoun, Craig, 28; and cosmopolitans and locals, 28; and definitions, 25–35; and detachment from time and space, 26; and difference, 25–33; and engagement with the Other, 84; and EU, 7; and federalism, 23, 25; and globalization, 26–35; and Hall, Stuart, 27; and Hannerz, Ulf, 28–29; and Huyssen, Andreas, 25–26; and hybridity, 124–26; and Kant, Immanuel, 26–27, 184; and memory, 28, 90, 91–93; and moorings, 6; and Nadolny, Sten, 44–46, 84–86; and nation, 31–32, 148–50; and native informant, 35–38; and new conceptual language, 26; and Nussbaum, Martha, 27; and Othering, 63–64; and Özdamar, Emine Sevgi, 87, 116–17; and Pamuk, Orhan, 146–47, 181–82; and postcolonialism, 31–33; and post-ethnicity, 27; and Robbins,

Bruce, 31, 33; and Tomlinson, John, 28–29; and universalistic order, 25–26; and Walkowitz, Rebecca, 41–42; and world citizenship, 28–29; and Zaimoğlu, Feridun, 118, 142–43
cosmopolitical claims, 4, 6, 9, 30–31, 33, 38, 146, 186; and *Abschaum*, 144–45; and aesthetics, 38–39; definition of, 33, 38; and dissidence, 186; and freedom, 33; and methodological core, 35–38; and ontologies of foreigner, 63–65; and Özdamar, Emine Sevgi, 87, 94–95, 116–17; and Pamuk, Orhan, 146–47, 181–82; and politics of representation, 29; and postcolonial theory, 36–38; and romanticism, 176; and self-evident differences, 199; and self-representation and validation, 119; and *Selim*, 45–46, 84–86; and *Seltsame Sterne*, 87, 116–17; and subaltern significations, 61–63, 91–93; and Zaimoğlu, Feridun, 118, 142–43
culture, 4, 14; and Appadurai, Arjun, 23–24; and culturalism, 7; and difference, 23–25, 48, 55–56, 80; and difficulty of dialogue, 23; and diversity, 16; and hybridity, 121–22, 124–25; and interlocutor, 119, 192–93; and nativism, 30; and transnationalism, 124–25

Dal, Güney, 188
Dangarembga, Tsitsi, 180
darstellen and *vertreten*, 29, 59–60, 84–85, 116
Demirel, Süleyman, 109
democratic iterations, 10
demos and *ethnos*, 9–11, 14, 24–25, 34, 38, 42, 54, 93, 146, 150, 211n4; and *Abschaum*, 145; and Adorno, Theodor W., 13; and definition of, 9–10; and diasporic memory, 93; and extra-constitutional contexts, 11; and *The New Life*, 146; and political membership, 10; and *Selim*, 54

Derrida, Jacques, 38–39, 62, 201n9, 210n1; and ethnocentric subject in *Of Grammatology*, 60; and foreigner, 44–45; and "Foreigner Question," 44–45; and hospitality and hostility, 44–45; and "On Cosmopolitanism," 184; and polis, 44–45; and "Politics of Friendship," 82–84
deterritorialization, 20–21, 88–89
Dharwadker, Vinay, 151
diaspora, 25–26
diasporic memory, 186; and cosmopolitanism, 25; and Huyssen, Andreas, 25–26, 90–93; and minority history, 90–92; and recuperation, 90–92
difference, 14, 22, 67, 133; and Appadurai, Arjun, 23–25; and Bhabha, Homi, 56; and cosmopolitanism, 32–33; and cosmopolitical claims, 5–7, 32–42; and Germany, 19, 25; and Turkey, 157–58
Durzak, Manfred, 52, 201n4

east and west, 96; as binaries, 181; as geocultural spaces, 6, 153; as parodied struggle, 156
ethnic/ethnicity, 2–4, 6, 59–60, 65, 67, 79, 87–88, 96, 104, 110, 119, 121, 123, 125–26, 130, 132–33, 136–40, 158, 176, 184, 190–95; and abjection, 125; and assimilation, 187; and Chow, Rey, 61–63; and collectivities, 2–4, 9, 24–25, 60–63; and colonies of Turks in Germany, 129; and hybridity, 125–26; and identities, 3–9, 12–14, 17–19, 88–91, 122–27, 190–91; and nationality, 35; and purloining in *Abshchaum*, 139–43; and ressentiment, 64–65
Europe, 1–4, 6–10, 49, 64, 80, 131, 193–92; and EU, 2, 7–9, 147; and North America, 2, 198–99
exclusion, 7, 14, 42–43, 183–84

Fachinger, Petra, 15, 213n1, 214n17; and Zaimoğlu, Feridun, 135–36
Fanon, Franz, 122
Fassbinder, Rainer W., 51
foreign-native, 25, 44–53
foreigners, 77; attacks on, 49; and citizens, 44–46; and culpability, 44; and empowerment, 45; as equitable subject of polity, 44; and "Foreignness of Languages," 54–57; and Hannerz, Ulf, 28–29; and ontological instability, 45; and relationship between guest and host, 44–46; and Tomlinson, John, 28–29; and willingness to engage with, 84–85
France, 2, 4, 37, 47, 190, 193, 210n1
Frankfurter Allgemeine Zeitung, 8
Frankfurter Rundschau, 48
Fremdarbeiter, 47
Federal Republic of Germany, 2–5, 38, 42, 46, 201n2; and colonialism 205n24; and integration of guest workers, 48–49; and new citizenship law, 5, 195–96; and Turkey, 37, 180; and Turks in Germany, 129
Friedman, Jonathan, 123
Friedman, Thomas L., 43
Frisch, Max, 49–50, 196, 206n3
frontiers, 1–8, 42–43

Gadamar, Hans Georg, 21–22; and Adelson, Leslie, 22, 204m17; and Benhabib, Seyla, 22, 204n17; and *Horizontverschmelzung*, 21; and interculturalism, 21–22; and Seyhan, Azade, 22–23, 204n17
Gandhi, Indira, 183
Gandhi, Mahatma, 193
Gaschke, Susanne, 127–29, 214n8
Gastarbeiter (guest workers), 2, 3, 4, 6, 14, 43, 48, 188–90, 196, 202n12; and cultural difference, 47–49; and German literature, 50–51; and globalization, 49–50; and host, 43, 44–46; and journalistic discussions in Germany, 46–49; and racial discrimination, 48–49; and *Selim*, 68–82; and *Seltsame Sterne*, 110; and social isolation, 47–49; and Zaimoğlu, Feridun, 132–33

Genç Kalemler, 156
Gerk, Andrea, 131
Germanisierung, 79
Germanistics, 19
Gilroy, Paul, 185
globalization, 1–2, 27–28, 30, 50, 124; and multiculturalism 2, 42
Goethe, Wolfgang von, 104, 149
Gökalp, Ziya, 39; and anti-cosmopolitanism, 165; and Turkish national identity, 156–60, 201n10, 215n7, 216n8
Gökberk, Ülker, 15, 85; "Culture Studies," 203n13, 207–8n8, and *Selim*, 52
Göktürk, Deniz, 15; and Bhabha, Homi, 55; "Spectacles of Multiculturalism," 189–90
Göle, Nilüfer, 99
Greber, Erika, 147
Gray Wolves organization, 160, 170
Grimm, Jacob and Wilhelm, 11, 175
Grumbach, Detlef, 130, 214n8
guest workers. *See* Gastarbeiter
Guha, Ranajit, 57
Gürsal, Cemal, 109

Haas, Robert, 120
Hansel, Jana, 107
Hassan, Jamalie, 88, 210n2; and Rushdie, Salman, 88
headscarf debate, 2
Heidelberger Manifesto, 78–80
Heinrich von Ofterdingen, 172–79
Hestermann, Sandra, 134–35, 139; and *Kanak Sprak*, 134–35
Hikmet, Nazim, 183
history: and memory, 147; as gossip, 151; slouching of, 39, 88–91, 93
Hoffmann, Dieter, 53
hospitality, 39, 41; and immigrants, 184–85, 198

Hulewicz, Witold, 179
Huntington, Samuel, 191
Huyssen, Andreas, 39, 204n19, 210–11n3, 213n26; and Chakrabarty, Dipesh, 90–93; and cosmopolitanism, 26, 116–17; and diasporic memory, 90–93
hybridity, 74; and authenticity, 38, 122–26; and borderline culture, 122–24; and choice and awareness, 123–25; and closet idealism, 124–25; and closure, 42; and colonialism, 122; and coming together of cultures of countries of birth and countries of residence, 123–24; and cosmopolitanism, 121; and criticism, 123–25; and critique by Cheah, Pheng, 124–25; and dependence on cultural specificities, 125–26; and diasporic aesthetics, 121–27; and essentialization, 126; and freedom from the given, 147; and immigrant cultures, 121–23; and literary examples, 123; and memory, 90–93; and native informant author, 126–27; and newness and Bhabha, Homi, 123; and subaltern signification, 121; and translocution, 123–24; and Turkish-German slang, 119–20
hypermasculinity, 137
hyphenated literature, 4, 7, 42, 96, 132, 146

Ib'n Arabi, 168, 170
identity, 14, 17–19, 84, 86, 89, 94, 181, 185, 188–89, 190–94, 210n1, 217n2
immigration, 11, 13, 97; and authors, 5; and difference, 129–30; and narrative, 146; and national imaginary, 146; and native informants, 95–102; and scholarship on women authors, 10, 95–102, 211; and status of authors and literature, 3
India, 80, 88–89, 170; and subaltern studies, 57; and partition, 88, 193

interculturalism, 14, 15–17, 19–21; and Adelson, Leslie, 15–16; and Benhabib, Seyla, 15–16, 22–23; and dialogue, 15–16; and evaluation of literature, 22; and Parekh, Bhikhu, 22–23; and Spivak, 88–89
interlocution, 54–60, 66–79, 123; and social worker, 129–30
Islam, 48, 74, 128–29, 130, 161, 168, 170, 176–77, 183–84, 195–96; and angles in Rilke's *Duino Elegies*, 178–79; and conservative Turks in Germany, 129; and ethnicity, 195; and immigration, 2; resurgence of, 42; and terrorism, 2

Jackson, Jesse, 194
Jäger, Lorenz, 8
Jakobson, Roman, 66–67
Jews, 108; and Wagner, Richard, 12

Kanak Sprak, 127–36, 214n18
Kanake, 127, 130–39; and homophobia, 140, 141–42; and hybrid aspirations, 141; and misogyny, 140
Kant, Immanuel: and Benhabib, Seyla, 10; and cosmopolitan right, 25–27; and Derrida, 184
Khan, Yahya, 183
Kohl, Helmut, 48
Kolat, Dilek, 127
Konuk, Kader, 15; and Özdamar, 99
Koran, 168–71, 177; and copying, 168–69; and misinterpretations, 169–71; and *Satanic Verses*, 170–71
Kristeva, Julia, 149; and abject 125, 214n6
Kuruyazici, Nilüfer, 15, 201n4, 203n14; and *Selim*, 52
Kymlicka, Will, 184

Lasker-Schüler, Else, 213n21; and *Seltsame Sterne*, 104–05
Lindenberger, Herbert, 192
Lorenzini, Maria, 193

Maier, Hans, 48
Manguel, Alberto, 120
Mani, B. Venkat, 142–43, 205n24, 213n25
Mann, Heinrich, 180
marginalization: of Turks in Germany, 20–21; of Turkish-German literature, 22
Marx, Karl, 94, 197
McGowan, Mary, 15, 203n14
memory, 38; and cosmopolitanism, 25–26; and history, 90–93, 116–17; and Huyssen, Andreas, 25–26, 90–93
Mignolo, Walter, 34–35, 37
Milosevic, Slobodan, 194
minority, 20–21, 61–66, 90, 104, 183–84, 193; and aesthetics, 30; and cosmopolitan thinking, 37; and culture, 8, 25, 184; and diasporic memory, 89–93; and experiences, 7; and history, 89–93; and literature, 4, 15 19, 93–102; and modernity, 7, 34; and recuperation, 93–117; scholarship on, 185; and women authors, 95–102
Mohanty, Satya P., 64–65, 85, 210n21
Morrison, Toni, 148
Mudimbe, Valentin Y., 120
Mühl, Otto, 105–06, 213n22
multiculturalism, 8, 14, 15, 19, 30, 66, 80, 82, 97, 184, 189–92, 194–97; and breakdown of, 185; and culturally derived differences, 185; death of, 197; and defiance, 135; and literature, 4, 15, 185; and minority studies, 192–93; and specter of, 197
Müller, Heiner, 112, 115

Nadolny, Sten, 5, 38, 189, 206–08n8; and cosmopolitan aspirations, 84–86; and *Das Erzählen*, 210n20; and narration, 85–86; and works, 51
narraphasia, 38, 65–66, 72–81; in *Selim*, 66–68
nation, 5, 6, 13; and community, 150–51; and *Geheimnis* of the Nation, 151; and literature, 20–22; and novels, 149; and Others, 9; and pedagogical and performative, 186; and scraps, 155
native informant, 29, 35, 36–37, 38, 42, 60–61, 72–73, 76, 95–96, 112, 119, 126, 133, 204n22; and cosmopolitanism, 29; and cosmopolitics, 29; and immigrant women authors, 95–99; and informance, 29; and Nadolny, 70–71; and Özdamar, 93–102; and post-Enlightenment autobiography, 97; and Zaimoğlu, 119
Nehru, Jawaharlal, 193
Neo-Nazis, 49
Neruda, Pablo, 183
Nesin, Aziz, 170
New German Critique, 19, 190
The New Life (*Yeni Hayat*), 146–47, 151–82; and anti-globalization, 160–65; and the book, 152, 154–56, 161, 164–72, 174–79; and cosmopolitanism, 171; and cosmopolitics, 181–82; and *demos* and *ethnos*, 146; and foreign goods, 164–65; and foreign products, 162–65; and givenness of the nation, 151–52; and great conspiracy, 151; and new authentic Turkishness, 158–60; and printed word, 163–64; and readership as membership to the nation, 154–55; and resident's intervention in the performative and the pedagogical, 151; and Rushdie, Salman, 169–70; and temporality of a nation, 163–64; and Turkish-German narrative, 146–47
non-German ethnicities, 3, 4, 5
non-migratory contexts, 7
non-Western cultures, 99

Ören, Aras, 1, 3, 4, 120; and *Bitte Nix Polizei*, 143
Orientalism and ethnic ressentiment, 84

otherness, 9, 15, 28–29, 72, 84, 96, 113, 126–27, 130, 184–85, 191–93, 203n15, 205n23; and cosmopolitanism, 27–29, 84; and double othering, 99; and fixity, 63; and othering, 63, 74; and otherness, 191–92; and purloined ethnicity, 127; and self-evident differences, 199; and Spivak, Gayatri Chakravorty, 59–61
Ottoman Empire, 155–56, 209n15, 215n7, 216n10; and Mugla, 74
overforeignization, 49
Özdamar, Emine Sevgi, 5, 6, 38, 87, 89–90, 94–95, 100–02, 189, 201n5, 205n23, 213n20; and autobiography, 101, 103; and critique and applause, 94–102; and German language, 94–95, 101–02; and identity, 89; and intellectual biography, 93–95; and memory, 100–17; and stereotypes, 94–95; and Turkey, 94–95, 108–10; and voice of minority, 89, 93–95; works, 94–102, 211n5, 211n6
Özel, Banu, 148

Packer, George, 2
Pamuk, Orhan, 5–7, 39, 146, 147, 152–54, 181–82, 199, 201n5, 215n11; and cosmopolitical claims, 166; and East and West, 147–48; and German Peace Prize, 147; and interview with *Tagesanzeiger*, 146; and print media, 147–48; and Rilke, 177–79; and script of new Europe, 147; and Turkish-German narrative, 146–47; and vagrant's disruption in the country of birth, 146; and western novel, 180; and works, 215n4
Parekh, Bhikhu, 19, 185
Pazarkaya, Yüksel, 49–50, 120
Peck, Jeffrey, 20
Pekdeger, Asaf, 127
performance, 29, 88–89, 93, 100–01, 116–17
Pollock, Sheldon, 34

postcolonialism, 36–38, 59–61, 128, 164; and German studies, 204n23
post-positivist realism, 64–65
Professor Unrat, 180
Puccini, Giacomo, 8

random access memory, 188–89
Rappe, Michael, 132, 214n14
rehearsal, 104, 105, 114
Reich-Reinicki, Marcel, 95
religion 5; and difference, 48; and fundamentalism, 43
Die Rheinische Post, 47
Rilke, Rainer Maria, 177; *Duino Elegies*, 178–79
Robbins, Bruce, 30–31, 33, 39
Robinson, Orrin, 188
rootlessness, 6
Rorty, Richard, 181
Rumsfeld, Donald, 2
Rushdie, Salman, 1, 2, 6, 170–71, 201n1; and *Satanic Verses*, 55, 122–23, 208n9; and *Midnight's Children*, 88; and *Step across this Line*, 1, 3, 6, 9
Rüth, Thomas, 129

Said, Edward, 52, 148, 191, 206n7
Schami, Rafik, 1, 3, 4; and Seyhan, Azade, 18
Schechner, Richard, 116
Schiller, Friedrich, 188
Schmidt, Helmut, 49
Schröder, Gerhard, 194
Scotland Yard, 170
Scum. The True Story of Ertan Ongun. See *Abschaum. Die wahre Geschichte von Ertan Ongun*
Second World War, 4, 37, 48, 50, 51–53, 104, 185, 193–94
Seeba, Hinrich, 15
Selçuk, 74
self, 9; and self-marginalizing postcolonial, 36; and representation, 119, 191–92
self-referentiality, 14

Selim, oder die Gabe der Rede (*Selim, or the Gift of Speech*), 51–86, 201n5, 206n5, 206n7, 209n14, 209n15, 209n16, 210n21; approaches to, 51–53; and constitutive elements, 52; and cosmopolitan aspirations, 84–86; and cosmopolitan history, 73–74; and cosmopolitanism, 73–74, 84–86; and cosmopolitical claims, 53, 84–86; and cultural interlocution, 53–54; and epistemic privilege, 53; and figure of the Turkish guest worker, 51–86; and German studies, 51; and Jews in Germany, 71; and locution, 54, 64–84; and multiculturalism, 74–80, 85–86; and narration, 65–86; and narraphasia, 65; and native informant, 70–71; and Orientalism, 65; and prejudices, 208n12; and reception in German newspapers, 51; and representation, 51–86; and stereotypes, 52–54, 62–63, 73–76, 135; and subaltern signification, 58–59, 65–85; and voice of the Other, 64–86

Seltsame Sterne Starren zur Erde (*Strange Stars Stare toward the Earth*), 38, 186; and affiliations with Turkey, 108–10; and Bahro, Rudolf, 114–15; and Berlin, 87; and Besson, Benno, 113; and Brecht, Bertolt, 113; and cosmopolitan memory, 116–17; and cosmopolitical claims, 103–04, 116–17; and country of birth, 107–10; and *darstellen*, 116; and East Berlin, 87, 94, 103–17; and experience, 87; and foreign language, 109–10; and Goethe, Johann Wolfgang von, 115; and Grandmother, 111; and Hamlet, 115–16; and history, 87; and impossibility of recuperation through language, 109–10; and Langhoff, Matthias, 114; and language, 103–04; and Marquadt, Fritz, 114; and memory work, 87; and minoritarian cosmopolitanism, 87; and Müller, Heiner, 115; and nostalgia, 87; and origin, 87; and recuperation, 87; and rehearsal, 87, 112–16; and structure, 102–03; and subordinated pasts, 105–09, 116–17; and Volksbühne 112–17

Senocak, Zafer, 90, 204n19, 211n3, 214n18

Seyhan, Azade, 15, 17–20, 94; and agency, 18; and allegorical transfigurations, 17; and border crossings, 18; and consumption of the foreign, 22; and displacement, 17; and Gadamer, Hans Georg, 22; and identity, 18; and *New German Critique*, 19, 190; and memory, 101–02; and paranational alliances, 23; and shared cultural memory, 18–19; and Turkish-German literature, 17; *Writing outside the Nation*, 17–19, 22–23, 101, 102, 211n6, 213n19

Shakespeare: and *Hamlet*, 115–16; and *Tempest*, 32

Sibelius, Jean, 8

Sieg, Katrin, 15, 17, 100, 144

Snow (*Kar*), 147

Sölçün, Sargut, 15

Spivak, Gayatri Chakravorty, 29, 30, 38, 97, 99, 185–86; and absolute interculturalism, 88; "Acting Bits, Identity Talk," 87–89, 210n1; and authentic voice of the Other, 59–61; and Bhabha, Homi, 64; "Can the Subaltern Speak?," 59–61, 64, 81; and Chow, Rey, 30, 61–62; and *Critique of Postcolonial Reason*, 61–6, 186, 204n22, 208n10; and Deleuze, Gilles, 59–60; and deterritorialization, 88–89; and disidentification/disaffiliation, 88–89; and experience, 87–89; "Explanation, Culture," 39; and intercultural translation, 88–89; and minority cultural politics, 88; and minority voice, 88; and native

informant, 59–61; and self-representation, 61; and transcoding of identity, 88–89; and voice of the Other,
59–61
Steinbach, Udo, 49
stereotypes, 52, 73, 75–76, 95
Stokes, Martin, 147
Strauß, Botho, 51
subaltern/subalternity, 56, 80, 119; and
cosmopolitanism, 34–35, 37; and
Cosmopolitical Claims, 57–58; and
cultural hybridity, 119; and ethnic
subject, 186; and past, 90–93, 116–17,
119, 186; and signification, 56–58,
59–63, 119, 147; and Zaimoğlu,
136–37; subalternity 186
Süddeutsche Zeitung, 47
Suleri, Sara, 96–97

Tawada, Yoko, 189
Taylor, Charles, 184
Tekin, Mehmet, 181
The Three-Penny Opera, 193
Theil, Stephan, 131, 214n11
Thomas, D. M., 181, 215n5
Tieck, Ludwig, 175
tolerance, 39
Tom Jones, 193
Toulmin, Stephen, 26
transatlantic relations, 196–97
transcultural literature, 181
trans-European space, 6
translatability, 23, 56–57
transnationalism, 150–51
Turkey, 5, 6–9; and Europe, 8–9, 147;
and European Union, 7–8, 201n6;
and feminism, 99; and guest worker,
51–81; and guest workers in Germany, 2–9, 46–49; and nation 5, 6;
and national literature, 15; and
national project, 146; pre-Ottoman,
74; and revolution, 156–60; and
Turkish figure as subaltern, 37; and
Turkish-German dialogue in
Pamuk, Orhan, 165, 172–80; and

Turkish-German Literature, 4, 9,
14–23, 202n12, 207n8; and Turkish-
German narrative, 146; and Turkish
minority in Germany statistics, 8;
and westernization and modernization 157–58; and women's writings,
212n16
Turks: and Germany, 2–9, 46–49,
127–30, 207n8, 214n8
Twain, Mark, 171

Überfremdung, 49
Überhoff, Thomas, 53

Verne, Jules, 171
Volksbühne, 211n5
von Arnim, Achim, 175
von Dirke, Sabine, 73, 85; and *Selim*, 52,
207n8, 209n14

Wagner, Richard, 11–12
Walkowitz, Rebecca, 40–41, 208n9
Wallraff, Günter, 71, 136, 214n17
Wanderarbeiter, 46
Weber, Max, 25
Weigel, Sigrid, 98–99, 190
Wellbery, David E., 187–91
Werbner, Pnina, 123
Widmann, Arno, 95
wrestling, 74, 210n17

"Yeni Hayat ve Yeni Kiymatlar," 157
Yeni Mecmua, 156
Yesilada, Karin, 15
Yüksel, Hacar, 127

Zaimoğlu, Feridun, 5, 38, 39, 127,
130–34, 186, 201n5, 205n23, 214n13,
214n15; and celebration in German
press, 132–34; and claims of authenticity, 118–19, 131–34, 136, 142–43; and
class, 119; and cosmos kanakistan,
133; and cultural assimilation-in-
difference, 134; and cultural hybridity, 134; and ethnic Other, 133–37;

and *Gastarbeiterliteratur*, 133–35; and hybridity, 127–37; and journalism, 120, 127–33; and literature of immigrants, 131–32; and multiculturalism, 131, 135; and Nadolny, 119; and narration, 119; and native authentic, 119; and otherness, 133–34; and scholarly discussions, 134–37; and self-referential claims, 131–37; and slang, 133; and spectacle, 120–21

Ziya, Mehmed, aka Gökalp, Ziya, 156
Zulima, 176–78
Zwangsgermanisierung, 48